MONEY SOURCES
FOR SMALL BUSINESS

How You Can Find Private, State, Federal, and Corporate Financing

William Alarid

Puma Publishing Co.

Santa Maria, California

Library of Congress Cataloging-in-Publication Data

Alarid, William M., 1936-
  Money sources for small business: how you can find private, state, federal, and corporate financing / William Alarid.
      p.   cm.
  Includes index.
  ISBN 0-940673-51-7 (pbk. : alk. paper) : $19.95
  1. Small business--Finance. 2. Small business--Finance--Directories. I. Title
  HD5724.T87 1991
  658.15'224--dc20   90-45299
                                                                          CIP

ACKNOWLEDGEMENTS

Many people helped make this book possible. Of particular note is the help given by Curt Scott of Crown Publishing. I'd like to also thank Gus Berle, Dan Poynter, Vendela Vida, Sam Dawson, Terri Nigro, plus Casey, Christy, David, and Corey.

INTRODUCTION

"Money Sources" is not only an interesting book for anyone planning to go into business or expanding the one he or she is in now, but a vital companion. If just one resource mentioned here opens a door for you, saves you untold hours of searching, and enables you to fulfill a dream, it will be worth the price of admission.

The "Capital Connection" is important to have. It is not the most important — the no. 1 requirement is management expertise — but it certainly ranks among the top necessities for any business person. Even billionaires (you know the Donald Trump story!) get into occasional cash crunches.

Liquidity is important. When starting up, you need money not only to pay rent, acquire inventory, fixtures, equipment, down payments on utilities, salaries for employees, payments for vehicles, memberships, tax set-asides, but also for the most important ingredient in the scenario — YOU. Then there is that other little item that bedevils even the most astute entrepreneurial planner: the unforeseen.

If you have a budget set for $50,000, let's say, add another 25 to 50 percent for two uncontrollable factors: (1) the many unforeseen, unexpected, uncontrollable increases in actual costs over projected costs, and (2) the delay in getting a new cash flow from your customers started. Unless you plan to run an all-cash business, figure on having enough reserve cash to SEE YOU THROUGH AT LEAST 60 DAYS of business operation.

In cash requirement planning, bear in mind two realities. (1) Any money you borrow must be paid back, usually with interest tacked on to it. Chances are that this money is backed by some solid collateral — such as your inventory, car, house, or other valuables. (2) You might not need as much money as you figured on. The less you can borrow, the less vulnerable your fragile new business will be.

Striking the right balance is vital to your business health. More financial mismanagement has sunk a new enterprise than perhaps any single cause after personal mismanagement.

What are the general sources for obtaining working capital with which to open a new business or expand an existing one?

- YOR — your own resources that start the majority of small enterprises, especially small service and consulting enterprises.
- FAF — friends and family, especially Dear Ol' Mom, people who know you best and are most available.
- Commercial banks which, after all, owe their successes to viable entrepreneurs like you (but who are very persnickety about your own fiscal involvement, your management expertise, your detailed business plan and your demonstrable ability to pay back the loan).
- Other money lenders such as; venture capitalists, strategic alliance partners, leasing options, grants, going public, Employee Stock Option Plans, state government sources, federal government sources, Certified Development Companies, Small Business Administration loan guarantees, credit unions, mutual funds, insurance companies, savings and loans, and even your own credit cards.

There you have almost a score of possibilities.

For enterprises that require less than $5,000,000, or even less than $500,000 — and that applies to the majority of start-up and expansion companies — any one of the foregoing traditional money sources provide viable options. If your capital connection is above those figures, then you need to be acquainted with Regulations 504, 505, and 506 of the SEC (known as Regulation D). For such really big money, you'd best get a knowledgeable attorney or certified accountant who can lead you through the minefields of major money management.

Even if it is true that "money makes the world go 'round," always remember that what makes the money go round is an astute and enterprising business person. What you borrow in the way of investment capital must be paid back. What must be paid back must usually carry interest. What must be paid back must first be earned in the competitive marketplace. And the capital that is borrowed in the first place must be accompanied by a highly credible business plan that spells out exactly what you plan to do, how you want to do it, and how the lender can share in your genius and hard work. And that applies equally to the hardnosed banker as it does to your brother-in-law.

Good luck.

Gustav Berle

Author, *Raising Start Up Capital for Your Company*
former National SCORE Director, Small Business Administration

Washington, DC

TABLE OF CONTENTS

CHAPTER 1

THE FUNDAMENTALS OF FINDING MONEY

Our thanks to the Small Business Administration for supplying this chapter.

SUMMARY

Some small business persons cannot understand why a lending institution refuse to lend them money. Others have no trouble raising funds, but they are surprised to find strings attached to their loans. Such owner-managers fail to realize that banks and other lenders have to operate by certain principles just as other types of business do.

This chapter discusses the following fundamentals of borrowing: (1) credit worthiness, (2) kinds of loans, (3) amount of money needed, (4) collateral, (5) loan restrictions and limitations, (6) the loan application, and (7) standards which the lender uses to evaluate the application.

INTRODUCTION

Inexperience with borrowing procedures often creates resentment and bitterness. The stories of three small business persons illustrate this point.

"I'll never trade here again," Bill Smith said when his bank refused to grant him a loan. "I'd like to let you have it, Bill," the banker said, "but your firm isn't earning enough to meet your current obligations." Mr. Smith was unaware of a vital financial fact—namely, that lending institutions have to be certain that the borrower's business can repay the loan.

Tom Jones lost his temper when the bank refused him a loan because he did not know what kind or how much money he needed. "We hesitate to lend," the banker said, "to business owners with such vague ideas of what and how much they need."

John Williams' case was somewhat different. He didn't explode until after he got the loan. When the papers were ready to sign, he realized that the loan agreement put certain limitations on his business activities. "You can't dictate to me," he said and walked out of the bank. What he didn't realize was that the limitations were for his own good as well as for the bank's protection.

Knowledge of the financial facts of business life could have saved all three of these businessmen the embarrassment of losing their tempers. Even more important, such information would have helped them to borrow money at a time when their businesses needed it badly.

IS YOUR FIRM CREDIT WORTHY?

The ability to obtain money when you need it is as necessary to the operation of your business as is a good location, the right equipment, reliable sources of supplies and materials, or an adequate labor force. Before a bank or any other lending agency will lend you money, the loan officer must feel satisfied with the answers to the five following questions:

1. What sort of person are you, the prospective borrower? By all odds, the character of the borrower comes first. Next is your ability to manage your business.
2. What are you going to do with the money? The answer to this questions will determine the type of loan, short or long-term. Money to be used for the purchase of seasonal inventory will require quicker repayment than money used to buy fixed assets.
3. When and how do you plan to pay it back? Your banker's judgment of your business ability and the type of loan will be deciding factors in the answer to this question.
4. Is the cushion in the loan large enough? In other words, does the amount requested make suitable allowance for unexpected developments? The banker decides this question on the basis of your financial statement which sets forth the condition of your business and on the collateral pledged.
5. What is the outlook for business in general and for your business in particular? Adequate Financial Data Is a "Must."

The banker wants to make loans to businesses which are solvent, profitable, and growing. The two basic financial statements used to determine those conditions are the balance sheet and profit-and-loss statement. The former is the major yardstick for solvency and the latter for profits. A continuous series of these two statements over a period of time is the principal device for measuring financial stability and growth potential.

In interviewing loan applicants and in studying their records, the banker is especially interested in the following facts and figures: General Information — Are the books and records up-to-date and in good condition? What is the condition of accounts payable? Of notes payable? What are the salaries of the owner-manager and other company officers? Are all taxes being paid currently? What is the order backlog? What is the number of employees? What is the insurance coverage? Accounts Receivable: Are there indications that some of the accounts receivable have already been pledged to another creditor? What is the Accounts Receivable turnover? Is the Accounts Receivable total weakened because many customers are far behind in their payments? Has a large enough reserve been set up to cover doubtful accounts? How much do the largest accounts owe and what percentage of your total accounts does this amount represent? Inventories: Is merchandise in good shape or will it have to be marked down? How much raw material is on hand? How much work is in process? How much of the inventory is finished goods?

Is there any obsolete inventory? Has an excessive amount of inventory been consigned to customers? Is inventory turnover in line with the turnover for other businesses in the same industry? Or is money being tied up too long in inventory? Fixed Assets: What is the type, age, and condition of the equipment? What are the depreciation policies? What are the details of mortgages or conditional sales contracts? What are the future acquisition plans?

WHAT KIND OF MONEY?

When you set out to borrow money for your firm, it is important to know the kind of money you need from a bank or other lending institution. There are three kinds or money: short term, term money, and equity capital.

Keep in mind that the purpose for which the funds are to be used is an important factor in deciding the kind of money needed. But even so, deciding what kind of money to use is not always easy. It is sometimes complicated by the fact that you may be using some of the various kinds of money at the same time and for identical purposes.

Keep in mind that a very important distinction between the types of money is the source of repayment. Generally, short-term loans are repaid from the liquidation of current assets which they have financed. Long-term loans are usually repaid from earnings.

Short-Term Bank Loans

You can use short-term bank loans for purposes such as financing accounts receivable, for say 30 to 60 days. Or you can use them for purposes that take longer to pay off—such as for building a seasonal inventory over a period of 5 to 6 months. Usually, lenders expect short-term loans to be repaid after their purposes have been served: for example, accounts receivable loans, when the outstanding accounts have been paid by the borrower's customers, and inventory loans, when the inventory has been converted into salable merchandise.

Banks grant such money either on your general credit reputation with an unsecured loan or on a secured loan. The unsecured loan is the most frequently used form of bank credit for short-term purposes. You do not have to put up collateral because the bank relies on your credit reputation.

Term Borrowing

Term borrowing provides funds which you plan to pay back over a fairly long time. Some people break it down into two forms: (1) intermediate—loans longer than 1 year but less than 5 years, and (2) long-term—loans for more than 5 years.

However, for your purpose of matching the kind of money to the needs of your company, think of term borrowing as a kind of money which you probably will pay back in periodic installments from earnings.

Equity Capital

Some people confuse term borrowing and equity (or investment) capital. However there is a big difference. You don't have to repay equity money. It is money you get by selling a part interest in your business. You take people into your company who are willing to risk their money. They are interested in potential income rather than in an immediate return on their investment.

HOW MUCH MONEY?

The amount of money you need to borrow depends on the purpose for which you need funds. Figuring out the amount of money required for business construction, conversion, or expansion—term loans or equity capital—is relatively easy. Equipment manufacturers, architects, and builders will readily supply you with cost estimates. On the other hand, the amount of working capital you need depends upon the type of business you're in. While rule-of-thumb ratios may be helpful as a starting point, a detailed projection of sources and uses of funds over some future period of time—usually for 12 months—is a better approach. In this way, the characteristics of the particular situation can be taken into account. Such a projection is developed through the combination of a predicted budget and a cash forecast.

The budget is based on recent operating experience plus your best judgment of performance during the coming period. The cash forecast is your estimate of cash receipts and disbursements during the budget period. Thus, the budget and the cash forecast together represent your plan for meeting your working capital requirements.

To plan your working capital requirements, it is important to know the "cash flow" which your business will generate. This involves simply a consideration of all elements of cash receipts and disbursements at the time they occur. These elements are listed in the profit-and-loss statement which has been modified to show cash flow. They should be projected for each month.

WHAT KIND OF COLLATERAL?

Sometimes, your signature is the only security the bank needs when making a loan. At other times, the bank requires additional assurance that the money will be repaid. The kind and amount of security depends on the bank and on the borrower's situation.

If the loan required cannot be justified by the borrower's financial statements alone, a pledge of security may bridge the gap. The types of security are: endorsers; co-makers and guarantors; assignment of leases; trust receipts and floor planning; chattel mortgages; real estate; account receivables; savings accounts; life insurance policies; and stocks and bonds. In the majority of states where the Uniform Commercial Code has been enacted, paperwork for recording loan transactions will be greatly simplified.

Endorsers, Co-makers, and Guarantors

Borrowers often get other people to sign a note in order to bolster their own credit. These endorsers are contingently liable for the note they sign. If the borrower fails to pay up, the bank expects the endorser to make the note good. Sometimes, the endorser may be asked to pledge assets or securities too.

A co-maker is one who creates an obligation jointly with the borrower. In such cases, the bank can collect directly from either the maker or the co-maker.

A guarantor is one who guarantees the payment of a note by signing a guaranty commitment. Both private and government lenders often require guarantees from officers of corporations in order to assure continuity of effective management. Sometimes a manufacturer will act as guarantor for customers.

Assignment of Leases

The assigned lease as security is similar to the guarantee. It is used, for example, in some franchise situations.

The bank lends the money on a building and takes a mortgage. Then the lease, which the dealer and the parent franchise company work out, is assigned so that the bank automatically receives the rent payments. In this manner, the bank is guaranteed repayment of the loan.

Warehouse Receipts

Banks also take commodities as security by lending money on a warehouse receipt. Such a receipt is usually delivered directly to the bank and shows that the merchandise used as security either has been placed in a public warehouse or has been left on your premises under the control of one of your employees who is bonded (as in field warehousing). Such loans are generally made on staple or standard merchandise which can be readily marketed. The typical warehouse receipt loan is for a percentage of the estimated value of the goods used as security.

Trust Receipts and Floor Planning

Merchandise such as automobiles, appliances, and boats, has to be displayed to be sold. The only way many small marketers can afford such displays is by borrowing money. Such loans are often secured by a note and a trust receipt.

This trust receipt is a legal paper for floor planning. It is used for serial-numbered merchandise. When you sign one, you: (1) acknowledge receipt of the merchandise, (2) agree to keep the merchandise in trust for the bank, and (3) promise to pay the bank as you sell the goods.

Chattel Mortgages

If you buy equipment such as a cash register or a delivery truck, you may want to get a chattel mortgage loan, by which you give the bank a lien on the equipment you are buying.

The bank also evaluates the present and future market value of the equipment being used to secure the loan. How rapidly will it depreciate? Does the borrower have the necessary fire, theft, property damage, and public liability insurance on the equipment? The banker has to be sure that the borrower protects the equipment.

Real Estate

Real Estate is another form of collateral for long-term loans. When taking a real estate mortgage, the bank finds out: (1) the location of the real estate, (2) its physical condition, (3) its foreclosure value, and (4) the amount of insurance carried on the property.

Accounts Receivable

Many banks lend money on accounts receivable. In effect, you are counting on your customers to pay your note.

The bank may take accounts receivable on a notification or a non-notification plan. Under the notification plan, the purchaser of the goods is informed by the bank that his or her account has been assigned to it and he or she is asked to pay the bank. Under the non-notification plan, the borrower's customers continue to pay you the sums due on their accounts and you pay the bank.

Savings Accounts

Sometimes, you might get a loan by assigning to the bank a savings account. In such cases, the bank gets an assignment from you and keeps your passbook. If you assign an account in another bank as collateral, the lending bank asks the other bank to mark its records to show that the account is held as collateral.

Life Insurance

Another kind of collateral is life insurance. Banks will lend up to the cash value of a life insurance policy. You have to assign the policy to the bank.

If the policy is on the life of an executive of a small corporation, corporate resolutions must be made authorizing the assignment. Most insurance companies allow you to assign the policy back to the original beneficiary when the assignment to the bank ends.

Some people like to use life insurance as collateral rather than borrow directly from insurance companies. One reason is that a bank loan is often more convenient to obtain and usually may be obtained at a lower interest rate.

Stocks and Bonds

If you use stocks and bonds as collateral, they must be marketable. As a protection against market declines and possible expenses of liquidation, banks usually lend no more than 75% of the market value of high grade stock. On Federal Government or municipal bonds, they may be willing to lend 90% or more of their market value.

The bank may ask the borrower for additional security or payment whenever the market value of the stocks or bonds drops below the bank's required margin.

WHAT ARE THE LENDER'S RULES?

Lending institutions are not just interested in loan repayments. They are also interested in borrowers with healthy profit-making businesses. Therefore, whether or not collateral is required for a loan, they set loan limitations and restrictions to protect themselves against unnecessary risk and at the same time against poor management practices by their borrowers. Often some owner-managers consider loan limitations a burden.

Yet others feel that such limitations also offer an opportunity for improving their management techniques.

Especially in making long-term loans, the borrower as well as the lender should be thinking of: (1) the net earning power of the borrowing company, (2) the capability of its management, (3) the long range prospects of the company, and (4) the long range prospects of the industry of which the company is a part. Such factors often mean that limitations increase as the duration of the loan increases.

WHAT KINDS OF LIMITATIONS?

The kinds of limitations which an owner-manager finds set upon the company depends to a great extent on the company. If the company is a good risk, only minimum limitations need be set. A poor risk, of course, is different. Its limitations should be greater than those of a stronger company.

Look now for a few moments at the kinds of limitations and restrictions which the lender may set. Knowing what they are can help you see how they affect your operations.

The limitations which you will usually run into when you borrow money are:

(1) Repayment terms.
(2) Pledging or the use of security.
(3) Periodic reporting.

A loan agreement, as you may already know, is a tailor-made document covering, or referring to, all the terms and conditions of the loan. With it, the lender does two things: (1) protects position as a creditor (keeps that position in as protected a state as it was on the date the loan was made, and (2) assures repayment according to the terms.

The lender reasons that the borrower's business should generate enough funds to repay the loan while taking care of other needs. The lender considers that cash inflow should be great enough to do this without hurting the working capital of the borrower.

Covenants — Negative and Positive

The actual restrictions in a loan agreement come under a section known as covenants. Negative covenants are things which the borrower may not do without prior approval from the lender. Some examples are: further additions to the borrower's total debt, non-pledge to others of the borrower's assets, and issuance of dividends in excess of the terms of the loan agreement.

On the other hand, positive covenants spell out things which the borrower must do. Some examples are:

(1) Maintenance of a minimum net working capital.

(2) Carrying of adequate insurance.

(3) Repaying the loan according to the terms of the agreement.

(4) Supplying the lender with financial statements and reports.

Overall, however, loan agreements may be amended from time to time and exceptions made. Certain provisions may be waived from one year to the next with the consent of the lender. **You Can Negotiate!**

Next time you go to borrow money, thrash out the lending terms before you sign. It is good practice no matter how badly you may need the money. Ask to see the papers in advance of the loan closing. Legitimate lenders are glad to cooperate.

Chances are that the lender may be flexible on the terms. Keep in mind also that, while you're mulling over the terms, you may want to get the advice of your associates and outside advisors. In short, try to get terms which you know your company can live with. Remember, however, that once the terms have been agreed upon and the loan is made (or authorized as in the case of SBA), you are bound by them.

THE LOAN APPLICATION

Now you have read about the various aspects of the lending process and are ready to apply for a loan. Banks and other private lending institutions, as well as the Small Business Administration, require a loan application on which you list certain information about your business.

The SBA form is more detailed than most bank forms. The bank has the advantage of prior knowledge of the applicant and his or her activities. Since SBA does not have such knowledge, its form is more detailed. Moreover, the longer maturities of SBA loans ordinarily will necessitate more knowledge about the applicant.

Before you get to the point of filling out a loan application, you should have talked with an SBA representative, or perhaps your accountant or banker, to make sure that your business is eligible for an SBA loan. Because of public policy, SBA cannot make certain types of loans. Nor can it make loans under certain conditions. For example, if you can get a loan on reasonable terms from a bank, SBA cannot lend you money. The owner-manager is also not eligible for an SBA loan if he or she can get funds by selling assets which his or her company does not need in order to grow.

Most loan applications are self-explanatory. However, some applicants have trouble with certain sections because they do not know where to go to get the necessary information. "Collateral Offered" is an example. A company's books should show the net value of assets such as business real estate and business machinery and equipment. "Net" means what you paid for such assets less depreciation.

If an owner-manager's records do not contain detailed information on business collateral, such as real estate and machinery and equipment, the bank sometimes can get it from your Federal income tax returns. Reviewing the depreciation which you have taken for tax purposes on such collateral can be helpful in arriving at the value of these assets.

If you are a good manager, you should have your books balanced monthly. However, some businesses prepare balance sheets less regularly. In filling out your "Balance Sheet as of _____, 19 _____, Fiscal Year Ends _____," remember that you must disclose the condition of your business within 60 days of the date on your loan application. It is best to get expert advice when working up such vital information. Your accountant or banker will be able to help you.

Again, if your records do not show the details necessary for working up profit and loss statements, your Federal income tax returns may be useful in getting together facts for the loan application.

Insurance

Information about the kinds of insurance a company carries is also needed. The owner-manager gives these facts by listing various insurance policies.

Personal Finances

The lender also must know something about the personal financial condition of the applicant. Among the types of information are: personal cash position; source of income including salary and personal investments; stocks, bonds, real estate, and other property owned in the applicant's own name; personal debts including installment credit payments, life insurance premiums, and so forth.

EVALUATING THE APPLICATION

Once you have supplied the necessary information, the next step in the borrowing process is the evaluation of your application. The loan processor looks for:

(1) The borrower's debt paying record to suppliers, banks, home mortgage holders, and other creditors.

(2) The ratio of the borrower's debt to net worth.

(3) The past earnings of the company.

(4) The value and condition of the collateral which the borrower offers for security.

The loan processor also looks for: (1) the borrower's management ability, (2) the borrower's character, and (3) the future prospects of the borrower's business.

Good Luck. Don't be discouraged if your first attempt is not successful. We've found that various money sources differ drastically in their policies.

CHAPTER 2

FEDERAL FINANCIAL AID

Before going into general business loans extensively it must be pointed out that there also are a myriad of federal funding options, especially for research and development contracts.

Usually, but not necessarily, there are research and development contracts for established high tech or specialized small companies. If you need detailed information on obtaining funds for a highly technical project, write us and ask for a copy of *The Small Business Guide To Federal Research and Development Funding Opportunities*. Information on how to order is in the back of this book.

THE SMALL BUSINESS ADMINISTRATION'S BUSINESS LOAN PROGRAMS

SBA loans have helped thousands of small companies get started, expand and prosper. By law, an applicant must first seek financing from a bank or other lending institution before using SBA loan assistance.

SBA Offers Two Basic Types of Business Loans

1. Guarantee loans are made by private lenders, usually banks, and guaranteed up to 90% by SBA. Most SBA loans are made under the guarantee program. The maximum guarantee percentage of loans exceeding $155,000 is 85%. SBA can guarantee up to $750,000 of a private sector loan.

There are three principal parties to an SBA guarantee loan: (1) SBA, (2) the small business applicant, and (3) the private lender. The lender plays the central role in the loan delivery system. The small business submits the loan application to the lender, who makes the initial review, and, if approved for submission to SBA, forwards the application and analysis to the local SBA office. If approved by the SBA, the lender closes the loan and disburses the funds.

2. SBA direct loans have an administrative maximum of $150,000 and are available only to applicants unable to secure an SBA-guaranteed loan. Before applying for an SBA direct loan, an applicant must first seek financing from his/her bank of account, and, in cities of over 200,000, from at least one other lender. Direct loan funds are very limited and, at times, available only to

certain types of borrowers (e.g. businesses located in high-unemployment areas, or owned by low-income individuals, handicapped individuals, Vietnam-era Veterans, or disabled Veterans).

How to Apply For a Loan

1. Prepare a current business balance sheet listing all assets, liabilities, and net worth. New business applicants should prepare an estimated balance sheet as of the day the business starts. The amount that you and/or others have to invest in the business must be stated.

2. Income (profit and loss) statements should be submitted for the current period and for the most recent three fiscal years, if available. New business applicants should prepare a detailed projection of earnings and expenses at least for the first year of operation (a monthly cash flow is recommended).

3. Prepare a current personal financial statement of the proprietor, or each partner or stockholder owning 20% or more of the corporate stock in the business.

4. List collateral to be offered as security for the loan along with an estimate of the present market value of each item as well as the balance of any existing liens.

5. State the amount of the loan requested and purposes for which it is to be used.

6. Take this material to your lender. If the lender is unable or unwilling to provide the financing directly, the prospects of using the SBA guarantee program should be explored. The lender should be encouraged to contact the nearest SBA field office if additional program information is needed. An SBA direct loan may be possible for credit-worthy applicants who are unable to obtain a guarantee loan, depending on availability of funds. Contact the nearest SBA field office for advice on the possibilities of a direct loan.

Terms of Loans

Working capital loans generally have maturities of five-to-seven years. The maximum maturity is 25 years; however, the longer maturities are used to finance fixed assets such as the purchase or major renovation of business premises. Interest rates in the guarantee program are negotiated between the borrower and the lender subject to SBA maximums. Generally, interest rates for loans with maturities of seven years or more cannot exceed 2-3/4% over New York prime, and loans with maturities of less than seven years cannot exceed 2 1/4% over New York prime. Interest rates on direct loans are based on the cost of money to the Federal Government and are calculated quarterly.

FEDERAL PROGRAMS YOU CAN USE

SMALL-BUSINESS LOANS FOR VERY SMALL COMPANIES

The Small Business Administration is implementing a new program to encourage lenders to make loans of less than $50,000. SBA administrator Susan B. Engeleiter has asked the American Bankers Associating and the National Association of Guaranteed Lenders to urge their members to cooperate in the small-loan program.

SBA says it expects that the availability of these loans will be especially helpful to women business owners. Women make up a very strong presence among owners of service businesses which have lower capital requirements than other types of firms.

For more information call the SBA's toll free number: 1-800-368-5855.

LOANS FOR BUSINESSES IN SMALL TOWNS

The Farmers Home Administration's **Business and Industrial Loan Program** guarantees up to 90% of principal and interest on loans made by commercial lenders to establish or improve businesses and industries, if they are used primarily to help preserve or create new employment opportunities for rural people. Loans may assist enterprises located in the countryside and towns or cities of up to a population of 50,000.

The money may be used for business acquisitions, construction, conversion, enlargement, repair, purchasing land, easements, buildings and/or equipment and supplies.

The FmHA has fewer rules than the SBA; for example, the FmHA will consider loans for publishing enterprises and the SBA will (usually) not.

Contact: Farmers Home Administration, Department of Agriculture, 14th & Independence Avenue, S.W., Washington, DC 20250. Phone (202) 447-4323.

LOANS FOR TEENAGERS

Youth Project Loans from the Farmers Home Administration are available to youngsters ages 10 through 20 in rural communities. It will finance nearly any kind of income-producing project. Youths have started landscaping companies, repair shops, catering services, roadside stands and art/crafts sales enterprises, among others. The money can be used for equipment, supplies, renting tools, buying livestock, and for operating expenses. Only small projects are financed.

Contact: Youth Project Loans, Farmers Home Administration, 14th & Independence Avenue, S.W., Washington, DC 20250. For a pamphlet describing the program call (202) 382-1632.

NONFARM ENTERPRISES ON FARMS

The **Farmers Home Administration** makes loans and gives technical and management assistance for businesses to supplement farm income. It can make loans up to $200,000 and guarantee bank loans up to $400,000. These loans have financed welding shops, service stations, grocery stores, barber shops, cabinetmakers, sporting goods stores, beauty shops, riding stables, repair services and restaurants, among others.

Applications of veterans receive preference. To be eligible one must be or intend to become the owner-operator of a family- sized farm or be a tenant on such a farm.

The loans may be used for buildings, land, buying or renting tools and equipment, furnishings, operating expenses, refinance debts, pay closing costs, purchase inventories or supplies, pay for organizing the enterprise, develop water and waste disposal systems for the enterprise and construct necessary roads.

Contact: Farmers Home Administration, 14th & Independence Avenue, S.W., Washington, DC 20250. Phone (202) 447-4323 and ask for the Nonfarm Enterprise Loan pamphlet.

A POTPOURRI OF FARMERS HOME ADMINISTRATION LOANS

The FmHA has loan programs for purchasing and developing farms, buying livestock and equipment, paying farm and home operating equipment, converting farms to outdoor recreation enterprises, constructing buildings and homes, providing rental housing, developing water and waste disposal systems, refinancing debts, and soil and water conservation.

Contact: Farmers Home Administration, Department of Agriculture, 14th & Independence Avenue, S.W., Washington, DC 20250. Phone (202) 447-4323.

LOAN GUARANTEES FOR AGRICULTURAL EXPORTS

The **Export Credit Guarantee Program** (GSM-102), run by the **Agriculture Department's Commodity Credit Corporation** is designed to expand U.S. agricultural exports by stimulating U.S. bank financing of foreign purchases on credit terms of up to 3 years. In every transaction, the foreign buyer's bank must issue an irrevocable letter of credit covering the port value of the commodity exported.

The **Credit Corporation's** guarantee will cover most of the amount owed to the U.S. bank in case the foreign bank defaults. The program operates in situations where credit is necessary to increase or maintain U.S. exports to a foreign market and where private financial institutions would be unwilling to provide financing without guarantee.

A secondary objective is to permit some countries with improved financial conditions to purchase on fully-commercial terms.

The **Intermediate Export Credit Guarantee Program** (GSM-103) is similar but provides coverage on credit terms in excess of three but not greater than ten years.

Under these programs, guarantee coverage may be made available on credits extended for freight cost and marine and war risk insurance costs associated with U.S. agricultural exports. The Credit Corporation announces availability of such coverage on a case-by-case basis.

Contact: Foreign Agricultural Service, Commodity Credit Corporation, Department of Agriculture, 14th & Independence Avenue, S.W., Washington, DC 20250. Phone (202) 447-3224.

GRANTS FOR INVENTIONS

The **ENERGY-RELATED INVENTIONS OFFICE** encourages innovation in non-nuclear energy technology by helping individual inventors and small R&D companies to develop promising energy-related inventions. It evaluates all submitted inventions and recommends those that are promising to the Department of Energy (DOE).

The evaluation criteria are: technical feasibility, degree of energy impact, commercial potential, and intrinsic technical merit. DOE then reviews the recommended inventions and, working closely with the inventor, determines the next reasonable step for the invention and how much money it will take. Most often, support takes the form of a one-time-only cash grant and technical assistance in developing linkages with the private sector.

Contact: Energy-Related Inventions Office, National Institute of Standards and Technology (formerly National Bureau of Standards), Department of Commerce, Building 202, Room 209, Gaithersburg, MD 20899. Phone (301) 975-5500.

FUNDS FOR FISHING

The **Commercial Fisheries Financial Assistance Programs** include the:
1. **Fisheries Obligation Guarantee Program** which provides a Federal Guarantee of financing of commercial fishing vessels and shoreside facilities.
2. **Capital Construction Fund Program** which defers Federal income taxes for agreement holders on commercial fishing operations to permit accumulation of capital for use in approved commercial fishing vessel acquisition or reconstruction projects.
Contact: National Oceanic and Atmospheric Administration, National Marine Fisheries Service, Department of Commerce, Financial Services Division, F/TWI, 1825 Connecticut Avenue, N.W., Washington, DC 20235. Phone (202) 673-5424.

IF YOUR FISHING BOAT OR GEAR IS DESTROYED

If your fishing boat is destroyed by a foreign vessel or if your fishing gear is damaged by an oil-related activity, the government may make direct payments to you.

a. Boat Destruction

In 1988, approximately 135 claims for fishing boat destruction totaling $1 million were paid. The claims ranged from $600 to $150,000.

The applicant must be a U.S. commercial fisherman and a U.S. citizen. The incident must have occurred within the U.S. Fishery Conservation zone or in an area where the United States has exclusive management authority. You need to keep affidavits, receipts, logbooks, and inventories to show you're a fisherman and owned the property for which compensation is claimed.

b. Gear Loss

If you lost gear because of an oil- or gas-related activity in any area of the Outer Continental Shelf, the government will pay for the gear plus 50% of the resulting economic loss.

In 1988 approximately 115 claims for gear damage, ranging from $500 to $25,000, were paid, totaling $700,000.

There are no restrictions on the use of these funds.

You must present financial statements, receipts, logbooks, and affidavits to establish you are a fisherman and owned the equipment for which compensation is claimed.
Contact: Financial Services Division, Attn: National Marine Fisheries Service, Department of Commerce, 1825 Connecticut Ave. N.W., Washington, DC 20235. Phone (202) 673-5421.

IF YOUR FISHING BOAT IS SEIZED

The **Department of State** will reimburse you if your fishing boat is seized by a foreign country on the high seas.

In addition, if the seizure occurs in waters claimed by the foreign country as territorial, but the claim is not recognized by the United States, the State Department will still pay.

Pre-registration and payment of a premium fee are necessary.

Losses payable are limited to the market value of the fish before seizure, market value of the boat and gear, and 50% of the gross income lost.

In 1988, 45 claims totaling $1.8 million were paid. Whether or not you preregister, the government will reimburse you for fines paid to a foreign government to secure the release of your boat.

Contact: Office of Fisheries Affairs, Bureau of Oceans and International Environmental and Scientific Affairs, Room 5806, Department of State, Washington, DC 20520. Phone Stetson Tinkham at (202) 647-2009.

MINORITY LOANS FOR DEPARTMENT OF ENERGY RESEARCH

The minority loan program was established to assist minority business enterprises in participating fully in DOE research, development, demonstration and contract activities. The financial assistance is in the form of direct loans, where DOE would provide funds to a minority business borrower from its appropriated funds.

The loans are to assist a minority business borrower in financing up to 75% of costs a borrower incurs in preparing a bid or proposal to attempt to obtain DOE contracts or agreements or first and second their subcontracts with DOE operating contractors.

The maximum amount of money that can be borrowed for any one loan is $50,000.

Contact: Minority Economic Impact Office, Department of Energy, 1000 Independence Avenue, S.W., Room 5B-110, Washington, DC 20585. Phone (202 586-1594.

FINANCING OF ARCHITECTURAL AND ENGINEERING OVERSEAS PROJECTS.

The **Export-Import Bank** (EXIM bank) provides financing to help U.S. architectural and engineering firms win foreign contracts for project-related feasibility studies and pre-con-

struction engineering services. Under the program, Eximbank, the U.S. Government agency charged with facilitating financing for U.S. exports, offers medium-term loans directly to the foreign purchasers of those services, and guarantees private financing for a portion of the local costs of the project. To qualify for the program, the contract must involve a project with the potential to generate additional U.S. exports worth $10 million or twice the amount of the initial contract, whichever is greater.

Contact: Export-Import Bank of the United States, 811 Vermont Avenue, N.W., Washington, DC 20571. Phone toll-free (800) 424-5201; firms in Alaska, Hawaii and Washington DC should call (202) 566-8860.

INSURANCE ON CREDIT TO FOREIGNERS

American companies often find that extending credit to foreign buyers is essential to expand or win business. But distance, unfamiliar legal procedures and unforeseen political or economic events make credit sales to foreign buyers riskier than similar sales to domestic customers.

Eximbank's Policies, offered through its agent, the **Foreign Credit Insurance Association (FCIA)**, makes it easier for companies, even those with little or no exporting experience, to get credit risk protection for their export credit sales.

Four policies are offered: **New-to-Export Policy, Umbrella Insurance Policy, Short-Term Multi-Buyer Policy,** and **Bank-to-Bank Letter of Credit Policy.** Products and services include consumables, raw materials, spare parts, agricultural commodities, capital goods, consumer durables and services.

The **Umbrella Policy** enables state and local government agencies, banks, export trading companies, freight forwarders and other financial and professional organizations to become administrators of short-term credit risk insurance covering the export sales of numerous exporters. These administrators assume responsibility for collecting premiums, reporting shipments, filling out forms and processing claims on behalf of the exporters insured under their **Umbrella Policy**.

This policy gives new exporters greater access to foreign credit risk protection and lessens their paperwork burdens. It also helps exporters get financing because the policy proceeds are assignable to any financial institution as collateral on a hold harmless basis. Administrators of Umbrella Policies benefit as well. The **Umbrella Policy** enables them to offer an important service to their small- and medium-size business customers.

The **New-to-Export Policy** assists companies which are just beginning to export or have an annual export sales volume of less than $750,000. The Short-Term Multi-Buyer Policy is available for any exporter. The Bank-to-Bank Letter of Credit Policy is available to any bank financing export sales on an irrevocable letter of credit basis.

Contact: Export-Import Bank of the United States, 811 Vermont Avenue N.W., Washington, DC 20571. Phone toll-free (800) 424-5201; firms in Alaska, Hawaii and Washington DC should call (202) 566-8860.

FIXED RATE LOANS FOR EXPORTS

In addition to the risks that a foreign obligator will not repay an export loan, a commercial bank providing export financing faces the risk that its cost of money will rise before the loan is repaid. For this reason, banks generally prefer to extend floating rate loans. Foreign purchasers, however, are frequently unwilling to accept a fluctuating interest rate risk in addition to the foreign exchange risk they bear on foreign currency loans.

Eximbank's **Medium-Term Intermediary Loan** program enables commercial lenders to offer fixed rate export loans to finance sales of U.S. companies' products and services. In cases where the business is not small, the exporter must face officially supported subsidized foreign competition.

Interest rates are fixed at the lowest rate permitted under the export credit guidelines followed by members of the **Organization for Economic Cooperation and Development (OECD)**.

The OECD rates are reviewed every six months and adjusted as necessary to reflect changes in prevailing interest rates. This program enables financing institutions unrelated to the exporter to borrow from Eximbank below the rate on the export loan, and is used to support sales of goods and services customarily sold on credit terms of one to five years, such as automobiles, trucks, construction equipment and feasibility studies. For more information ask about **Intermediary Loans**.

Contact: Export-Import Bank of the United States, 811 Vermont Avenue N.W., Washington, DC 20571. Phone Larry Luther toll-free at (800) 424-5201; firms in Alaska, Hawaii and Washington DC should call (202) 566-8860.

GET A REVOLVING LINE OF CREDIT FOR EXPORTS

The **Export Revolving Line of Credit Loan Program (ERLC)** is designed to help more small businesses export their products and services abroad. Any number of withdrawals and repayments can be made as long as the dollar limit of the line is not exceeded and the repayments are made within the stated maturity period, not to exceed 18 months.

Proceeds may be used only to finance labor and materials needed for manufacturing or wholesaling for export, and to penetrate or develop foreign markets.

Through this program, SBA can guarantee up to 85% of a bank line of credit (up to a maximum of $500,000) to a small business exporter. On amounts under $155,000 SBA can guarantee up to 90% of the loan.

Applicants must qualify as small under SBA's size standards and meet the other eligibility criteria for all SBA loans. In addition, an applicant must have been in business (not necessarily in exporting) for at least 12 full months prior to filing an application.

ERLC loans are available only under the **SBA's Guarantee Plan.** A prospective applicant should review the export financing needs of the business with their bank. If the bank is unable or unwilling to make the loan directly, the possibilities of a participation with SBA should be explored. The participation of a private lender is necessary in order to consummate an ERLC.

Contact: Export Revolving Line of Credit Loan Program (ERLC), Small Business Administration, 1441 L Street N.W., Washington, DC 20416.

ANOTHER SOURCE OF EXPORT LOAN GUARANTEES

The **SBA-EXIM Co-Guarantee Program** provides for co-guarantees to small business exporters and export trading companies. The co-guarantees shall extend to loans in principal amounts ranging from $200,000 to $1 million on a per-borrower basis and shall cover 85% of the loan amount.

The terms and conditions of co-guarantees, except where otherwise provided, are determined by SBA rules and regulations for **Export Revolving Line of Credit (ERLC)** loans.

Proceeds can be used only to finance labor and materials needed for manufacturing or wholesaling for export, and to penetrate or develop foreign markets.

Contact: Small Business Administration, 1441 L Street, N.W., Washington, DC 20416.

YET ANOTHER SOURCE OF LOAN GUARANTEES; THIS ONE HAS INSURANCE FOR EXPORTERS TOO

The **Overseas Private Investment Corporation** (a government agency) offers the **Contractors and Exporters Program** to improve the competitive position of American contractors and exporters seeking to do business in the developing nations. OPIC offers specialized insurance and financing services.

Many developing countries require foreign firms to post bid, performance or advance payment guaranties in the form of standby letters of credit when bidding on or performing overseas contracts. OPIC's political risk insurance for contractors and exporters protects against the arbitrary or unfair drawing of such letters of credit.

In addition, contractors and exporters may obtain insurance against the risks of currency inconvertibility, confiscation of tangible assets and bank accounts, war, revolution, insurrection and civil strife, and losses sustained when a government owner fails to settle a dispute in accordance with the provisions of the underlying contract.

OPIC also offers a special loan guarantee program for small business contractors to assist with their credit needs. This plan provides an OPIC guarantee of up to 75% of a stand-by letter of credit that is issued to a financial institution on behalf of a small-business contractor.

Contact: Overseas Private Investment Corporation, 1615 M Street, N.W., Washington, DC 20527. Phone toll-free (800) 424- 6742; for businesses within Washington, DC call 457-7010.

WORKING CAPITAL GUARANTEES FOR EXPORTERS

Exporting is an important opportunity for many American companies. Sometimes, however, small and medium-size businesses have trouble obtaining the working capital they need to produce and market goods and services for sale abroad.

Despite their credit worthiness, these potential exporters find commercial banks and other lenders reluctant to offer them working capital financing. Some companies have already reached the borrowing limits set for them by their banks.

Others do not have the type or amount of collateral their banks require. That's why the **Export-Import Bank** of the United States developed the program. **Eximbank** does not lend to exporters directly. Instead, it encourages commercial banks and other lenders to make working capital loans by guaranteeing that, in the event of default by the exporter, Eximbank will repay most of the loan.

For more information ask about the Working Capital Guarantee Program.

Contact: Export-Import Bank of the United States, 811 Vermont Avenue N.W., Washington, DC 20571. Phone toll-free (800) 424-5201; firms in Alaska, Hawaii and Washington DC should call (202) 566-8860.

MONEY AND INSURANCE FOR INVESTING IN OVERSEAS VENTURES

American investors planning to share significantly in the equity and management of an overseas venture can often utilize OPIC's finance programs for medium- to long-term financing.

To obtain OPIC financing, the venture must be commercially and financially sound, within the demonstrated competence of the proposed management, and sponsored by an investor having a proven record of success in the same or closely related business.

OPIC's financing commitment of a new venture may extend to, but not exceed, 50% of the total project cost. A larger participation may be considered for an expansion of a successful, existing enterprise.

Currently OPIC provides financing to investors through two major programs. Direct loans, which are available only for ventures sponsored by, or significantly involving, U.S. small businesses or cooperatives, and Loan guaranties, which are available to all businesses regardless of size.

OPIC will issue a guarantee under which funding can be obtained from a variety of U.S. financial institutions. The guarantee covers both commercial and political risks.

While private investors generally have the capability to assess the commercial aspects of doing business overseas, they may be hesitant to undertake long-term investments abroad, given the political uncertainties of many developing nations. To alleviate these uncertainties, OPIC insures U.S. investments against three major types of political risks.

Inconvertibility coverage protects an investor against the inability to convert into U.S. dollars the local currency received as profits, earnings, or return of capital on an investment. OPIC's inconvertibility coverage also protects against adverse discriminatory exchange rates.

Expropriation protects the investor not only against classic nationalization of his enterprise or the taking of property, but also a variety of situations which might be described as 'creeping expropriation.'

Coverage also is provided against political violence for loss due to bellicose actions (war, revolution, insurrection) and politically motivated civil strife.

Contact: Overseas Private Investment Corporation, 1615 M Street N.W., Washington, DC 20527. Phone toll-free (800) 424-6742; for businesses in Washington, DC, call 457-7010.

ASSISTANCE IN OBTAINING CAPITAL FOR SMALL BUSINESS INNOVATIVE RESEARCH

A system is available to identify potential sources of capital that may help SBIR awardees commercialize their research and development activities. This system is a free service that provides a list of potential investors such as venture capitalists, corporations, and state government programs.

The database is searchable by technology and industry areas, thereby allowing the office to identify the sources of capital most likely to be interested in a particular company.

This system was also designed to assist SBIR awardees seeking Phase II awards which require that special consideration be given to proposals demonstrating Phase III non-Federal capital commitments.

Contact: Innovation, Research, and Technology Office, Small Business Administration, 1441 L Street N.W., Room 500, Washington, DC 20416. Phone (202) 653-6458.

MONEY FOR POLLUTION CONTROL

Businesses may be eligible for pollution control financing if they are unable to obtain private financing on terms or at rates comparable to businesses which do not fit the SBA definition of a small business.

Loan proceeds may be used for aspects of constructing and placing into operation any eligible facility which the SBA determines is likely to prevent, reduce, abate, or control noise, air, or water pollution.

SBA has several options for the kinds of financing instruments that can be used. Lenders can also generate funds for the loans by using marketable securities such as taxable bonds and debentures within authorized loan limits. The principal is not to exceed $5 million.

Contact: Small Business Administration, Pollution Control Financing Staff, 1441 L Street N.W., Washington, DC 20416. Phone (202) 653-2548.

GRANTS FOR BROADCASTING STATIONS

The **Public Telecommunications Facilities Program** provides grants to assist in the planning and construction of public telecommunications facilities. Special emphasis is placed on extending public broadcasting signals to currently unserved areas. Construction grants are awarded as matching grants up to 75% of the total cost. Planning grants are awarded up to 100% of the funds necessary for planning a project.

Special consideration is given to women and minorities.

Contact: Public Telecommunications Facilities Program, National Telecommunications and Information Administration, U.S. Department of Commerce, Washington, DC 20230. Phone Dennis Connors at (202) 377-5802.

EQUITY LOANS

Chapters Five and Six have more details on equity loans. Equity investments and long-term loans are available from small business investment companies (SBICs) and section 301(d) small business investment companies which are privately owned firms licensed by the SBA and partly funded by the Federal Government.

Loans must be of at least five years maturity, and interest rates, which are subject to negotiation, cannot exceed 15%. SBICs and 301(d)s generally emphasize income-generating investments, such as convertible debentures and straight long-term debt. They tend to be most active in providing growth capital to established businesses, and are active in financing high-technology, start-up enterprises.

The applicant should prepare a business plan that describes its operations, financial condition, and financing requirements — detailing information on products, new product lines, patent positions, market and competitive data, sales and distribution, key personnel, and other pertinent factors.

Your nearest SCORE office can be of help in preparing the proper business plan. See the section on SCORE, (Service Corps of Retired Executives). Note that Section 301(d) SBICs finance only socially or economically disadvantaged small business.

Contact: Small Business Administration, Office of SBIC Operations, Room 810, 1441 L Street N.W., Washington, DC 20416. Phone (202) 653-6584.

SAVE MONEY ON TAXES, BECOME A FOREIGN SALES CORPORATION

A **Foreign Sales Corporation (FSC)** is a corporation set up in a qualifying foreign nation or U.S. possession that obtains an exemption on corporate taxes on a portion of the profits earned on exports or services. Usually 15% of the profits are tax-free.

There are "regular" FSCs and Small FSCs; Small FSCs' rules are easier to cope with.

To get a brochure on the rules and some applications call Helen Burroughs at (202) 377-3277 or write the Office of Trade Finance, U.S. Department of Commerce, International Trade Administration, Washington, DC 20230.

STARTING A FEDERAL CREDIT UNION

The **National Credit Union Administration** will explain how to get started, help prepare the charter application, assist in start-up operations and provide depositor insurance.

For established credit unions in low-income communities it also offers direct loans.

The guidelines for eligibility are that you can start a credit union if you have an association with at least 300 members, have an employee group of 200 or more, or live in a rural community with 500 or more families. In 1987, 315 new federal credit union charters were granted.

For more information ask for the Credit Union Information Package. Contact: National Credit Union Administration, 1776 G St. N.W., Washington, DC 20456. Phone (202) 357-1000. For information on loans phone Mr. Floyd Lancaster at (202) 357-1140.

ECONOMIC INJURY DISASTER LOANS

The **Disaster Assistance Division** of the **Small Business Administration** can help if your business concern suffers economic injury as a result of natural disasters. If the business was within the disaster area, see the next entry, Physical Disaster Loans.

In 1987, 585 of these loans were made for $43 million. The terms are up to 30 years for repayment with a $500,000 limit.

The funds are for paying current liabilities which the small concern could have paid if the disaster had not occurred. Working capital for a limited period can be provided to continue operations until conditions return to normal.

For more information request the pamphlet Economic Injury Disaster Loans for Small Business.

Contact: Disaster Assistance Division, Small Business Administration, 1441 L Street N.W., Washington, DC 20416. Phone (202) 653-6879.

PHYSICAL DISASTER LOANS

The **Disaster Assistance Division** of the **Small Business Administration** can help if your business is physically damaged by a natural disaster such as a hurricane, flood, or tornado. If your business is not physically damaged, but suffers economically, see the preceding section, Economic Injury Disaster Loans.

In 1988, 22,000 loans were made for $350 million. In general the terms are for 30 years, with a limit of $500,000, although if high unemployment will result, the amount can be higher. The SBA will establish an on-site office to help with processing and disbursement.

For more information request the pamphlet Physical Disaster Loans.

Contact: Disaster Assistance Division, Small Business Administration, 1441 L Street N.W., Washington, DC 20416. Phone (202) 653-6879.

IF YOU NEED A PERFORMANCE BOND AND CAN'T GET ONE

Small contractors may find, for whatever reasons, bonding unavailable to them. If so, the Small Business Administration is authorized to guarantee to a qualified surety up to 90% of losses incurred under bid, payment, or performance bonds issued to contractors on contracts valued up to $1 million. The contracts may be for construction, supplies, or services provided by either a prime or subcontractor.

In 1987, 10,382 contractors were helped. The loan guarantees for 1989 were over $1 billion dollars.

Contact: Office of Surety Guarantees, Small Business Administration, 4040 N. Fairfax Dr., Arlington, VA 22203. Phone Howard Huegel at (703) 235-2900.

START A SMALL AIRLINE

If you'd like to provide air services to small towns, the **Department of Transportation** may be able to help. It subsidizes service to approximately 150 communities that would not otherwise have air access. The payments cover costs and return on investment. The annual payments range from $90,000 to $400,000 per destination. Approximately twenty-eight million dollars was paid in 1988.

Contact: Director, Office of Aviation Analysis, P-50, Department of Transportation, 400 Seventh St. S.W., Washington, DC 20590. Phone (202) 366-1030.

FLOOD INSURANCE

The **Federal Insurance Administration** enables persons and small businesses to purchase insurance against losses from physical damage to buildings and their contents. The premium rate is generally lower than a normal actuarial rate, reflecting a subsidy by the Federal Government. Maximum coverage is $250,000 for small business structures and $300,000 for the contents.

It has a large number of booklets available, which explain the program, design guidelines for floor damage reduction, and how to understand floor insurance rate maps, etc.

Contact: Federal Insurance Administration, FEMA, Washington, DC 20472. Phone David Cobb at (202) 646-2774.

EMERGENCY LOANS FOR FARMERS AND RANCHERS

The **Farmers Home Administration** has loans to assist family farmers, ranchers and agriculture operators to cover losses suffered from major disasters. Loans may be used to repair, restore, or replace damaged property and supplies and, under some circumstances, to refinance debts.

The maximum loan is $500,000; the interest rate is 4.5%. In 1987, 2,548 loans totaling $113 million were made.

Contact: Farmers Home Administration, Department of Agriculture, Washington, DC 20250. Phone (202) 382-1632.

LOANS FOR NON-PROFIT CORPORATIONS

The **Farmers Home Administration** has loans, loan guarantees, and grants to rural development and finance corporations that improve business, industry and employment in rural areas through the stimulation of private investment and foundation contributions.

The non-profit corporation may serve profit or nonprofit businesses but they must be local. The corporation must be authorized to do business in at least three states.

For more information, contact: Administrator, Farmers Home Administration, Department of Agriculture, Washington, DC 20250. Phone (202) 447-7967.

MONEY FOR NOT GROWING STUFF

If your green thumb has turned yellow, this is for you. For not growing cotton, corn, sorghum, barley, oats, wheat, or rice, the **Department of Agriculture** will reward you. What's the catch? You must do this by reducing the amount you usually produce.

Contact: Commodity Analysis Division, Agricultural Stabilization and Conservation Service, P.O. Box 2415, U.S. Department of Agriculture, Washington, DC 20013. Phone (202) 447-6734.

SMALL FOREST PROJECTS

If you own 1,000 acres or less of forest land capable of producing industrial wood crops, the **Forestry Incentives Program** may be of interest. The government will share up to 65% of the cost of tree planting, timber stand improvement, and site preparation. In 1989 approximately eight million dollars in cost-share assistance was provided.

Contact: Conservation and Environmental Protection Division, Department of Agriculture, P.O. Box 2415, Washington, DC 20013. Phone (202) 447-6221.

MORTGAGE INSURANCE

If you rent housing to low or middle income people, the elderly, in urban renewal areas, or are a credit risk because of low income, the **Department of Housing and Urban Development** may be able to help by providing mortgage insurance.

Contact: Insurance Division, Office of Insured Multi-family Housing Development, Department of Housing and Urban Development, Washington, DC 20410. Phone (202) 755-6223.

GRANTS FOR DESIGNERS

Grants for architecture, landscaping, fashion, design, interior decorating, and urban design are available from the **National Endowment of the Arts**.

Examples of projects that have been funded are: an urban design plan for the revitalization of a city waterfront district, a design competition for a museum of fine arts, adaptive reuse of unused school buildings, and the potential uses for vacant and derelict land in American cities.

In 1989 a total of over 4 million dollars was awarded. Ask for the booklets *National Endowment for the Arts, Guide to Programs and Design Arts Guidelines*.

Contact: Director, Design Arts Program, National Endowment for the Arts, 100 Pennsylvania Ave. N.W., Washington, DC 20506. Phone (202) 682-5437.

MONEY FOR SHIPS

The Department of Transportation's **Maritime Administration** will provide loan guarantees to promote the construction of ships for foreign and domestic commerce.

The vessels must be designed for research or for commercial use in coastwide or intercoastal trade, on the Great Lakes, on bays, rivers, lakes, etc., of the U.S., in foreign trade, or as floating drydocks. Any ship not less than five net tons (other than a towboat, barge, scow, lighter, canal boat or tank vessel of less than 25 gross tons) is eligible.

The ship owner must provide 25% of the total cost. These guarantees have been used to build large ships such as tankers, ocean-going liners, dredges, jack-up drilling rigs, and container ships. Numerous smaller ships including ocean-going and inland tugs and barges have also been funded.

Contact: Associate Administrator for Maritime Aids, Maritime Administration, Department of Transportation, Washington, DC 20590. Phone (202) 366-0364.

LOCAL DEVELOPMENT COMPANY LOANS

Groups of local citizens whose aim is to improve the economy in their area can get a **Certified Development Company Loan**. Loan proceeds may be used for land, buildings, construction, expansion, renovation, modernization, machinery, and equipment.

The Certified Development Company (504) Program operates from an entirely different philosophy than other SBA programs. Its purpose is to provide long-term financing for the expansion of policies regarding the use of business or personal businesses to expand or locate in the desired area. The program's concept differs from the "lender of last resort" philosophy inherent in many of SBA's other lending activities. Also, the Certified Development Company Program uses different size standards than SBA's regular business loan program and can offer longer loan maturities. The program can boast genuine community support and involvement because it requires at least 25 members per development company and a tightly defined area of operation

How to Set Up A Certified Development Company

Establishing a certified development company in your community is not difficult. You should:

Identify the area to be served by the certified development company.

Identify individuals interested in joining an organization that will play an important role in the economic development of their community. Certified development company membership (25 members are required) must include representation from all of the following groups: a local government, a private lending institution, a community organization, or a business organization.

Identify the officers and directors (there must be a minimum of five) including a president, a vice-president, a secretary and a treasurer. At least one private lending institution must be represented on the board. The board of directors is required to meet bimonthly and actively participate in management decisions such as the making and servicing of loans by the development company.

Identify the individuals or organizations who will provide the financial and management services that SBA requires for each participating certified development company.

Have a lawyer draw up the articles of incorporation and bylaws for the certified development company based on sample forms obtained from the SBA

Prepare a membership list with the following information:

Name, address, telephone number, occupation and percentage of ownership or voting control of each member.

Name, address, telephone number, occupation of the individual or organization performing each staff capability required by the certified development company. Identify the specific function provided by each individual and their related experience.

Certification Process

Applications for certification as a certified development company will be submitted on form 1246 to the SBA field office servicing the area in which the prospective certified development company is located. The SBA field office will forward the application, along with its recommendation, to the Associate Administrator for Financial Assistance, Washington, DC, for final determination of eligibility. Qualified companies shall receive a certificate evidencing eligibility for participation in this program. The following material must be submitted to SBA in the development company's application for certification:
— Articles of incorporation
— Bylaws
— Resolution from the board of directors that gives SBA the authority to Certify applicant
— List of officers and directors
— List of members
— List of staff capabilities and individuals who perform those functions
— Statement that no member controls more than 10% of the development company's stock or voting membership
— SBA form 912 on officers and directors
— Resume on officers, directors and individuals performing staff functions
— Organizational chart on operating structure of the certified development company
— The certified development company's operating plans

— The certified development company's area of operation and information on the place of business
— Financial statements

Application Information Required from The Certified Development Company

All exhibits must be signed and dated

A history and description of the business

A statement detailing the exact uses of the loan proceeds

A statement of the anticipated benefits from the proposed financing

SBA Form 912 (Personal History Statement) on all officers and/or directors and owners of 20% or more of the SBC affiliated stock

A balance sheet and profit and loss statement for the previous three years

A current balance sheet and a current operating statement (not over 90 days old)

A pro forma balance sheet and projected operating statement for two years

A monthly cash flow for the first 12 months of operation or three months beyond the break-even point

The names of affiliates and/or subsidiary firms

Resumes of the principals

A list which contains the original date and amount, present balance owed, interest rate, monthly payment, maturity and security for each loan or debt that your business currently has, indicating whether the loan is current or delinquent

If your business is a franchise, include a copy of the franchise agreement

Current personal financial statement for each proprietor, partner, officer and each stockholder with 20% or more ownership of the business — (Form 413)

Resolution from the Board of Directors, if a corporation, authorizing the small business concern to borrow

It should be noted that the small business concern receiving assistance may be required to submit periodic financial statements to SBA

Contact: Office of Economic Development, Small Business Administration, Room 720, 1441 L Street N.W., Washington, DC 20416. Phone (202) 653-6416.

CHAPTER 3

STATE AND LOCAL MONEY SOURCES

State financial programs have become the prime source for small business financing. Most states have a program; if you don't see one for your state listed on the following pages, check with your local chamber of commerce to see if one has recently been initiated.

Besides loans, most states have numerous other programs that may be applicable to your business. Examples include:

(1) Contracting with the state to provide services.
(2) Selling products to the state.
(3) Obtaining export assistance.
(4) Participating in a business support program.

State agencies may give you financial backing even if you've been turned down by banks or venture capitalists as the agencies come to the realization that small businesses create the most jobs. In addition, as you may have noticed by now, banks prefer to lend large amounts to one person rather than small amounts to many people. For this reason, many states have become aggressive in lending small amounts of money to lots of people. So far, state agencies tend to be less risk-conscious than traditional institutions. Some states use lottery money as the source of funding.

In some cases the states have passed legislation which attracts private institutions such as BIDCOs (Business and Industrial Development Corporations).

ALABAMA

Loans For All Businesses

The state has a loan program available to all businesses. Contact: Mr. Joe S. Knight, Executive Director, **Southern Development Council,** 671 S. Perry Street, Suite 500, Montgomery, AL 36104. (205) 264-5441.

Alabama Development Office

The **Alabama Development Office** provides technical and management training programs as well as financing through Industrial Revenue Bonds (IRBs). Through IRBs, businesses can receive financing for land, buildings, and equipment. The office is responsible for the Alabama

Industrial Development Program, which provides technical services such as screening of personnel, upgrading of skills, and on-the-job training free of charge to businesses. In addition, the office has an office of small business advocacy and a one-stop permit application office for state business licenses.

Contact: Mr. Jack Hammontree, Director, or Mr. David Rumbarger, Deputy Director, Alabama Development Office, 135 S. Union Street, Montgomery, AL 36130. (205) 263-0048.

ALASKA

Assistance for Assuming Existing Business Loans

The **Division of Investment** offers a program that assists entrepreneurs to assume existing small business loans. Applicants must demonstrate financial responsibility and good character, must have sufficient collateral, and must demonstrate knowledge of Alaska's business climate. Other factors considered are the business's potential for growth, its ability to repay the loan, and its potential to create more jobs and provide additional services to the community.

If the existing loan is for a building that was built, purchased, or refinanced under the state's small business loan program (AS 45. 95. 010-080), the building must be at least 50-percent occupied by the applicant. Applicants must be Alaskan residents 18 years old or older.

Corporations, partnerships, limited partnerships, or any other association of applicants must be 100-percent owned by a resident or residents of Alaska.

Contacts: Mr. Greg Winegar, Regional Loan Manager, Division of Investments, Department of Commerce and Economic Development, P.O. Box DI, Juneau, AK 99811. (907) 465-2510.

Mr. Bob Richardson, Regional Loan Manager, Division of Investments, Department of Commerce and Economic Development, 3601 C Street, Suite 740, Anchorage, AK 99503. (907) 562-3779.

Umbrella Bond Program

The **Umbrella Bond Program** is designed to provide long-term financing for business projects to obtain buildings, plants, property, and equipment. Any business located in the state may apply. Businesses may obtain indirect loans up to $10 million plus whatever portion the originating lender will retain. (The minimum originating lender participation amount is 10% for loans of $1 million or less; 20% for loans over $1 million.) Interest depends on the cost of the bonds.

Contact: Mr. Bert Wagnon, Executive Director, Alaska Industrial Development and Export Authority, 1577 C Street, Suite 304, Anchorage, AK 99501. (907) 274-1651.

Alaska Business Development Center

The **Alaska Business Development Center (ABDC)** began as a part of the Alaska Native Foundation in the early 1970s and incorporated independently in 1979. Since that time, ABDC has used a variety of state, federal and other funding sources. ABDC was awarded a contract by the Alaska Department of Commerce and Economic Development to operate small business support centers in Anchorage and Juneau. Services are not limited to minority businesses.

Contacts: Mr. Gary Selk, President, The Alaska Business Development Center, 143 E. 9th, Suite 250, Anchorage, AK 99501. (907) 279-7427.

Mr. Ron Walt, Site Manager, The Alaska Business Development Center, 2201 N. Jordan Avenue, Juneau, AK 99801. (807) 789-3660.

Funds for Rural Development

Alaska's **Department of Community and Regional Affairs** assists businesses through its training and rural development programs. The Rural Development Initiative (REDI) provides technical and financial assistance for economic and community development.

Contact: Ms. Judith A. Holden, Block Grant Administrator, Rural Development Division, Department of Community and Regional Affairs, P.O. Box B, Juneau, AK 99811. (907) 465-4708.

ARIZONA

Small Business Financing Programs

The responsibility for Arizona state small business programs resides with the **Arizona Department of Commerce.** The department offers assistance to companies in various growth phases, packages expansion financing for established companies, assists businesses establishing operations in Arizona, and helps with export financing and other export logistics. The Guide to Establishing a Business in Arizona, published by the Department of Commerce, provides information on registering a business, licensing requirements, taxation, environmental regulations, labor regulations, sources of funds for business development, and a list of sources for additional information.

Contact: Ms. Lois Yates, Acting Director, Arizona Department of Commerce, 1700 W. Washington Street, Phoenix, AZ 85007. (602) 542-5371.

Small business financing programs are administered by the Department of Commerce to encourage the start-up and expansion of businesses. The staff analyzes loan requests and assembles application packages on behalf of small businesses for submission to the funding sources. A revolving loan program is administered for businesses in economically distressed counties of the state. Financing available through the agency includes SBA 503/504 loans and 7(a) loans, U.S. Department of Commerce and Economic Development Administration revolving loan funds, and the U.S. Department of Housing and Urban Development's Community Development Block Grant loan funds.

Contacts: Mr. Jim Gullyes, Division Manager, Community Development and Finance Division, Arizona Department of Commerce, 1700 W. Washington Street, Phoenix, AZ 85077. (602) 255-4967.

Mr. John Lopach, Program Manager for the Community Finance Secretary, Arizona Enterprise Development Corporation, 1700 W. Washington Street, Phoenix, AZ 85007. (602) 255-4967.

Statewide SBA 504 Certified Development Company

The Arizona **Enterprise Development Corporation** was certified by the SBA to operate on a statewide basis. It offers financing to independently owned businesses with a net worth of less than $6 million under the SBA's Section 504 loan program. A 504 loan is a guaranty loan that requires a 10-percent cash down payment by the loan applicant. The SBA will guarantee the funds advanced by the corporation up to the lesser of 90% of the loan or $750,000. The interest rate for a 504 loan is the market rate.

Contacts: Ms. Patty Duff, Assistant Vice-President, Arizona Enterprise Development Corporation, 1700 W. Washington Street, Phoenix, AZ 85007. (602) 255-5705. Mr. John Lopach, Program Manager for Community Finance Secretary, Arizona Enterprise Development Corporation, 1700 W. Washington Street, Phoenix, AZ 85007. (602) 255-4967.

ARKANSAS

Intermediate and Long-Term Financing

The **Arkansas Capital Corporation** is organized as a non-profit institution and funded by the state. The corporation provides intermediate and long-term financing for fixed assets, land, and working capital. The average loan is between $350,000 and $500,000.

Contact: Mr. George H. Eagen, Executive Vice-President, Arkansas Capital Corporation, 800 Pyramid Place, 221 W. Second Street, Little Rock, AR 72201. (501) 374-9247.

Small Business Innovation Research Grants Assistance Program

The **Small Business Innovation Research Grants Assistance Program** assists small businesses in Arkansas to obtain federal research and development funds.

Contact: Mr. Chuck Myers, Research Program Manager, Arkansas Science and Technology Authority, 100 Main Street, Suite 450, Little Rock, AR 72201. (501) 371-3554.

The Seed Capital Investment Program

The Seed Capital Investment Program fosters the formation and development of innovative technology-based business enterprises that will stimulate the economy of Arkansas through increased employment and leveraging of private investment.

Contact: Mr. James T. Benham, Vice President Finance, Arkansas Science and Technology Authority, 100 Main Street, Suite 450, Little Rock, AR 72201. (501) 371-3554.

CALIFORNIA

Department of Commerce

Within the California Department of Commerce, the **Office of Small Business (OSB)** provides the following services to small businesses: advocacy, seminars, general information, management and technical counseling, and loan programs. It helps small businesses deal with regulatory agencies, provides guidance on license requirements, and acts as a link to the resources needed to solve business problems.

Among the loan programs coordinated through the Office of Small Business are the following:

- Through the **Small Business Loan Guarantee Program**, loan guarantees are available to small firms unable to obtain financing at reasonable cost and terms. Guarantees are issued by affiliated regional corporations up to $350,000 or 90%, whichever is less, for a maximum term of seven years. Most are short-term loans under $100,000, revolving lines of credit, or agricultural loans.

- In the **New Product Development Program**, qualified affiliated regional corporations are authorized to make royalty-based investments in small firms to bring to market new products and processes that are beyond the theoretical development stage. Implementation procedures and regulations are being developed.

- **Energy Reduction Loans** are available to eligible small businesses for the purchase and installation of energy-saving equipment or devices. Implementation procedures and regulations are now being developed.

- The **Hazardous Waste Reduction Loan Program** provides loans for small firms to finance the acquisition and installation of hazardous waste reduction equipment and processes. Implementation procedures and regulations are being developed.

- Through the **Farm Loan Program**, eligible rural development corporations may provide loans to farmers using funds allocated by the state. A portion of these loans may be guaranteed by an agency of the federal government. The effective date for this program was April 1, 1988.

Contacts: Mr. Richard Nelson, Executive Director, or Ms. Anne Roberts, Deputy Director, Office of Small Business, Department of Commerce, 1121 L Street, Suite 501, Sacramento, CA 95814. (916) 445-6545.

The **Office of Local Development** and the public and private sectors work together to diversify and strengthen local economies and provide jobs for local residents. The office promotes economic development as an ongoing function of local government by providing case studies, handbooks, slide shows, and other information on topics such as downtown revitalization, the streamlining of the permit process, and the formation of local development corporations. The office also provides direct loan development through the state's revolving loan programs and some limited loan application packaging assistance.

Financing mechanisms from the Office of Local Development include the following:

- The **Enterprise Zone Loan Program** is designed to strengthen local economies through job creation and retention. It is limited to declared enterprise zones. The maximum loan amount is $350,000 and the term can be as long as 20 years.

- Through the **Community Development Block Grant-Nonentitlement Program**, eligible cities with populations of fewer than 50,000 and counties with populations of fewer than 200,000 may obtain funds for a variety of activities that benefit small businesses, including the acquisition, rehabilitation, and construction of public works facilities, housing clearance and rehabilitation, and economic development.

- The **Small Business Revitalization Program** provides loan packaging assistance for eligible businesses applying for assistance from the Small Business Administration and the U.S. Department of Housing and Urban Development.

- The **Sudden and Severe Economic Dislocation Program** provides predevelopment grants and business loans within eligible areas that have experienced major plant closures and employment losses within the last year. Contacts: Mr. Al Gianini, Director, or Mr. Brian McMahon, Deputy Director, Office of Local Development, Department of Commerce, 1121 L Street, Suite 600, Sacramento, CA 95814. (916) 322-1398.

Business and Industrial Development Corporations

Business and Industrial Development Corporations (BIDCOs) provide financial assistance to California firms in cooperation with the U.S. Small Business Administration, pursuant to section 7(a) of the U.S. Small Business Act. They are publicly chartered and privately funded corporations for small business development, regulated by the State Banking Department.

Contacts: Mr. Richard Nelson, Executive Director, or Ms. Anne Roberts, Deputy Director, Office of Small Business, Department of

Commerce, 1121 L Street, Suite 501, Sacramento, CA 95814. (916) 445-6545.

SAFE-BIDCOS

The **State Assistance Fund for Energy, (California) Business and Industrial Development Corporation (SAFE-BIDCO)** is a state-owned non-profit corporation. Like other BIDCOs, it makes loans in conjunction with SBA's guarantee program. It can also assist small firms working with the state's Export Finance Office or the seven regional development corporations that provide state guarantees for loans.

Firms are eligible for SAFE-BIDCO loans if they (1) are involved with an energy product or project, (2) export California products, or (3) are owned by women or minorities. Terms are flexible: loans can range from $25,000 to $550,000 for five to twenty years. These loans can help a firm acquire assets, provide working capital, or restructure an existing debt. SAFE-BIDCO works with many other agencies to boost economic development, job creation, minority opportunity, energy conservation, and export growth.

Contact: Mr. Paul O. Cormier, President, State Assistance Fund for Energy, California Business and Industrial Development Corporation, 1014 2nd Street, 3rd Floor, Sacramento, CA 95814. (916) 422-3321 or toll-free (800) 343-7233.

California Pollution Control Financing Authority

Created in 1973, the **California Pollution Control Financing Authority** is an independent state agency. Companies that most fully comply with air and water quality regulations or have waste disposal projects are eligible for tax-exempt financing. The authority will fund the cost of a project including land, buildings, equipment, engineering, and related professional expenses.

Contact: Mr. Douglas Chandler, Executive Secretary, California Pollution Control Financing Authority, 915 Capitol Mall, Room 280, Sacramento, CA 95814. (916) 445-9597.

Alternative Energy Source Financing Authority

Established in 1980, the **Alternative Energy Source Financing Authority** assists companies using new energy projects developed by private businesses.

Contact: Mr. Keith Seegmiller, Acting Executive Secretary, Alternative Energy Source Financing Authority, 915 Capitol Mall, Room 280, Sacramento, CA 95814. (916) 445-9597.

California Export Finance Program

The **California Export Finance Office** (CEFO), a unit of the **California State World Trade Commission**, provides both working capital (preshipment) and accounts receivable (post-shipment) loan guarantees to assist in the financing of California exports. Applicants must have a solid export order in hand and at least one year of experience.

CEFO can guarantee up to 85% of a qualified loan, with a maximum guarantee of $350,000, for as long as 360 days. Past CEFO guarantees have supported transactions ranging in size from $25,000 to $5 million. A preshipment guarantee can provide working capital needed to finance the cost of labor, material, and other expenses leading to an export sale. A post-shipment guarantee enables an exporter to extend terms to a foreign buyer.

The CEFO became operational in mid-1985. To date, the office has supported over $52 million in California export sales. A recent pilot agreement with the U.S. Small Business Administration created a joint loan guarantee arrangement by the two agencies that can provide for a working capital loan of up to $822,000.

Contacts: Mr. Tom Hodge, Marketing Research Specialist, California Export Finance Office, 107 S. Broadway, Suite 8039, Los Angeles, CA 90012. (213) 620-2433.

Ms. Sally Hugh, Marketing Specialist, California Export Finance Office, World Trade Center 250-S, San Francisco, CA 94111. (415) 557-8912.

COLORADO

Loans for New and Expanding Businesses

The **Office of Business Development** works to attract businesses seeking new locations and to retain the state's existing businesses. Local business development loans, established through grants from the **Colorado Department of Local Affairs**, are available for new or expanding businesses. The loans can provide 20 to 40% of the total amount of financing, but are not available in every part of the state.

Contact: Mr. John Greuling, Director, Office of Business Development, Office of Economic Development, 1625 Broadway, Suite 1710, Denver, CO 80202. (303) 892-3840.

Programs for Housing and Exporters

Colorado Housing and Finance Authority (CHFA), a quasi-government corporation, was established in 1973 to finance housing through the issuance of tax-exempt securities. In 1982, the Colorado General Assembly authorized CHFA to develop and operate programs to assist small business. Currently, CHFA offers the Quality Investment Capital (QIC) program, the bank participation (ACCESS) program, and the Colorado Export Credit Insurance program.

The QIC program is funded by the Colorado State Treasurer and is administered by CHFA to provide fixed-rate financing for small business loans guaranteed by the SBA.

ACCESS is a small business financing tool for fixed assets, created through participation in a bank-generated first mortgage funded as part of an SBA 504 financing package. ACCESS benefits to borrowers include:

- Fixed-rate loans for 20 years.

- Fixed rates for all qualified projects at 10.5%; industrial, manufacturing, or wholesale distribution projects may be eligible for a rate of 9.95%.

- A minimum loan amount of $100,000. There is no maximum.

Colorado, through CHFA, was the first state to offer exporters a way to insure their foreign receivables under the umbrella policy of the Foreign Credit Insurance Association (FCIA). FCIA is an agent of the Export-Import Bank of the United States; this insurance is backed by the U.S. Government. A Colorado Export Credit insurance policy will cover 90% of commercial risk and 100% of political risk, based on the gross invoice amount.

Contact: Mr. Michael Marez, Director, Commercial Programs Division, Colorado Housing and Finance Authority, 777 Pearl Street, Denver, CO 80203-3716. (303) 861-8962.

Quality Agricultural Loan

The **Colorado Agricultural Development Authority** (CADA) offers additional financing to Colorado agricultural producers through its Quality Agricultural Loan (QAL) program. The QAL program is a source of funds administered by CADA to make competitive fixed-rate financing for up to seven years to state farmers and ranches. Loans are made by the existing lending community, utilizing the Farmers Home Administration (FmHA) guaranteed loan program. Once a lender has received a loan guarantee from the FmHA, CADA can purchase the guaranteed portion of the loan. The maximum allowable operating loan, including refinancing of original debt, is $400,000. FmHA will no longer consider farm ownership loans.

Contact: Mr. Bob McLavey, Administrative Officer, Colorado Department of Agriculture, Colorado Agricultural Development Authority, 1525 Sherman Street, Room 406, Denver, CO 80203. (303) 866-2811.

SBA 503/504 Certified Development Companies

Five Colorado development companies, located in Denver, Colorado Springs, and Pueblo, are lending to small and medium-sized businesses at fixed rates for terms of 10 or 20 years. Companies must create one job for every $15,000 they receive in financing. A 504 loan is funded through the sale of a debenture that is guaranteed by the U.S. Small Business Administration for up to $750,000 or 40% of the total cost of land, buildings, and equipment. City and County of Denver: Ms. Julie Bender, Economic Development Specialist, Denver Urban Economic Development Corporation, 303 W. Colfax Avenue, Suite 1025, Denver, CO 80204. (303) 575-5540. Pueblo County: Dr. Tom Autobee, President, Southern Colorado Local Development Company, 108 E. Pitkin Avenue, Pueblo, CO 81004. (303) 544-7133. El Paso County: Ms. Marian Swanger, Acting Executive Director, Old Colorado City Development Company, 1112 W. Colorado Avenue, Colorado Springs, CO 80904. (303) 578-6962.

Statewide Contact: Mr. John Burger, Executive Director, Community Economic Development Company of Colorado, 1801 California Street, Suite 2840, Denver, CO 80202. (303) 893-8989.

CONNECTICUT

Exporters Revolving Loan Fund

The International Division encourages both foreign and domestic companies to locate or invest in Connecticut. The division promotes trade through a trade lead program, publishes a licensing and joint venture brochure, sponsors trade missions, and participates in trade shows. Also available are an Exporters Revolving Loan Fund to encourage export opportunities for small to medium-sized companies, as well as other incentive programs.

Contact: Mr. Gary H. Miller, Director International Division, Connecticut Department of Economic Development, 210 Washington Street, Hartford, CT 06106. (203) 566-3842.

Capital Formation for Small Business

The **Connecticut Development Authority** is a public agency established to assist in capital formation for small business. The authority is governed by a board of directors that includes the state treasurer, the commissioner of economic development, and the secretary of the **Office of Policy and Management**. The authority assists business through the following programs: the **Umbrella Bond Program**, the **Mortgage Insurance Program**, the **Naugatuck Valley Revolving Loan Program**, the **Connecticut Growth Fund**, and the **Comprehensive Business Assistance Fund**.

The **Connecticut Growth Fund** provides up to $1 million of fixed asset or working capital financing to businesses with sales of $10 million or less on terms of 5 to 20 years.

The **Comprehensive Business Assistance Fund** provides up to $500,000 of financing to businesses affect by natural or economic disaster and up to $250,000 of financing to certain targeted businesses with sales of $3 million or less.

The **Naugatuck Valley Revolving Loan Program** provides supplemental financing in amounts up to $200,00 to industrial businesses in the Naugatuck Valley area and certain other areas of Connecticut.

Through the **Umbrella Bond Program** the authority issues bonds on behalf of small firms to cover small amounts.

Under the **Credit Insurance Program** the Authority has the ability to insure both bonds and privately financed loans. The program is especially effective in helping small and medium-sized firms, because the insured portion of the loans is backed by the full faith credit of the state. The Authority is responsible for the statewide SBA 503 program.

Contact: Mr. Richard L. Higgins, Executive Director, Connecticut Development Authority, 217 Washington Street, Hartford, CT 06106. (203) 522-3730.

Risk Capital Investments for New Products

A quasi-public, nonprofit organization, the **Connecticut Product Development Corporation** makes risk capital investments in Connecticut firms developing new products. Up to 60% of development costs is provided in exchange for royalties, typically 5%, on the sale of sponsored products. Capitalized by general obligation bonds of the state, the goal of the organization is self-sufficiency based on royalty income. Loans of up to $300,000 at favorable interest rates for terms up to six years are offered to provide working capital for market introduction of new products. Loans must be matched dollar-for-dollar from the private sector.

Contact: Mr. Burton A. Jonap, Vice President, Connecticut Product Development Corporation, 78 Oak Street, Hartford, CT 06106. (203) 566-2920.

DELAWARE

Special Financing Programs for Businesses

The **Business Finance Division** offers several special financing programs for businesses. Financing representatives can assist businesses in processing finance applications, a procedure which can be completed in nine weeks when the borrower's needs are not unusual.

Contact: Mr. Darrell J. Minott, Director of Business Finance, Delaware Development Office, 99 Kings Highway, P.O. Box 1401, Dover, DE 19903. (302) 736-4271.

Statewide Financial Assistance to New or Expanding Businesses

By issuing industrial revenue bonds (IRBs), the Delaware Economic Development Authority is able to provide statewide financial assistance to new or expanding businesses. IRBs are purchased by investors at low interest rates because interest from the bonds is exempt from federal and state income taxes for Delaware residents. Business owners may thereby obtain long-term financing at interest rates below the prime rate. Bond proceeds may be used for the acquisition of land, buildings, and equipment. Organizations qualifying as 501(c)(3) may utilize bond proceeds for working capital. Projects eligible for IRB financing include the following:

- Manufacturing projects, including office and warehouse space as long as it is a related part of the overall manufacturing facility.

- Agriculture-related projects involving the acquisition of equipment to be used for farming purposes by an individual who has not at any time had any direct or indirect ownership interest in substantial amounts of farmland.

- Projects supporting the exempt activities of 501(c)(3) organizations.

Contact: Ms. Lee K. Porter, Bond Administrator, Delaware Economic Development Authority, 99 Kings Highway, P.O. Box 1401, Dover, DE 19903. (302) 736-4271.

DISTRICT OF COLUMBIA

The District of Columbia offers businesses a wide range of financing programs. The District-wide SBA 503/504 loan program is operated through the Washington, DC **Local Development Corporation**, which is staffed by the **Office of Business and Economic Development**. SBA 503/504 loans are offered for fixed-asset financing for terms of up to 25 years and for amounts of up to $500,000 or 40% of total project cost, whichever is less. Eligible uses of funds include the purchase of land, buildings, machinery, and equipment, building renovation and construction, and leasehold improvements.

The OBED offers several direct loan programs. The revolving loan fund offers small and medium-sized businesses direct, short-term loans in conjunction with private lenders. Typical uses are for short-term financing for equipment and inventory purchases. The OBED also offers the **Participation Loan Program** (PLP), designed to broaden the spectrum of businesses eligible for financing. PLP direct loans are for periods of one to 20 years, depending on the use of funds.

Contact: Ms. Pamela Vaughn-Cooke-Henry, Chief, Financial Services Division, Office of Business and Economic Development, 1111 E Street N.W. , Suite 700, Washington, DC 20004. (202) 727-6600.

The **Neighborhood Commercial Services Division** of OBED, under its **Neighborhood Commercial Revitalization Program** (NCRP), offers special loans through its **Facade Improvement Loan Program** to revitalize neighborhood commercial corridors. A unique technical assistance component is provided by OBED to assist loan recipients from the design stage through completion of construction.

Contact: Mr. Victor Selman, Acting Chief, Neighborhood Commercial Services Division, Office of Business and Economic Development, 1111 E Street N.W. , Suite 700, Washington, DC 20004. (202) 727-6600.

Economic Development Finance Corporation

The **Business Purchase Assistance Program** (BPAP) is a new effort to directly stimulate business and commercial revitalization in the District's neighborhood commercial corridors. The BPAP includes two programs: the **Real Property Acquisition Loan Program** (RPA) and the **Business Acquisition and Expansion Loan Program** (BAE). The RPA provides loans for the acquisition of primarily vacant real property in certain targeted areas of the District. The BAE provides loans for acquiring for-profit corporations, partnerships, or proprietorships.

Contact: Mr. Michael Gallie, President, District of Columbia Economic Development Finance Corporation, 1660 L Street N.W., Suite 308, Washington, DC 20036. (202) 775-8815.

FLORIDA

The **Community Development Section** encourages business and economic development in small Florida communities by providing technical assistance for industrial recruitment and assisting in incubator development. The Section administers a retention and expansion program to assist communities in specific areas of need by providing departmental staff to serve as consultants to communities. The section can also help organize local venture capital pools and encourage support of an entrepreneurship club network consisting of lawyers, bankers, accountants, venture capitalists, entrepreneurs, and others who support and promote entrepreneurship.

Contact: Ms. Bridgett Merrill, Supervisor, Bureau of Business Assistance, Florida Department of Commerce, G-26 Collins Building, Tallahassee, FL 32399-2000. (904) 488-9357.

The **Finance Section** helps businesses locate financing alternatives to meet their needs, assists communities in locating financing for economic development efforts and projects, and administers the Economic Development Transportation Fund, which makes financing available for public road improvements needed to support business starts or expansions.

The Section also assists with loan packaging for the SBA 504 program and provides information on the SBA 7(a) loan program. The SBA 504 loan program provides results in job creation. The 7(a) loan program provides user financing for start-up, expansion, and property.

The **Florida First Capital Finance Corporation** (FFCFC), a nonprofit organization certified to issue debentures, offers financial assistance to Florida businesses in conjunction with the U.S. Small Business Administration's 504 loan program. The Florida Department of Commerce provides loan packaging assistance. An SBA 504 loan may be used to buy land, construct buildings, buy existing buildings, buy machinery and equipment, modernize, renovate and restore an existing facility including leasehold improvement. The borrower must not have a net worth over $6 million or an average net profit for the previous two years of $2 million, and within two years of loan closing must create one job for every $15,000 provided.

Contact: Mr. Mark Dowis, Bureau of Business Assistance, Florida Department of Commerce, G-26 Collins Building, Tallahassee, FL 32399-2000. (904) 487-0463.

The **Entrepreneurship Network Program** encourages the affiliation of venture capitalists, bankers, lawyers, accountants, business consultants, successful entrepreneurs, university resource people, and others who provide assistance to entrepreneurs. Currently, 20 such local organizations are located throughout the state.

Contact: Mr. Maury Hagerman, Development Representative, Bureau of Business Assistance, Florida Department of Commerce, G-26 Collins Building, Tallahassee, FL 32399-2000. (904) 488-9357.

The **Florida High Technology Innovation Research and Development Fund** is a $1.5-million venture capital pool with up to $50,000 in equity financing for research and development of new and existing high-tech businesses in the state. Patterned after the federal Small Business Innovation Research program, this fund encourages innovation in designated high-tech areas.

Contact: Mr. Ray Iannucci, Executive Director, Florida High Technology and Industry Council, Room 501A, Collins Building, 107 W. Gaines Street, Tallahassee, FL 32399-2000. (904) 487-3136.

The **Florida Black Business Investment Board**, also created by the Florida Small and Minority Business Act of 1985, concentrates on obtaining financial assistance for Florida's black-owned and black-operated firms. The state appropriated $5 million for this purpose. Direct loans are provided.

Contact: Mr. Cleve Warren, Executive Director, Florida Black Business Investment Board, 315 S. Calhoun Street, Barnett Bank Building, Suite 490, Tallahassee, FL 32301. (904) 487-4850.

GEORGIA

The **Rural Development Initiative** began operations in August 1986, and serves six rural counties in south central Georgia. The organization works with industry and trade groups to encourage economic development in rural areas, and it has helped finance business start-ups and expansions.

The Rural Development Initiative is funded by the state legislature and the counties it serves.

Contact: Mr. R. A. Foss, Executive Director, Rural Development Initiative, P.O. Box 28, Soperton, GA 30457. (912) 529-3367.

In 1980, the governor and the General Assembly established the **Advanced Technology Development Center** (ATDC), part of the State University System, located on campus at the Georgia Institute of Technology. The ATDC encourages high-technology growth in the state by supporting technology-based entrepreneurs and small businesses, helping existing businesses with new product development, assisting in the formation of venture capital, and providing educational programs. A consortium of Emory University, the University of Georgia, the Georgia institute of Technology, and the Advanced Technology Development Center has been established. The ATDC serves as the focal point of these efforts and provides the staff of coordinate research at the three universities.

Contact: Dr. Richard T. Meyer, Director, Advanced Technology Development Center, 430 10th Street N.W., Suite N-116, Atlanta, GA 30318. (404) 894-3575.

HAWAII

Department of Business and Economic Development

The **Small Business Information Service** (SBIS) is primarily an information and referral service providing data on government requirements, training and consulting services, business plan writing assistance, market research, alternative financing, and other resources available to small firms. The SBIS was established in 1984.

SBIS has in operation a business permits center to facilitate the business registration and permit application process. This "one-stop" center provides information on required permits and accept completed applications and fees. The center also maintains information on applicable state and federal laws and county ordinances, and on financial assistance programs available for commercial activities.

Contacts: Mr. Dennis Ling, Coordinator, Small Business Information Service, 250 South King Street, Honolulu, HI 96813. (808) 548-7645.

Mr. Tom Smyth, Division Head, Business Services Division Department of Business and Economic Development, P.O. Box 2359, Honolulu, HI 96804. (808) 548-4608.

The **Financial Assistance Branch** has two programs to assist small business: the **Hawaii Capital Loan Program**, and the **Innovation Development Loan Program**.

The **Hawaii Capital Loan Program** provides loans of up to $1 million to business owners unable to secure financing from conventional sources. The interest rate is 7.5% with a maximum term of 25 years. Since the program's inception in 1964, 416 loans have been made for a total of $19. 4 million.

The **Hawaii Innovation Development Loan Program** has funding available for the development of new products or inventions. However, relatively few have applied for assistance through the program, and none have qualified. The loan terms are 7.5%, with a $50,000 ceiling and a maximum term of 10 years.

Contact: Ms. Doreen Shishido, Chief Financial Assistance Branch, Department of Business and Economic Development, 250 South King Street, Honolulu, HI 96813. (808) 548-4616.

Agricultural Loan Division

Within the Department of Agriculture is the **Agricultural Loan Division**, which directly promotes agricultural development by providing or facilitating loans to qualified farmers through a series of programs, including the Regular Agricultural Loan Program, the New Farmer Loan Program, the Emergency Loan Program, the Orchard Loan Program, the Hawaii Agricultural Products Program and the Aquaculture Loan Program.

Contact: Mr. Richard Morimoto, Administrator, Agricultural Loan Division, Department of Agriculture, P.O. Box 22159, Honolulu, HI 96822. (808) 548-7126.

IDAHO

The Idaho Department of Commerce offers a variety of services to small firms, including: site location, information on state and private financial assistance, **Community Development Block Grants; Industrial Revenue Bonds, Idaho Travel Council Grants**, information on regulations, permits, and licensing; international trade assistance; travel and tourism promotion, and management and technical assistance programs.

Contact: Mr. Gordon Thompson, Administrator, Economic Development Division, Idaho Department of Commerce, 700 West State Street, Boise, ID 83720. (208) 334-2470.

Venture Capital

The **Economic Development Division** works with private investors to create a venture capital group for investment within the state. Special emphasis is placed on assisting companies in the state's traditional industries using high technology equipment and methods. Idaho also has an industrial revenue bond program.

Contact: Mr. Gordon Thompson, Administrator, Economic Development Division, Idaho Department of Commerce, 700 West State Street, Boise, ID 83720. (208) 344-2470.

The **Division of Science and Technology** cooperates with several high technology firms in Idaho in an effort to attract more high-tech companies to the state and to obtain venture capital.

Contact: Mr. Rick Tremblay, Administrator, Division of Science and Technology, Idaho Department of Commerce, 700 West State Street, Boise, ID 83720. (208) 334-2470.

ILLINOIS

Department of Commerce and Community Affairs, Small Business Assistance Bureau

The **Small Business Innovation Research (SBIR) Program** stimulates technology innovation, encourages small innovative firms to participate in government research, and provides for the conversion of research results into commercial applications. SBIR money is awarded in three phases. Seventy-five Illinois companies have won SBIR awards; many of those companies are multiple awardees.

Contact: Mr. Peter Ramirez, Manager, Business Development Division, Small Business Assistance Bureau, Illinois Department of Commerce and Community Affairs, 620 East Adams, Springfield, IL 62701. (217) 785-6160.

The **Business Finance and Energy Assistance Division** contributes to economic development in the state by promoting and assisting in the growth and development of small business concerns. The principal objectives of the division are to foster increased employment opportunities, expand business and industry, and reduce energy costs by providing free energy audits. The division offers financial assistance through the following programs:

- The **Build Illinois Small Business Development Loan Program** provides direct financing to small businesses at below-market interest rates in cooperation with private-sector lenders. Funds can be used for working capital, the lease or purchase of land and buildings, construction or renovation of fixed assets, and the lease, purchase or installation of machinery and equipment. Debt refinancing or contingency funding is not allowed. Loans cannot exceed 25% of the cost of the business expansion. The maximum loan amount for any one project is $750,000.

- The Build Illinois Small Business Development **Micro Loan Program provides direct financing to small businesses at a below-market interest rate in cooperation with private-sector lenders. The purpose of the program is to help small businesses create or retain jobs and assist businesses to expand. The **Micro Loan Program** may provide up to 25% of the total project cost, or a maximum of $100,000. Debt refinancing is not permitted.

- The **Equity Investment Fund Program** is designed to stimulate the development of technology-based companies by providing equity financing to companies with significant job creation potential. The fund can provide up to one-third of the anticipated costs, but not more than $250,000 investment in any one business. The product or service should be commercialized within 24 months.

- The **Business Innovation Fund Program** provides financial aid to businesses, using a university's assistance to advance technology, create new products, or improve

manufacturing processes. Businesses may qualify for up to $100,000 in assistance for projects matched with private resources.

- The **Minority and Women Business Loan Program** provides direct financing to small businesses at below-market interest rates in cooperation with private-sector lenders. The purpose of the program is to help minority and women-owned businesses create or retain jobs. Principal and interest repayments for the loans will be used to establish and maintain a state revolving loan fund for use by other minority and women-owned businesses.

- The **Energy Conservation Interest Write-Down Program** can assist a small business in securing an attractive low-interest loan for energy-saving improvements. Funds may be used for a retrofit or upgrading of an existing structure or equipment. The department will make a one-time prepayment of 50% of the interest cost of the loan or $10,000, whichever is less. Free audits are also available.

Contact: Mr. Richard LeGrand, Manager, Business Finance and Energy Management Division, Small Business Assistance Bureau, Illinois Department of Commerce and Community Affairs, 620 East Adams, Springfield, IL 62701. (217) 785-2708.

INDIANA

Grant and Loan Programs

The **Business and Financial Services Division** is the money mover of the economic development programs. It administers grant and loan programs and channels public and private funding for infra-structure development and other economic development activities.

Contact: Mr. Charles P. Preston, Director, Business and Financial Services Division, Indiana Department of Commerce, One North Capitol Avenue, Suite 700, Indianapolis, IN 46204. (317) 232-8782.

The **International Trade Division** was established to help Indiana businesses take advantage of overseas export opportunities. The staff is available to match export opportunities with specific Indiana firms and to provide export counseling. Financial assistance is available for firms participating in overseas trade shows. The division also organizes trade missions and hosts foreign delegations visiting the state.

Contact: Mr. Phillip M. Grebe, Director, International Trade Division, Indiana Department of Commerce, One North Capitol Avenue, Suite 700, Indianapolis, IN 46204-2288. (317) 232-8845.

Indiana Statewide Certified Development

The **Indiana Statewide Certified Development Corporation** makes fixed-rate 504 plan loans to small businesses for the purchase of land and buildings (including new construction), machinery and equipment, and renovation/leasehold improvements. To be eligible, a small business must be located in Indiana; be a for-profit corporation, partnership, or proprietorship; have a new worth under $6 million; and have an average net profit, after taxes, of less than $2 million per year for the last two years. The maximum loan is $500,000 at a rate of approximately 0.75% over Treasury bonds, issued in maturities of 10 or 20 years.

Contact: Ms. Jean Wojtowicz, Secretary, Indiana Statewide Certified Development Corporation, 2506 Willowbrook Parkway, Suite 110, Indianapolis, IN 46205. (317) 253-6166.

Risk Financing

The **Indiana Community Business Credit Corporation** is a privately owned company in which Indiana financial institutions pool funds for the use of Indiana businesses unable to secure complete financing from conventional sources. This is a source of supplemental, risk-oriented financing. The minimum size project is $300,000 and a participating lender must provide at least 50% of the financing.

Contact: Ms. Jean Wojtowicz, Secretary, Indiana Community Business Credit Corporation, 2506 Willowbrook Parkway, Suite 110, Indianapolis, IN 46205. (317) 255-9704.

State-Sponsored, $10 Million Capital Fund

The **Corporation for Innovation Development** (CID) is a privately owned, state-sponsored, $10 million capital fund. Organized in 1981, CID began making investments in 1983. To date, CID has invested in 15 businesses, all in Indiana. Businesses are varied and include service, manufacturing, and technology firms. CID is the lead investor in over half of its deals and also shares investments with other venture capital funds. It has a seven-member board of directors composed of Indiana business leaders experienced in new business development and venture capital investing.

Contact: Mr. Don Taylor, Vice President, Corporation for Innovation Development, 201 North Illinois Street, Suite 1950, Indianapolis, IN 46204. (317) 237-2350.

Applied Research Ventures

The **Indiana Corporation for Science and Technology** (CST) is a partnership of businesses, government agencies, and universities. Established in 1982 to help strengthen the economy of the state through the use of science and technology, CST is a private, not-for-profit company governed by a 25-member board of directors. CST has a capital base of state funds, which the corporation invests in applied research ventures. Entrepreneurs, business persons, researchers, industrialists, and educators are encouraged to apply for funding to support research and development proposals which will result in technology-intensive products, processes, and services of significant commercial value.

Contact: Mr. Robert S. Fryer, Director of Communications, Indiana Corporation for Science and Technology, One North Capitol Avenue, Suite 925, Indianapolis, IN 46204. (317) 635-3058.

Institute for New Business Ventures

The **Indiana Institute for New Business Ventures**, a not-for-profit private corporation, was created to support the development of growth-oriented enterprises throughout the state. The institute links entrepreneurs with the management, technical, and financial resources necessary to start and successfully operate high-growth companies. The institute also conducts conferences and workshops addressing the challenges of managing and financing growing business enterprises. It is governed by a nine-member board of directors, appointed by the governor, equally representing the public, private, and university sectors.

Contact: Mr. Ilene F. Schankerman, Conference Coordinator, Indiana Institute for New Business Ventures, One North Capitol Avenue, Suite 420, Indianapolis, IN 46204. (317) 634-8418.

IOWA

Low-Interest Loans for New or Expanding Small Businesses

The new **Self-Employment Loan Program** assists low-income entrepreneurs by providing low-interest loans for new or expanding small businesses. The loans may not exceed $5,000 and the rate of interest may not exceed 5% simple interest per annum.

Contact: Ms. Sharon Dreyer, Training Liaison, Bureau of Business and Industry Training, Iowa Department of Economic Development, 200 East Grand Avenue, Des Moines, IA 50309. (515) 281-7237.

The **Iowa Product Development Corporation** (IPDC) turns ideas into new products and jobs. The Corporation was created in 1983 by the General Assembly to improve the state's economy by investing in Iowa innovation. Last year, IPDC investments helped create nearly 200 new jobs. IPDC funding comes from state appropriations and lottery funds. The funds are an investment, not a loan. Venture contracts include a payback schedule from royalties on new product sales. As proceeds are reinvested, the IPDC's fund will become self-sustaining so other Iowa business ventures can be helped.

Contact: Mr. Dan Dittemore, President, Iowa Product Development Corporation, Iowa Department of Economic Development, 200 East Grand Avenue, Des Moines, IA 50309. (515) 281-5292.

The **Targeted Small Business Loan and Equity Grant Program** was created by the legislature in 1987. The purpose of the program is to assist in the creation and expansion of minority- and women-owned businesses in Iowa. Eligible applicants must meet criteria established for small businesses and for targeted small businesses. The program provides for loans, loan subsidies, or equity substitution grants for eligible small businesses. Applications are accepted any time and are awarded on a competitive basis as funds allow.

Contact: Mr. John Seay, Targeted Small Business Loan and Equity Grant Program, Iowa Department of Economic Development, 200 East Grand Avenue, Des Moines, IA 50309. (515) 281-3585.

The purpose of the **Financing Rural Economic Development** (FRED) program is to increase business development and employment opportunities in rural Iowa. The FRED program attempts to fill the assistance gap for small rural businesses. The program is a well-rounded approach designed to address the special needs of small and rural businesses. Specifically, the program provides: technical assistance, advice and counseling to both economic development specialists and business owners / entrepreneurs; training for business owners and entrepreneurs; and financial assistance—primarily subordinate debt financing—to expanding and / or diversifying businesses and to newly formed businesses.

FRED combines federal, state, and private funds to create a revolving loan fund. The fund offers loans to small businesses in rural communities with populations of less than 20,000. Assistance is available to existing and new businesses with 50 or fewer employees.

Contact: Mr. Kent Powell, Development Finance Specialist, Iowa Department of Economic Development, 200 East Grand Avenue, Des Moines, IA 50309. (515) 281-3752.

The **Community Economic Betterment Account** (CEBA), established to invest proceeds of the Iowa lottery in local economic development projects, has helped create and retain more than 10,000 jobs, with an investment of approximately $12 million. All cities, counties, or merged area schools are eligible to apply on behalf of local enterprises that are expanding, modernizing, or relocating.

Key criteria for approval of applications are the number of jobs created, the cost per job for the CEBA funds involved in the project, and significant community interest and involvement. The funds are used to buy down principal or interest on business loans, to acquire land or buildings for construction or reconstruction, to purchase equipment, to prepare industrial sites, and to assist in other business financing.

Contact: Mr. Michael Miller, Chief, Bureau of Business Grants and Loans, Financial Assistance Division, Iowa Department of Economic Development, 200 East Grand Avenue, Des Moines, IA 50309. (515) 281-4167.

Iowa's **Community Development Block Grant** (CDBG) from the U.S. Department of Housing and Urban Development (HUD) is divided among three programs: the Economic Development Set-Aside (EDSA), which receives 25% of the allocation; the Public Facilities Set-Aside, which receives 10% of the allocation; and the regular CDBG program, which receives the majority of the annual federal dollars distributed. Community improvements such as public works projects, housing rehabilitation, and job-generating expansions are financed by the CDBG program in all counties and cities, except the nine largest Iowa cities, which receive funds directly from HUD. CDBG funds are awarded on a competitive basis.

Contacts: Mr. Michael Miller, Chief Bureau of Business Grants and Loans, Financial Assistance Division, Iowa Department of Economic Development, 200 East Grand Avenue, Des Moines, IA 50309. (515) 281-4167.

The Iowa **Small Business New Jobs Training Program** is coordinated through the state's 15 community colleges. New or expanding Iowa companies can be reimbursed for up to 50% of new employee salaries and fringe benefits for up to one year of on-the-job training. The program is initially financed by a loan, which is paid off by the diversion of incremental property taxes and a portion of the state withholding tax on the new jobs. The loan amount may not exceed $75,000.

Contacts: Ms. Dory Briles, Chief, Bureau of Business and Industry Training, Iowa Department of Economic Development, 200 East Grand Avenue, Des Moines, IA 50309. (515) 281-3600.

Low-Interest Loans

The **Linked Deposit Program** was established in 1988 to assist in financing targeted small businesses. Fifteen million dollars in low-interest loans are available for lending through Iowa financial institutions by the office of the treasurer. Loan applications from targeted small businesses may be for the purchase of land, machinery, equipment, licenses, patents, or trademarks, but not inventory.

Contact: Mr. Michael Tramontina, State Treasurer's Office, Capitol Building, Des Moines, IA 50319. (515) 281-6859.

Iowa Small Business Loan Program

The purpose of the **Iowa Small Business Loan Program** is to assist the development and expansion of small businesses in Iowa through the sale, by the Iowa Finance Authority, of bonds and notes exempt from federal income tax. A small business is defined as having fewer than 20 employees or less than $3 million in sales. The loans may be used for purchasing land, construction, building improvements, or equipment. Funds cannot be used for working capital, inventory, or operations. The maximum loan is $10 million.

Contact: Mr. Larry Tuel, Executive Director, Iowa Finance Authority, 200 East Grand Avenue, Des Moines, IA 50309. (515) 281-4058.

The **Iowa Business Development Credit Corporation** (IBDCC) stimulates economic development through loans to new or established firms in conjunction with banks, insurance companies, savings and loan associations, and other financial institutions.

Counseling also is available in finance, marketing, and management. Loan proceeds may be used to purchase land, purchase or construct buildings, machinery, equipment, and inventory, or as working capital. A portion may be used to retire debt. Nonprofit enterprises, lending or financial institutions, and firms able to acquire funds at reasonable rates from other sources are ineligible. Loans up to $500,000 are available.

The IBDCC received U.S. Small Business Administration (SBA) certification in May 1981 thereby becoming the nation's first statewide Certified Development Company. This certification allows the IBDCC to offer the SBA 503/504 loan program to businesses in every Iowa community. The IBDCC provides long-term, fixed-asset financing at a fixed rate of interest, slightly below market rate.

Contact: Mr. Don Albertson, Executive Vice President, Iowa Business Development Credit Corporation, 901 Insurance Exchange Building, Des Moines, IA 50309. (515) 282-2164.

KANSAS

Kansas Department of Commerce

The **Division of Existing Industry Development** promotes the growth, diversification, and retention of business and industry in Kansas.

Because almost all Kansas businesses are small, much of the division's activity centers around small business assistance. The small business program staff identifies and addresses the needs of existing and start-up businesses. The division provides assistance both directly and through a statewide business assistance network, channeling appropriate resources for business planning, technical help, financing, or other business problems.

Contacts: Mr. R. S. (Jack) Montgomery, Director, Mr. Bradley J. Mears, Assistant Director, Ms. Carol Burch, Manager of Field Representatives, Division of Existing Industry Development, Kansas Department of Commerce, 400 S.W. 8th, 5th Floor, Topeka, KS 66603-3957. (913) 296-5298.

Seed Capital

In order in increase the availability of risk capital in Kansas, the state grants Kansas income tax credits to investors in both certified venture capital companies and certified local seed capital pools. Both of these programs are to provide financing assistance to Kansas small businesses which may not be able to secure conventional financing.

The Department of Commerce recognizes the need for a formalized referral service for businesses requiring risk capital beyond what is available from informal networks. Currently the department is developing a network of venture capital resources for businesses looking for risk capital.

Contact: Mr. Rich Bailey, Venture Capital Specialist, Division of Existing Industry Development, Kansas Department of Commerce, 400 S.W. 8th, 5th Floor, Topeka, KS 66603-3957. (913) 296-5298.

Programs within the **Division of Community Development** that benefit small businesses include the **Community Development Block Grant** (CDBG) programs, programs for rural communities, and the Enterprise Zone Program.

Kansas provides approximately 50% of its CDBG allotment for non-entitlement areas to economic development projects involving job creating enterprises. The funds are awarded to

eligible communities, which in turn lend or grant the funds to eligible businesses.

Contact: Mr. David Bossemeyer, Economic Development Specialist, Division of Community Development, Kansas Department of Commerce, 400 S.W. 8th, 5th Floor, Topeka, KS 66603-3957. (913) 296-3004.

Kansas Venture Capital, Inc.

Kansas Venture Capital, Inc., is a licensed small business investment company which is to be capitalized with $10 million of private investment and eventually $10 million of state funds. This venture capital company was created to focus on investments solely in qualified Kansas-based businesses.

Contacts: Mr. Rex Wiggins, President, Kansas Venture Capital, Inc. 8700 Monrovia, Suite 214, Lenexa, KS 66215. (913) 888-5913. Mr. Larry High, Executive Vice President, Kansas Venture Capital, Inc. Bank IV Tower, Suite 1030, Topeka, KS 66603. (913) 233-1368.

Kansas Development Finance Authority

The **Kansas Development Finance Authority** was created in 1987 and is dedicated to improving access to capital financing for state agencies, political subdivisions, public and private organizations, and business enterprises through the issuance of bonds.

Contact: Mr. Allen Bell, President, Kansas Development Finance Authority, London State Office Building, Suite 113, 900 S.W. Jackson, Topeka, KS 66612. (913) 296-6747.

SBA 503/504 Certified Development Companies

In Kansas, there is no statewide 503/504 program. Instead, the state is served by local and regional certified development companies, which provide financial packaging services for businesses utilizing state and U.S. Small Business Administration financing programs. The state provides supplemental funding to these organizations in recognition of the service they provide.

Contact: Mr. Ronald Nicholas, President, Kansas Association of Certified Development Companies, 100 Military, Suite 214, P.O. Box 1116, Dodge City, KS 67801. (316) 227-6406.

Kansas Funds for Kansas Farmers and Small Business

This program provides for linked deposits to local banks to grant low-interest loans to financially distressed farmers and small business owners.

Contact: Mr. Lyell Ocobock, Executive Officer, Kansas Pooled Money Investment Board, 900 S.W. Jackson, Suite 304 North, Topeka, KS 66612-1220. (913) 296-3372).

KENTUCKY

Low-Interest State Loans

Low-interest state loans are available in Kentucky to partially finance manufacturing and certain non-manufacturing projects, as defined by statute. The **Kentucky Development Finance Authority** within the **Cabinet for Economic Development**, makes loans to supplement private financing.

Contact: Mr. James Jones, Executive Director, Kentucky Development Finance Authority, 2400 Capital plaza Tower, Frankfort, KY 40601. (502) 564-4554.

Loans for up to 40% of the costs of expansion by qualifying Kentucky small businesses are available through the **Commonwealth Small Business Development Corporation**, a nonprofit corporation operated by the **Kentucky Cabinet for Economic Development**. The loans assist qualified small businesses unable to obtain

financing on reasonable terms without government aid.

Contact: Ms. Theresa Middleton, President, Commonwealth Small Business Development Corporation, Kentucky Development Finance Authority, 2400 Capital Plaza Tower, Frankfort, KY 40601. (502) 564-4320.

The **Crafts Guaranteed Loan Program** provides loans up to $20,000 to qualified craftspersons.

Contact: Ms. Theresa Middleton, Executive Staff Advisor, Kentucky Development Finance Authority, 2400 Capital Plaza Tower, Frankfort, KY 40601. (502) 564-4554.

LOUISIANA

The new Louisiana Economic Development Corporation is the single review agency for all loan and grant programs of the Department of Economic Development.

Programs include: the **Small Business Innovation Research (SBIR) Matching Grant Program**, the **Venture Capital Co-investment Program**, the **Venture Capital Match Program**, the **Minority Venture Capital Match Program**, the **Minority and Women's Business Development Program**, and the **Small Business Equity Program**.

Contact: Mr. Arnold M. Lincove, Executive Director, Louisiana Economic Development Corporation, P.O. Box 94185, Baton Rouge, LA 70804-9185. (504) 342-5388.

MAINE

Direct Loan and Loan Guarantee Programs

The **Finance Authority of Maine** (FAME) assets business development and job creation by administering a variety of direct loan and loan guarantee programs for small and larger businesses, as well as project grants for research and innovation. FAME programs include loan insurance funds, grants, targeted lending, and taxable and tax-exempt bonds.

Contact: Mr. David McLaughlin, Director of Lending, Finance Authority of Maine, 83 Western Avenue, P.O. Box 949, Augusta, ME 04330. (207) 623-3263.

The purpose of the **Linked Investment Program** is to assist Maine farmers in obtaining operating loans at lower interest rates and to encourage greater private lending in agriculture. The Maine legislature authorized the state treasurer to invest up to $4 million of state funds in financial institutions at reduced interest rates. The financial institutions use the funds to provide operating loans to Maine farmers at comparatively lower rates of interest.

The loans are approved and made by lenders according to their own policies; the state treasurer makes compensating payments to the lenders to provide the interest rate savings. The Finance Authority of Maine will assist the state treasurer in administering this program.

To be eligible, an applicant's principal source of income must be derived from raising crops or livestock. The maximum investment is $250,000 per borrower. Loans are for operating funds for purchases of seed, chemicals, fertilizer, feed, veterinary services, labor, and other production inputs.

Contacts: Mr. Stanley Provus, Chief Executive Officer, Finance Authority of Maine, 83 Western Avenue, P.O. Box 949, Augusta, ME 04330. (207) 623-3263.

Mr. Sam Shapiro, Treasurer, State of Maine, State House Station #39, Augusta, ME 04333. (207) 289-2771.

MARYLAND

Loans to Small and Minority-owned Businesses

Maryland's **Small Business Development Financing Authority**, established in 1978, provides loans to small and minority-owned businesses. The Authority provides short-term financing for government contracts and long-term guarantees on financing for equipment and working capital. It also operates a surety bond guarantee program for small businesses, and an equity participation investment program for potential minority franchises.

Contacts: Mr. Stanley W. Tucker, Executive Director, Mr. David Robinson, Industrial Assistance Officer, Department of Economic and Employment Development, Redwood Towers, 217 East Redwood Street, 10th Floor, Baltimore, MD 21202. (301) 333-6975.

Maryland Office of International Trade

Established in 1986, the **Maryland Office of International Trade** helps Maryland firms sell their products and services in the international marketplace through counseling, seminars, trade shows, and grant programs.

Contact: Mr. Harold Zassenhaus, Executive Director, Maryland Office of International Trade, World Trade Center, 401 East Pratt Street, Baltimore, MD 21202. (301) 333-4295.

MASSACHUSETTS

Small and Entrepreneurial Business Development Program

Direct federal funding of research and development (R&D) in the amount of $450 to $500 million is available to small businesses through the **Small Business Innovation Research (SBIR) Program**. The 12 participating federal agencies are required to set aside 1.25% of their extramural R & D budgets for small business. The **Small and Entrepreneurial Business Development Program** disseminates SBIR information to increase the number of awards granted to Massachusetts companies.

Contact: Director, Small and Entrepreneurial, Business Development Division, Massachusetts Office of Business Development, 100 Cambridge Street, 13th Floor, Boston, MA 02202. (617) 727-4005.

Community Development Finance

The **Community Development Finance Corporation** is a public corporation that invests in business enterprises sponsored by community development corporations (CDCs) in economically depressed areas of Massachusetts. New and existing businesses are selected through review of business plans and community impact evaluations. To qualify, businesses should show that they will increase full-time employment in the CDC target area; that they are unable to meet their capital needs from traditional sources; and that they have a reasonable expectation of success. Eligible activities for these businesses include commercial, industrial, or real estate ventures or other economic development activity undertaken in the target area.

Contact: Mr. Milton Benjamin, Acting President, Community Development Finance Corporation, 131 State Street, Suite 600, Boston, MA 02109. (617) 742-0366.

Investment Incentives

The **Massachusetts Industrial Finance Agency** (MIFA) is a state agency that promotes the expansion of small businesses in Massachusetts through the use of investment incentives. MIFA issues tax-exempt industrial revenue bonds (IRBs) for industrial development projects involving land acquisition, plant construction, expansion, or renovation, or equipment purchase.

MIFA also may approve IRBs issued by local industrial development financing authorities. IRBs may finance up to 100% of the project cost, although borrowers are subject to a $10-million capital expenditure limit. Pollution control projects and qualified solid waste disposal facilities are exempt from the $10-million ceiling.

Contact: Mr. Brian Carty, Executive Director, Massachusetts Industrial Finance Agency, 400 Atlantic Avenue, Boston, MA 02210. (617) 451-2477.

Venture Capital

The **Massachusetts Technology Development Corporation** (MTDC) is an independent, publicly-funded venture capital organization that makes investments in new and expanding technology-based companies in Massachusetts. MTDC finances companies that have the capacity to expand and generate new jobs but have been unable to obtain conventional financing for expansion.

The corporation works with private sector investors, such as venture capital firms, banks, and SBICs, which often invest two to four times the amount of capital MTDC provides. Initial investments typically total $100,000 to $250,000, and are made as debt, equity or a combination.

The debt portion of the financing is usually a long-term, unsecured, subordinated note at a favorable interest rate with a partial moratorium on principal repayment. Typical equity participation is through the purchase of common or preferred stock.

While the investment program has been MTDC's principal activity, its management assistance program also aids emerging companies by referring them to appropriate alternative sources of funding. A written business plan is the only required form of application.

Contact: Mr. John F. Hodgman, President, Massachusetts Technology Development Corporation, 131 State Street, Suite 215, Boston, MA 02109. (617) 723-4920.

Massachusetts Business Development Corporation

The **Massachusetts Business Development Corporation** (MBDC) is a private corporation under state charter that provides loans to private, for-profit and nonprofit firms. Loans may be used for the purchase or construction of fixed business assets (land, plant, or equipment) and for working capital. Loan terms are similar to those for conventional loans, although MBDC allows for floating interest rates and longer terms (as much as 20 to 25 years) and can provide up to 100% of financing, depending on need.

Contact: Mr. Kenneth J. Smith, President, Massachusetts Business Development Corporation, One Liberty Square, Boston, MA 02109. (617) 350-8877.

MICHIGAN

The **Michigan Strategic Fund** (MSF) is designed to increase investment in Michigan firms and to create jobs in Michigan. The fund consolidates and streamlines existing state programs and adds new, more flexible programs to meet the needs of Michigan's changing business environment.

The MSF provides fixed-rate, long-term financing; issues industrial revenue bonds; provides royalty-based equity financing; and offers financial services to Michigan businesses.

The fund's economic development tools offer financial assistance for product development and financing for new seed capital loans. The MSF also administers state support for export finance, minority businesses, start-up capital, working capital loans, and three non-profit research and development institutes.

Contact: Mr. Peter Plastrik, President, Michigan Strategic Fund, Michigan Department of Commerce, P.O. Box 30234, Lansing, MI 48909. (517) 373-7550.

In November 1982, the **Michigan Certified Development Company** (MCDC) was formally approved by the U.S. Small Business Administration to operate statewide as a Section 504 Certified Development Company. The MCDC works with local economic development professionals with loan packaging skills. Projects packaged by local professionals are referred to the MCDC for approval. The Michigan Strategic Fund provides staff support.

Contact: Ms. Edie Allen, Michigan Strategic Fund, Department of Commerce, P.O. Box 30234, Lansing, MI 48909. (517) 373-6378.

Loan assistance programs are available through the **Manufacturing Development Group** to assist businesses in developing, structuring, and locating financing.

Contact: Mr. Greg Main, Director, Manufacturing Development Group, Michigan Department of Commerce, Law Building, Lansing, MI 48909. (517) 373-0601.

Financing for New Products

Through the **Michigan Product Development Corporation**, new and emerging firms are assisted in bringing products to market. Financial proposals are prepared by the Michigan Product Development Corporation and submitted to the Michigan Strategic Fund for financing.

Contact: Mr. Rick Beer, President, Michigan Product Development Corporation, 23935 Research Drive, Farmington Hills, MI 48024. (313) 474-3314.

Pension Fund/Venture Capital

Michigan has liberalized its public retirement fund laws, making it possible for public pension funds to invest 2 to 5% of their portfolios as venture capital in small businesses. The fund will invest in firms with excellent potential for growth, profitability, and equity appreciation.

While all types of businesses are considered, the firm should have a unique product, service, or market position to give it a competitive edge. Joint investments with other institutions are also considered.

Contact: Mr. Paul E. Rice, Administrator, Venture Capital Division, Department of Treasury, Treasury Building, Lansing, MI 48922. (517) 373-4330.

MERRA (Michigan Energy and Resource Research Association) Small Business Development Center

The **State Research Fund** (SRF), established in 1982, provides grants to Michigan businesses and individuals who cooperate with Michigan educational institutions to develop prototypes in targeted areas of technology.

Contact: Mr. Mark Clevey, Vice President, Small Business R&D, MERRA SBDC, 1200 Sixth Street, Suite 328, Detroit, MI 48226. (313) 964-5030.

MINNESOTA

Minnesota Department of Trade and Economic Development

The **Community Development Division** provides information concerning a number of programs that assist Minnesota communities and small firms:

- **Minnesota Development Program.** This program provides funds for agricultural and economic development in the state. Funds may be used for the acquisition of land, buildings, machinery, equipment, building construction and renovation, and development costs. Working capital is not an eligible use of funds.

The Minnesota Agricultural and Economic Development Board issues revenue bonds backed by a state reserve.

- **Rural Development Board.** The board can award up to $1 million in challenge grants to six designated regional organizations around the state. These regional organizations use the challenge grants, matched with private funds, to provide loans to new and expanding businesses. Loans cannot be for less than $5,000 or more than $100,000.

- **OMNI.** A private financing corporation, OMNI provides subordinated mortgage financing to industry and manufacturing enterprises. Funds may be used for the acquisition of land, buildings, machinery and equipment, building renovations and other fixed asset purchases. Proceeds from the sale of OMNI debentures are used to provide fixed-rate financing for up to 40% of any project or $500,000, whichever is less. A local lending institution is required to provide 50% of the financing for the project. The remaining 10% is financed in the form of equity by the company.

- **Minnesota Enterprise Zone Program.** This program uses state and local tax credits to reduce businesses' costs of operating in Minnesota. It consists of two parts: the Border Cities Program, which helps retain existing businesses, and the Competitive Zone Program, which helps municipalities attract new and expanding businesses.

Contact: Robert Benner, Deputy Commissioner, Community Development Division, Minnesota Department of Trade and Economic Development, 900 American Center Bldg., 150 East Kellogg Blvd. St. Paul, MN 55101. (612) 297-2515

The **Minnesota Trade Office**'s primary mission is to promote and help develop exports and reverse investments that can have a positive effect on the Minnesota economy. The office's efforts are concentrated on small business, which creates 80% of new jobs, but less than 10% of total exports.

The **Export Finance Division** provides financial assistance through guaranteed loans, individual counseling, insurance coverage, and information on a variety of financing programs.

Contact: Mr. James Gambone, Director of Planning and Communications, Minnesota Trade Office, Minnesota Department of Trade and Economic Development, 1000 Minnesota World Trade Center, 30 East Seventh Street, St. Paul, MN 55101-4902. (612) 297-4283.

MISSISSIPPI

Loans and Loan Guarantees to New and Expanding Small Businesses

The **Department of Economic Development** provides assistance to the state's businesses and industries, including loans and loan guarantees to new and expanding small businesses, and an outreach program to publicize the business services available to Mississippi firms.

A statewide **Certified Development Company**—the Certified Development Company of Mississippi, Inc.—started with over $4 million in state funds. It administers two funding programs for Mississippi small businesses: the SBA 503

Loan and the Mississippi Small Business Loan Guarantee.

Mr. E. F. (Buddy) Mitcham, Director, Finance Division, Mississippi Department of Economic Development, P.O. Box 849, Jackson, MS 39205. (601) 359-3039.

Venture Capital Clearinghouse

Business Service Bureau staff also organized and put in operation the **Mississippi Venture Capital Clearinghouse** (MVCC). The purpose of the MVCC is to introduce entrepreneurs to individual investors and venture capital companies interested in start-up and early-stage financing. A confidential computer matching process is used to compare entrepreneur and investor criteria.

Contact: Mr. Clay Lewis, Manager Business Counseling Division, Business Service Division, 3825 Ridgewood Road, Jackson, MS 39211. (601) 982-6513.

MISSOURI

Seed Capital

The **Department of Economic Development** works with several high technology initiatives in the state. The **Missouri Corporation for Science and Technology**, a private, nonprofit corporation, advises the governor on science- and technology- related economic development issues. Four innovation centers in the state provide facilities, equipment, and technical services to new advanced-technology businesses. New legislation will provide seed capital through these centers to innovative high technology companies.

Contact: Mr. John Johnson, Manager, High Technology Program, Missouri Department of Economic Development, Truman State Office

Building, P.O. Box 118, Jefferson City, MO 65102. (314) 751-3906.

The **Finance Program** of the Missouri Department of Economic Development works with the Missouri Industrial Development Board (MIDB) to provide loan guarantees to selected businesses.

The MIDB may use its development fund—consisting of state appropriations, contributions, and reserve participation fees—to guarantee loans made through a participating lender for qualified projects. Qualified projects include facilities, equipment, improvements to facilities, and certain export trade activities such as consulting, advertising, marketing, product research, legal assistance, and warehousing.

The Finance Program also takes applications for the state treasurer's time deposit program, which offers bank funds for development of projects through the deposit of state funds. The Finance Program represents the state on the board of Rural Missouri, Inc., administers Missouri's Industrial Development Revenue bond Allocation Program, and provides manufacturing companies with additional funding through the Composite Bond Program.

Contacts: Mr. Mike Downing, Manager, Finance Program, Missouri Department of Economic Development, Truman State Office Building, P.O. Box 118, Jefferson City, MO 65102. (314) 751-0717.

MONTANA

Department of Commerce, Business Assistance Division

The **Business Assistance Division** of the Department of Commerce provides comprehensive services that constitute the direct technical assistance component of the "Build Montana" economic development program.

Technical assistance for development finance is available to businesses in the areas of financial analysis, financial planning, loan packaging, industrial revenue bonding, state and private capital sources, and business tax incentives. The program also is designed to work with businesses and financial institutions to encourage the use of various public-sector programs, including **Community Development Block Grants**, **Economic Development Administration Grants**, **Small Business Administration Loan Guarantees**, and the **Montana Board of Investments' In-State Investment Funds**.

Contacts: Mr. Barry Roose, Finance Officer, Ms. Delrene Rasmussen, Finance Officer, Business Assistance Division, Department of Commerce, 1424 Ninth Avenue, Helena, MT 59620. (406) 444-3923.

Beginning Farm Loan Program

The **Beginning Farm Loan Program** provides loans for the purchase of agricultural land or depreciable assets to qualified beginning farmers and ranchers and provides for a state tax deduction to the seller of land to a first-time farmer.

Contact: Mr. Michael Murphy, Administrator, Beginning Farm Loan Program, Montana Department of Agriculture, Agriculture Livestock Building, Capitol Station, 6th and Roberts Avenue, Helena, MT 59620. (406) 444-2402.

Loans for Youths

The **AG Finance Program** provides low-interest loans to rural youth, youth organizations, and first-time or beginning farmers.

Contact: Mr. Lee Boyer, Manager AG Finance, Montana Department of Agriculture, Agriculture Livestock Building, Capitol Station,

6th and Roberts Avenue, Helena, MT 59620. (406) 444-2102.

The **Board of Investments' Office of Development Finance** manages a series of small business loan programs. The board's responsibility is to strengthen and diversify the state's economy through prudent investments in qualifying Montana businesses. The board's programs are designed to make available long-term, fixed rate financing to businesses for a variety of needs.

Coal tax loans are limited to investments in businesses that will bring long-term benefits to the Montana economy. Priority is given to businesses that will create jobs without displacing existing jobs in other Montana businesses. While a minimum or maximum loan limit has not been established, loans of $500,000 to $3 million are targeted.

Through the **Federal Guaranteed Loan Program**, the board may fund a small business loan by purchasing the guaranteed portion of any federally backed loan, such as those guaranteed through the Small Business Administration, the Farmers Home Administration, or the Economic Development Administration. Financing can be used toward working capital, inventory, equipment, real property, or similar items. The interest rate to the board is set at 110% of the rate for U.S. Treasury bonds of a like or similar maturity for monthly payment loans and 115% for annual payment loans.

Through the **Business Loan Participation Program**, the board may fund a small business loan by purchasing from the originating lender up to 80% of the loan amount. Unencumbered land, buildings, and equipment may be financed through this program. The financial institutions service the entire loan and receive a servicing fee in addition to the board's quoted interest rate. The board participates in the security for the loan proportionately to the board's share of the loan.

The **Economic Development Linked Deposit (EDLD)** program offers businesses extended-term, fixed rate financing for working capital, inventory, or real property. The board places a long-term deposit at the pre-established rate with the financial institution originating the qualifying business loan. The proceeds of the deposit must be used to finance a long-term fixed rate loan to the applicant business. The rate and terms to the borrower are linked to the rate and terms of the EDLD.

The **Montana Capital Company Program** is designed to make private venture or equity capital available within the state. Through the program, the state offers a 50-percent tax credit incentive (up to $150,000) to investors in qualified Montana capital companies, which in turn must invest these funds in small Montana firms. The capital companies must be approved by the **Montana Economic Development Board**.

Available tax credits are limited to $5 million through 1989 and are allocated to capital companies in the order that they become "qualified" and have actual investors with at least $200,000 in equity capital.

Contact: Mr. Robert M. Pancich, Administrative Officer, Board of Investments, 555 Fuller Avenue, Helena, MT 59601. (406) 442-1970.

SBA 503/504 Certified Development Companies

There is one certified development company in Montana. The **Montana Community Finance Company** is certified under the Small Business Administration's SBA 504 program, and lends to small and medium-sized businesses at fixed rates for terms of 10 to 20 years. Companies must create one job for every $15,000 they receive in financing. A 504 loan is funded through the sale of a debenture that is guaranteed by the Small Business Administration for up to $750,000 or 40% of the total cost of land, buildings, and equipment.

Contact: Mr. Dick Fossum, Director, Montana Community Finance Corporation, P.O. Box 916, Helena, MT 59624. (406) 443-3261.

Community Development Block Grant Program

Montana's **Community Development Block Grant Program** is a competitive grant program designed to assist cities, towns, and counties with populations of fewer than 50,000 in meeting their greatest community development needs, with particular emphasis on assisting persons of low and moderate income. The program awards approximately $5 million annually in grants to local governments for a variety of economic development, housing, and public facility projects. At least 10% of funds awarded are set aside for economic development projects.

Contact: Mr. Newell B. Anderson, Administrator, Local Government Assistance Division, Department of Commerce, Cogswell Building, Room C-211, Capital Station, Helena, MT 59620. (406) 444-3757.

NEBRASKA

The **Community Development Block Grant Program** (CDBG) is a federal program administered by the state to help small cities address economic development issues such as chronic unemployment through business district revitalization and industrial development. Some job creation activities for low and medium-income residents must be a part of each CDBG project. The state awards CDBG funds to local governments, which make direct fixed asset loans and loan guarantees to local business and industry.

Revolving Loans and Loan Guarantees

The federal **Economic Development Administration** (EDA) of the U.S. Department of Commerce has two loan programs. One involves revolving loans offered through a local **Economic Development District** or similar nonprofit entity. These are direct loans and loan guarantees. The other is a program of loan guarantees from EDA for funds secured from private lending institutions. There is a minimum of $500,000 for this loan guarantee program. Eligible projects must create one job for every $10,000 invested and must be located in an economic development area designed by EDA.

Contact: Mr. Kevin Cogdill, Development Finance Consultant, Small Business Division, Nebraska Department of Economic Development, P.O. Box 94666, Lincoln, NE 68509. (402) 471-4167.

Financial Assistance for Rural Infrastructure

The **Community Development Division** offers financial assistance for rural infra-structure and technical assistance for local rural development programs.

Contact: Mr. Greg Hoover, Director, Community Development Division, Nebraska Department of Economic Development, P.O. Box 94666, 301 Centennial Mall South, Lincoln, NE 68509. (402) 471-3762.

Low Cost Financing for Manufacturing, Farms, Health Care, and Residential Development

The **Nebraska Investment Finance Authority** (NIFA) is an independent, nonprofit, quasi-state agency that provides lower cost financing for manufacturing facilities, certain farm property, and residential and health care development. NIFA seeks to encourage private financing to stimulate economic activity in Nebraska.

NIFA has no taxing authority and receives no state appropriations; it borrows money by issuing notes and bonds. Interest paid is lower than market rate, but is tax-deductible. NIFA established a Small Industrial Development Bond Program to help small Nebraska-based companies — those with fewer than 100 employees or less than $2. 5 million in gross salaries — to participate in bond financing of between $25,000 and $250,000. Fees charged are less than typical of bond issues.

Contact: Mr. Morris Reynolds, Deputy Director of Agricultural Development and Hospitals. Nebraska Investment Finance Authority, Gold's Galleria, 1033 "O" Street, Suite 218, Lincoln, NE 68508. (402) 477-4406.

SBA 503/504 Certified Development Companies

The **Business Development Corporation of Nebraska** (BDCN) is a statewide Certified Development Company Certified by the U.S. Small Business Administration. Through the SBA 504 program, the BDCN helps to provide small businesses with long-term, low interest, fixed asset financing.

A private lending institution provides up to 50% of total project costs at conventional interest rates. The SBA provides up to 40% (not to exceed $500,000), at an interest rate 0.75–1% above long-term. Treasury bond rates. To be eligible for an SBA 504 loan, a firm's net worth must not exceed $6 million and net profits after taxes for the two prior years must have averaged less than $2 million.

Contact: Mr. Alan Eastman, Program Manager, Business Development Corporation of Nebraska, 139 South 52nd Street, Lincoln, NE 68510. (402) 483-0382.

NEVADA

Statewide Certified Development Company

The **Nevada State Development Corporation** (NSDC) offers three programs: SBA 503/504 fixed asset loans, SBA 7(a) loans, and the American Development Finance Enterprise Capital Fund.

SBA 503/504 Fixed Asset Loans are long-term, fixed rate, low-down-payment, second-mortgage financing for real estate and fixed assets to owner-operated businesses. As a Certified Development Company, the NSDC is authorized by the U.S. Small Business Administration to offer and package loans and obtain private sector, first-mortgage financing and SBA second-mortgage approval on a statewide basis.

SBA 7 (a) loans provide SBA guarantees for up to 90% of loans made by banks to businesses for a wide range of financing purposes. The program provides assistance to borrowers in packaging their loan requests and in locating a bank to make the loan.

American Development Finance is a non-profit corporation established to offer financial and technical services for economic development. The **Enterprise Capital Fund** is a taxable commercial-paper facility established to finance business expansion projects.

Contact: Mr. Harry H. Weinberg, President, Nevada State Development Corporation, 350 South Center, Suite 310, Reno, NV 89501. (702) 323-3625.

Department of Commerce

The **Industrial Development Revenue Bond Program** was introduced through the Commerce Department in 1981, as a mechanism to help companies expand or build new facilities through the use of tax-exempt financing. In

1987, the program was restricted so that manufacturing concern could use composite tax-exempt bonds for its programs. The program offers low-cost, long-term, tax-exempt financing of up to $10 million to encourage new facilities or expansion that is compatible with Nevada's plan for economic development and diversification.

The **Venture Capital Bond Program**, established in 1987, enables the Department of Commerce to issue up to $100 million in bonds to fund venture capital projects in Nevada. Studies are underway to determine what needs exist in this area and whether the bonds can be marketed.

Contact: Mr. John E. Chrissinger, Deputy Director, Department of Commerce, 201 South Fall Street, Suite 321, Carson City, NV 89710. (702) 885-4250.

Office of Community Services

The **Small Business Revitalization (SBR) Program** was introduced in January 1983. SBR encourages private lender participation in creative loan packaging, drawing on a variety of public programs. Among these programs are the U.S. Small Business Administration's 504 loan and 7 (a) loan guarantee programs and the **Nevada Revolving Loan Fund**. SBR also gives Nevada small businesses access to low-cost, long-term financing to encourage their expansion and diversification into job creating activities. Eighty-seven loans totaling over $38 million have stimulated the creation of over 1,100 jobs.

Contact: Mr. Darrol Brown, Small Business Representative, Nevada Office of Community Services, 1100 East William Street, Suite 116, Carson City, NV 89710. (702) 885-5978.

Nevada Financial Development Corporation

Established in 1980, the **Nevada Financial Development Corporation** (NFDC) promotes growth and development of business and industry. It is a privately owned, non-depository financial organization operating in conjunction with the SBA, Farmers Home Administration, Federal Aviation Administration, U.S. Department of Energy, and other federal government loan guarantee programs.

The NFDC provides credit for 5-to 15-year terms to supplement and assist conventional lending sources in meeting the long-term financial needs of Nevada businesses. The corporation's activities are statewide. It operates under Chapter 670 of the Nevada Revised Statutes.

Contact: Mr. Timothy Collins, President, Nevada Financial Development Corporation, 350 South Center Street, Suite 380, Reno, NV 89501. (702) 323-3033.

NEW HAMPSHIRE

New Hampshire Industrial Development Authority

The **New Hampshire Industrial Development Authority** (IDA) assists businesses in all areas of finance, including guaranteeing mortgages, establishing credit, and securing loans. Up to $18 million is available to the authority to carry out its various programs. With the permission of the governor and council, the authority may borrow up to an additional $1 million to protect the interests of the state in any project previously financed. The IDA provides the following services:

- **Industrial Development Revenue Bond Financing.** Under New Hampshire law, the **Industrial Development Authority** is authorized to issue tax-free industrial development revenue bonds (IRBs) to provide 100-percent financing for industrial and pollution control facilities. Bond proceeds may be used to purchase land, to construct and equip a new facility to be used for manufacturing, or to acquire machinery and equipment. They may also be used to construct facilities for the disposal of waste material, small-scale power facilities for producing electric energy, water-powered electric generating facilities, or facilities for the collection, purification, storage, or distribution of water for use by the general public.

- **Guarantee Plan for Real Estate**. The Authority may guarantee first mortgage loans made by financial institutions to manufacturing industries that acquire, construct, or reconstruct facilities. One hundred-percent financing is available to out-of-state companies seeking to relocate in new Hampshire, as well as to New Hampshire companies expanding operations in the state. The state secures up to 50% of such loans, enabling financial institutions legally to lend money for the entire cost of a facility. There is a guarantee limit of $5 million for any single project, and loan terms may not exceed 25 years.

- **Guarantee Plan for Machinery and Equipment**. Up to 35% of a loan for new machinery and equipment may be guaranteed with 10-year maximum repayment terms. There is a guarantee limit of $600,000 for any single project.

Contact: Ms. Marilyn E. Jewell, Acting Executive Director, Industrial Development Authority, Four Park Street, Room 302, Concord, NH 03301. (603) 271-2391.

NEW JERSEY

Minority Business Financing

The primary function of the **Office of Minority Business Enterprise** is to assist minority business owners in financing, procurement, and management training. To further these goals, the Office issues Early Alert bulletins to advise minority business owners of new contracting opportunities, conducts seminars throughout the state, and provides a variety of consultative and problem-solving services.

Contact: Mr. Lee L. Davis, Chief, Office of Minority Business Enterprise, New Jersey Department of Commerce, Energy, and Economic Development, 20 West State Street, CN 835, Trenton, NJ 08625. (609) 292-0500.

The **Local Development Financing Fund** (LDFF) was established to provide supplementary financial assistance to qualifying commercial and industrial projects. The purpose of the enabling legislation is to provide long-term financing to such projects on a competitive basis.

The primary objectives of the program are (1) to award up to $45 million to businesses located in urban aid cities and meet the mandated competitive criteria; (2) to create and preserve employment; (3) to increase the municipality's tax base; and (4) to promote economic and physical revitalization to the qualifying municipalities.

Contact: Mr. Stephen C. Brame, Director, Office of Urban Programs, New Jersey Department of Commerce, Energy, and Economic Development, 20 West State Street, CN 829, Trenton, NJ 08625. (609) 633-6659.

The SAC Office administers the **Financial Assistance Grant Program** to counties and municipalities. Through this program, local entities establish innovative programs designed to increase the participation of small, women-owned, and minority-owned businesses in local procurement programs.

Contact: Mr. Anthony Vergara, Chief Set-Aside and Certification Office, New Jersey Department of Commerce, Energy, and Economic Development, 20 West State Street, CN 835, Trenton, NJ 08625. (609) 984-9835.

Below-Market-Rate Financing for Manufacturing Facilities, Land Acquisition, and Business Equipment and Machinery Purchases

The **New Jersey Economic Development Authority** (NJEDA) is a state business financing authority that uses tax-exempt private activity bonds to provide below-market-rate financing for manufacturing facilities, land acquisition, and business equipment and machinery purchases. It also issues taxable bonds to provide financing for manufacturing, distribution, warehousing, research, commercial, office, and service uses.

In addition, NJEDA has a **guaranteed loan program**, a **direct loan program**, a **pre-shipment working capital loan program for exporting**, and a **loan program directed to small retail businesses** in urban centers.

Contacts: Loans or guarantees: Mr. Eugene J. Bukowski, Director of Finance, New Jersey Economic Development Authority, Capital Place One, CN 990, Trenton, NJ 08625. (609) 292-0187.

SBA 503/504 Certified Development Company

The **Corporation for Business Assistance** (CBA) in New Jersey is designated by the U.S. Small Business Administration as a Section 503/504 Certified Development Company, with authority to operate statewide. The Office of Small business Assistance works with CBA by advising small business owners on how to participate in the program and by assisting them in the preparation of 503/504 loan packages. Loan applications are reviewed, processed, and recommended by the New Jersey Economic Development Authority.

Contact: Mr. Eugene J. Bukowski, Secretary, Corporation for Business Assistance in New Jersey, Capital Place One, CN 990, Trenton, NJ 08625. (609) 633-7737.

Financial Assistance for Farmers and Agribusinesses

The **Division of Rural Resources** of the New Jersey Department of Agriculture fosters the agriculture economic development of rural areas of the state through such services as financial assistance for farmers and agribusinesses.

Contact: Ms. Karen Kritz, AG Development Specialist, Division of Rural Resources, New Jersey Department of Agriculture, CN 330, Room 203, Trenton, NJ 08625. (609) 292-5511.

NEW MEXICO

Risk Capital for Sound Business Ventures

The New Mexico **Business Development Corporation** (BDC) is a state-chartered, privately owned corporation that provides risk capital for sound business ventures. Funding is available for new product and market development or for the purchase of equipment needed to expand or modernize. The BDC works with local and regional banks, savings and loan associations, and credit unions.

Contacts: Mr. Keith Dotson, CEO and President, Mr. Mark Peterson, Loan Officer, New Mexico Business Development Corporation, 6001 Marble, N. E. , Suite 6, Albuquerque, NM 87110. (505) 268-1316.

NEW YORK

New York State Job Development Authority

The **New York State Job Development Authority** (JDA) is the state's economic development bank. The JDA assists companies wishing to expand or build new facilities, thereby retaining existing jobs or creating new employment opportunities. Nearly every type of business is eligible for JDA assistance. (Loans or loan guarantees to retail establishments, hotels, or apartment buildings are not made under this program.)

Under the direct loan program, JDA may lend up to 40% of a project's costs for construction, acquisition, rehabilitation, or improvement of industrial or manufacturing plants and research and development facilities. The authority also provides loan guarantees of up to 80% of a project's costs for a maximum of 20 years.

Other programs offered by JDA include a **rural development loan fund**, a **long-term economic development fund**, an **export program**, and a **regional economic development partnership program**.

The **Bonding Assistance Experimental Program** (BAX) reflects the policy of the State of New York to assist minority, women, and small business owners to participate fully in the economic activity of the state and, more specifically, to do business with the state itself.

The program is designed to provide assistance in securing bonds on construction contracts of less than $500,000. Originally limited to contracts let by the state's Office of General Services, the program has been expanded to include contracts for public projects let by any state agency, authority, or public benefit corporation, and by cities, towns, and villages.

Contact: Mr. Robert Dormer, President, Job Development Authority, 605 Third Avenue, New York, NY 10158. (212) 818-1700.

SBA 503/504 Certified Development Company

The **Empire State Certified Development Corporation** is formally approved by the U.S. Small Business Administration as a Section 503/504 Certified Development Company, with authority to operate on a statewide basis.

Contact: Mr. Gerald Demers, Senior Loan Officer, Empire State Certified Development Corporation, 41 State Street, Albany, NY 12207. (518) 463-2268.

New York Business Development Corporation

The **New York Business Development Corporation** (NYBDC), a private corporation, makes term loans available to small businesses. The NYBDC coordinates both the SBA Section 503/504 Certified Development Corporation and a new loan program, the New York State/U.S. Small Business Administration Initiative. With an initial capitalization of $100 million coming from New York State employee pension funds, the Initiative program is a revolving loan fund for small business.

In order to safeguard the pension funds, the Initiative is required to have guarantees attached to at least 50% of the loans it makes. The U.S. Small Business Administration will provide these guarantees as each loan package is processed and approved.

Contact: Mr. Robert W. Lazar, President and Chief Executive Officer, New York Business Development Corporation, 41 State Street, Albany, NY 12207. (518) 463-2268.

New York Science and Technology Foundation

The **Corporation for Innovation Development** (CID) program is a venture capital fund for technology-based start-ups and young, growing business ventures in New York State. The corporation was partly funded by the U.S. Department of Commerce and was recently recapitalized by the state. It focuses on ventures with innovative products or services ready for introduction to a rapid growth market. The CID program will invest up to $250,000 in a business, but any investments must be matched by loans or investments from other sources.

Contact: Mr. Graham Jones, Executive Director, New York State Science and Technology Foundation. 99 Washington Avenue, Suite 1730, Albany, NY 12210. (518) 474-4349.

NORTH CAROLINA

Small Business Development Division

The **Small Business Development Division** of the North Carolina Department of Commerce provides information and assistance to business owners and prospective entrepreneurs. Information and assistance more frequently requested pertains to financing, taxes, regulations, marketing, education, and training.

In addition to working with individual small businesses, the division sponsors and co-sponsors workshops and conferences on such subjects as basic business management, taxes, advertising, and selling to government.

The division conducts buyer-supplier exchanges in various regions of the state to enable small businesses and industries to meet directors of purchasing of larger manufacturers. These events are held for new and expanding industries, as well as existing ones.

A business clearinghouse provides an ongoing service to businesses and investors, including a confidential listing of businesses for sale, investments needed, and investors interested in doing business in North Carolina. The same matching process applies to joint ventures, mergers, and contract manufacturing. The division provides staff support to the North Carolina Small Business Council.

Contact: Mr. William Lane, Assistant Secretary, Small Business Development Division, North Carolina Department of Commerce, Dobbs Building, Room 2019, 430 North Salisbury Street, Raleigh, NC 27611. (919) 733-7980.

Grants to Establish Incubator Facilities

The **North Carolina Technological Development Authority** was established by the New Technology Jobs Act of 1983. The authority makes grants to establish incubator facilities for small firms, and to oversee the North Carolina Innovative Research Fund, which provides equity financing for the research activities of new and existing small businesses.

Contact: Mr. E. Brent Lane, Director, North Carolina Technological Development Authority, Room 4216, 430 North Salisbury Street, Raleigh, NC 27611. (919) 733-7022.

Institute for Private Enterprise

The **Frank H. Kenan Institute for Private Enterprise** was established in 1985 at the University of North Carolina at Chapel Hill. As a national center for private enterprise research, the institute focuses on entrepreneurial development, new venture management, and development of course-work for use in business schools across the country.

The **Investment Contacts Network**, a program of the institute, is a confidential computerized matching service that brings together entrepreneurs with private and professional venture investors.

Contact: Mr. Rollie Tillman, Director, Institute for Private Enterprise, The University of North Carolina at Chapel Hill, Frank Hawkins Kenan Institute of Private Enterprise, CB 3440, Chapel Hill, NC 27599-3440. (919) 962-8201.

NORTH DAKOTA

Bank of North Dakota

The **Bank of North Dakota** is the nation's only state-authorized and -operated bank. The bank offers several unique lending programs for promoting agriculture, commerce, and industry within the state.

The **Small Business Loan Program** is designed to assist new and existing businesses in securing competitive financing with reasonable terms and conditions. Loans are restricted to non-farming small businesses located within the state. The maximum loan is $250,000, and applications must be made through a lead financial institution. The lead institution may charge the borrower an interest rate of up to 2% above the Bank of North Dakota's floating rate.

The **Risk Loan Program** is designed to assist new and existing businesses in obtaining loans with a higher degree of risk than would normally be acceptable to a lending institution. The bank's participation percentage is negotiated on a loan-by-loan basis up to $500,000. A lead lender must apply for and service the loan, and may not charge more than 2% above the bank's base rate. The Export Loan Program, newly established in the Bank of North Dakota, will make low interest rate loans available to foreign importers who want to buy North Dakota products.

Contact: Mr. Eric Hardmeyer, Commercial Loan Officer, Bank of North Dakota, 700 East Main Avenue, Box 5509, Bismarck, ND 58502. (701) 224-5685, (800) 472-2166, Ext. 5685 (in-state).

SBA 503/504 Certified Development Companies

The **Fargo Cass County Economic Development Corporation** is the only certified develop-ment company in North Dakota, and has been expanded to cover 34 counties. The company, located in Fargo, lends to small and medium-sized businesses at fixed rates, for terms of 10 or 20 years.

Small businesses must create one job for every $15,000 they receive in financing. A 504 loan is funded through the sale of the deben-ture, guaranteed by the U.S. Small Business Administration for up to $750,000 or 40% of the total cost of land, buildings, and equipment.

Contact: Mr. Toby Sticka, Executive Vice President, Fargo Cass County Economic Development Corporation, Box 2443, 320 N. 45th Street, Fargo, ND 58108-2443. (701) 237-6132.

OHIO

Minority Development Loan Program.

This program offers qualified minority busi-nesses below-market financing for fixed assets, land, buildings, and equipment. To be eligible, enterprises must engage in manufacturing, dis-tribution, commerce, or research. For the 1988-89 biennium, the state budgeted $5 million for this program.

Contacts: Ms. Marsha Harton, Executive Director, Minority Development Finance Com-mission, Ohio Department of Development, P.O. Box 1001, Columbus, OH 46266-0101. (614) 644-7708, (800) 282-1085 (toll-free, in-state), (800) 848-1300 (toll-free, out-of-state).

Mr. Richard Crockett, Loan Officer, Ohio Department of Development, P.O. Box 1001, Columbus, OH 43266-0101. (614) 644-7708, (800) 282-1085 (toll-free, in-state), (800) 848-1300 (toll-free, out-of-state).

OKLAHOMA

Oklahoma Department of Commerce

The **Capital Resources Division** is designed to assist Oklahoma companies gain access to the capital they need to grow and prosper. The division's central program is the **Capital Resources Network**. This program provides financial specialists to help businesses and analyze their financing needs and to work closely with local economic development staff to help them package proposals for their local companies. The division also administers several other programs, including;

- Oklahoma Innovation Network Public / Private Partnership Incentive, and Jobs Development Incentive Program

- Inventor's Assistance Program

- Programs authorized by Oklahoma's Small Business Incubator Incentives Act

Finally, the division is responsible for assisting in the development of new loan and investment programs, sponsored by both public and private organizations.

Contact: Mr. Robert Heard, Director, Capital Resources Division, Department of Commerce, 6601 Broadway Extension, Oklahoma City, OK 73116-8214. (405) 843-9770.

Finance Authorities

Two statewide entities that deal in business finance are the **Oklahoma Development Finance Authority** and the **Oklahoma Industrial Finance Authority**. Both issue notes and bonds to fund business projects. Interest earnings on the notes or bonds can be either taxable or tax-exempt.

Contacts: Mr. Carl Clark, Director, Oklahoma Development Finance Authority, 205 N.W. 63rd Street, Suite 270, Oklahoma City, OK 73116. (405) 848-9761.

Mr. Jay Casey, President, Oklahoma Industrial Finance Authority, 205 N.W. 63rd Street, Suite 260, Oklahoma City, OK 73116. (405) 521-2182.

OREGON

The **Oregon Business Development Fund** (OBDF), created by legislation in April 1983, provides financing to small and medium-sized firms expanding their operations or locating in the state. Loans of up to $250,000 are made for land, buildings, fixed assets, or working capital. The maximum term is 25 years, with the rate fixed at one percentage point below U.S. Treasury bond rates.

The fund was capitalized with $2 million in federal Economic Development Administration funds and $667,000 from the state lottery. The fund is administered by the state's **Economic Development Department** (EDD).

The EDD also is the state coordinator for an industrial revenue bond program designed to help businesses expand. EDD is offering a new pooled industrial revenue bond program to increase access to small borrowers.

Contacts: Mr. Mark D. Huston, Manager, Mr. Barrett MacDougall, Senior Finance Officer, Business Finance Section, Oregon Economic Development Department, 595 Cottage Street N. E., Salem, OR 97310. (503) 373-1240.

The **Oregon Certified Development Company** is a statewide company providing Small Business Administration "504" financing to eligible small businesses. It works closely with local certified development companies throughout the state.

Contact: Mr. Mark D. Huston, Manager, Financial Services Division, Oregon Economic Development Department, 595 Cottage Street N. E., Salem, OR 97310. (503) 373-1240.

Investment Capital for Early-Stage Business Finance

The **Oregon Resource and Technology Development Corporation** (ORTDC) was created by the Oregon legislature to provide investment capital for early-stage business finance (see capital) and applied research and development projects that can lead to commercially viable products.

Seed capital investments are limited to $500,000 per enterprise. Applied research investments are limited to $100,000 and must be matched through cash or in-kind services. As of May 1988, ORTDC had made two research and development and 15 seed capital investments. The corporation's total capitalization is $8. 5 million.

ORTDC is co-sponsoring the **Northwest Capital Network**, a computer-based network which will link entrepreneurs needing capital to private investors seeking investment opportunities.

Contact: Mr. John Beaulieu, President, ORTDC, One Lincoln Center, Suite 430, 10300 S.W. Greenburg Road, Portland, OR 97223. (503) 246-4844.

Minority- and Women-Owned Business Programs

Fifteen percent of funds in the **Oregon Business Development Fund** (see description above) are reserved for minority- and women-owned businesses. The Economic Development Department actively encourages applications from women-and minority-owned businesses.

Contact: Mr. Barrett MacDougall, Senior Finance Officer, Business Finance, Oregon Economic Development Department, 595 Cottage Street N. E., Salem, OR 97310. (503) 378-6359.

PENNSYLVANIA

Department of Commerce

The **Office of Enterprise Development** administers the programs of the **Appalachian Regional Commission** (ARC) and the **Enterprise Development Program** (EDP) in Pennsylvania.

The program goal is to accelerate the creation of jobs by assisting small entrepreneurial enterprises to develop new markets for Pennsylvania products. Through the EDP, seven **Local Development Districts** (LDDs) serve Pennsylvania's 52 Appalachian counties and link resources to support local business expansion and job creation. Each LDD is active in finance, federal procurement assistance, export outreach, business incubators, job training, and advanced technology.

Contact: Mr. Paul Hallacher, Director, Office of Enterprise Development, Department of Commerce, 402 Forum Building, Harrisburg, PA 17120. (717) 783-8950.

Long-Term, Low-Interest Business Loans

The **Pennsylvania Industrial Development Authority** (PIDA) was established in 1956 to make long-term, low-interest business loans to firms engaged in manufacturing or industrial enterprises. Current policy targets PIDA funds to small and advanced technology businesses, enterprise zones, and minority- and women-owned businesses.

A qualified business may receive up to $1.5 million, with interest rates ranging from 3% to 7.5%, depending upon the unemployment rate in the critical economic area where the project is located. PIDA defines a small business as one employing fewer than 50 persons.

PIDA requires that at least one full-time job, or its equivalent, be created for every $15,000 of financing provided. This job creation target must be met within three years of occupancy of the project site.

Contact: Mr. Gerald Kapp, Director, Pennsylvania Industrial Development Authority, Department of Commerce, 481 Forum Building, Harrisburg, PA 17120. (717) 787-6245.

The **Ben Franklin Partnership** (BFP) programs promote advanced technology in an effort to make traditional industry more competitive in the international marketplace and to spin off new small businesses on the leading edge of technological innovation. The BFP's four **Advanced Technology Centers** represent consortia of business, labor, research universities and other higher education institutions, and economic development groups. Each center provides:

- Joint applied research and development efforts, in concert with the private sector, in specified areas such as robotics, biotechnology, and CAD-CAM.

- Assistance to higher education institutions to provide training and retraining in technical and other skills essential to firm expansions and start-ups.

- Entrepreneurial assistance services, which include: linking research, financial, and human resources; assisting in the preparation of business plans and feasibility studies; and providing small business incubator and technology transfer services.

Other services offered by the BFP include;

- The **Small Business Incubator Program**

- **five privately managed seed venture capital funds**

- research seed grants up to $35,000 for small businesses seeking to develop or introduce advanced technology into the marketplace.

Contact: Mr. Jacques Koppel, Executive Director, Ben Franklin Partnership, Department of Commerce, 463 Forum Building, Harrisburg, PA 17120. (717) 787-4147.

Financing for projects approved through the **Revenue Bond and Mortgage Program** are borrowed from private sources through a local **Industrial Development Authority** (IDA). Because the authority is recognized as a political subdivision, the lender (except those affected by the Tax Reform Act of 1986) does not pay taxes on the interest earned from the loan, and the borrower has the benefit of an interest rate lower than conventional rates.

Businesses can use the funds to acquire land, buildings, machinery, and equipment. Business borrowers of commercial, industrial, and specialized loans under the program must create a minimum number of new jobs within three years of the loan's closing.

Contact: Ms. Shirley Lloyd, Division Manager, Revenue Bond and Mortgage Program, Department of Commerce, 479 Forum Building, Harrisburg, PA 17120. (717) 783-1108.

The **Pennsylvania Capital Loan Fund** (PCLF) provides low-interest loans to businesses for capital development projects that will result in long-term net new employment opportunities.

The PCLF is capitalized with federal funds from the **Appalachian Regional Commission** and the **Economic Development Administration**, and with state appropriations. Recent statutory changes have expanded the program to provide assistance to manufacturers of apparel products and to small business enterprises that are increasing their participation in foreign export markets.

Eligibility criteria, terms, fees, and rates differ, depending on the funding source and class of the loan.

Contact: Mr. Jim Graham, Division Manager Pennsylvania Capital Loan Fund, Department of Commerce, 494 Forum Building, Harrisburg, PA 17120. (717) 783-1768.

The **Pennsylvania Economic Development Financing Authority** (PEDFA) pools bond issues for both tax-exempt and taxable bonds to provide loans to industrial and commercial development authorities for economic development projects. PEDFA fills a financing gap for tax-exempt small issues as a result of the Tax Reform Act of 1986 and provides competitive rates for taxable and tax-exempt bond issues.

Among the eligible users are manufacturing, industrial, and commercial enterprises, and specialized facilities.

Contact: Mr. Frank Tokarz, Division Manager, Pennsylvania Economic Development Financing Authority, Department of Commerce, 479 Forum Building, Harrisburg, PA 17120. (717) 783-5831.

Minority Business Loans

The **Pennsylvania Minority Business Development Authority** (PMBDA) provides low-interest, long-term loans and equity guarantees to assist in the start-up or expansion of minority-owned businesses. The maximum loan amount is $100,000 per applicant, not to exceed 75% of the total required financing. The project must show that one job will be created or preserved for every $15,000 requested.

For advanced technology firms and manufacturing companies located in the state's designated enterprise zones or redevelopment areas, loans may be made up to $200,000, for a maximum of 20 years. Interest rates are 50% of the prime lending rate as of the date approved by PMBDA.

In 1985, PMBDA established the Surety bond and Working Capital Program to guarantee up to 90% of bid and performance bonds needed by a minority business enterprise to obtain a contract with a state agency, and to provide short-term loans to minority contractors with

the state for working capital. A portion of the proceeds will be used for all forms of financial and technical assistance to aid in the start-up or expansion of minority-owned businesses.

Contact: Mr. Aqil A. Sabur, Executive Director, Pennsylvania Minority Business Development Authority (PMBDA), 461 Forum Building, Harrisburg, PA 17120. (717) 783-1127.

Agricultural Entrepreneur Development Fund.

The **Agriculture Entrepreneur Development Fund** was established in July 1987. It provides grants of $10,000 to $100,000 to small agricultural enterprises desiring to move into processing to create value-added products.

Contact: Mr. Steven M. Crawford, Executive Assistant to the Secretary, Department of Agriculture, 2301 North Cameron Street, Harrisburg, PA 17110. (717) 787-4626.

PUERTO RICO

The Government Development Bank for Puerto Rico

One of the **Primary functions of the Government Development Bank** (GDB) for Puerto Rico is to foster economic development in both the public and private sectors. Responsibility within the bank for private-sector economic development rests principally with the private financing department, which lends to commercial, industrial, and service firms that contribute to the Puerto Rican economy. The GDB's loan section consists of three divisions: The Credit Administrative Division, the Credit Analysis Division, and the Special Loans Division.

Real estate, machinery, and equipment can be used as collateral for loans. Personal or corporate guarantees are required. In all cases, the bank seeks guarantees from the U.S. Small Business Administration, the Farmers Home Administration, or another agency of the federal government.

Contact: Mr. Hiram Melendez, Senior Vice President, Government Development Bank of Puerto Rico, GPO Box 42001, San Juan, PR 00940. (809) 722-2525.

The Economic Development Bank for Puerto Rico

The **Economic Development Bank for Puerto Rico** began operations in May 1986. The fund lends to manufacturing and commercial concern under more flexible lending and collateral terms than the Government Development Bank. The maximum amount the fund may lend on direct loans is $1. 5 million, and on guaranty loans up to $1 million.

Contact: Mr. Ramon Pena, Banco de Desarrollo Economico Para Puerto Rico, P.O. Box 5009, Hato Rey, PR 00919-5009. (809) 766-4300.

RHODE ISLAND

One-Stop Clearinghouse for Financing Packages

Several financing programs are offered through the **Department of Economic Development**. The agency serves as a one-stop clearinghouse for financing packages, assisting qualified companies with all steps from the initial contact with financial institutions to assembling the project in final form for approval.

Contact: Mr. Virgil A. Nolan, Director of Financial Services, Rhode Island Department of Economic Development, 7 Jackson Walkway, Providence, RI 02903. (401) 277-2601.

The **Rhode Island Port Authority and Economic Development Corporation** provides financial aid through tax-exempt revenue bonds for construction, acquisition, or renovation of industrial plants or equipment.

Contact: Mr. Virgil A. Nolan, Director of Financial Services, Rhode Island Department of Economic Development, 7 Jackson Walkway, Providence, RI 02903. (401) 277-2601.

The **Rhode Island Industrial Building Authority** issues mortgage insurance on financing obtained through banks or other financial institutions. Insured loans can be used for construction of new facilities or renovation of existing buildings and for the purchase of new machinery. The authority can also insure tax-exempt revenue bonds.

Contact: Mr. James Sullivan, Manager, Rhode Island Industrial Building Authority, Rhode Island Department of Economic Development, 7 Jackson Walkway, Providence, RI 02903. (401) 277-2601.

The **Revolving Loan Fund** provides for manufacturing, processing, and marine resource development up to 25% of project costs. These loans can be for either fixed assets or working capital, for new or existing businesses.

Contact: Mr. Robert Donovan, Project Supervisor, Rhode Island Department of Economic Development, 7 Jackson Walkway, Providence, RI 02903. (401) 277-2601.

Rhode Island Business Investment Fund

The **Rhode Island Business Investment Fund** is a cooperative effort between the state, the U.S. Small Business Administration, and local banks. Loans are provided for fixed assets and working capital. Interest rates are tied to the U.S. Treasury note rate and enable businesses to borrow at a fixed rate.

Contact: Mr. Jerome F. Williams, Deputy General Treasurer, State of Rhode Island, Office of the General Treasurer, 198 Dyer Street, Providence, RI 02903. (401) 277-2287.

Ocean State Business Development Authority

The **Ocean State Business Development Authority** (OSBDA) is a Certified Development Company as designated by the U.S. Small Business Administration. The authority focuses on administering the SBA 504 program, which provides financing at favorable rates and terms to small businesses for expansion projects. By combining long-term bank debt with the sale of SBA-guaranteed debentures, OSBDA can offer terms and blended rates approaching those available to larger companies.

Contact: Mr. Henry A. (Bud) Violet, President, Ocean State Business Development Authority, 7 Jackson Walkway, Providence, RI 02903. (401) 277-2601.

Venture Capital Club, Inc., may be a place to start for those seeking capital, technical, marketing, or management assistance, or other resources to start a business or expand an existing one. The Venture Capital Club brings together entrepreneurs, investors, and prospective joint venture partners. Club meetings begin with a brief presentation on a topic related to venture formation, development, and financing, followed by brief individual presentations of business ideas or investment goals. Information is available from the Small Business Development Center.

Contact: Mr. Douglas Jobling, State Director, Rhode Island Small Business Development Center, Bryant College, 450 Douglas Pike, Smithfield, RI 02917-1284. (401) 232-6111.

Grants to Businesses for Applied Research

The **Rhode Island Partnership for Science and Technology** is a research institute that offers grants to businesses for applied research in conjunction with universities, colleges, or hospitals in the state. The partnership seeks major innovative projects with a minimum research budget of $200,000 that offer potential for profitable commercialization.

The partnership will fund up to 60% of a research project and no less than 33%. The research funding must be spent at the universities, colleges, or hospitals working with the institution.

Contact: Mr. Bruce Lang, Executive Director, Rhode Island Partnership for Science and Technology, 7 Jackson Walkway, Providence, RI 02903. (401) 277-2601.

State Supported SBIR Program

A new Rhode Island program provides four categories of support to qualified **Small Business Innovation Research** (SBIR) applicants. Free consulting is provided by the **Rhode Island Small Business Development Center** to help applicants develop proposals. A Rhode Island company that submits a valid Phase 1 SBIR proposal to the federal government may receive a $1,000 grant to help defray the cost of preparing the application. A matching grant of 50% (up to a maximum of $2,500) is available to Phase I recipients who use as a consultant a faculty member of a Rhode Island university or college.

A Rhode Island Phase I SBIR grant recipient who submits a Phase II proposal is eligible to receive a matching state grant of 50% of the Phase I award, up to a maximum of $25,000.

Contact: Mr. Bruce Lang, Executive Director, Rhode Island Partnership for Science and Technology, 7 Jackson Walkway, Providence, RI 02903. (401) 277-2601.

SOUTH CAROLINA

Loans and Capital Formation

An 11-member, quasi-public **Jobs Economic Development Authority** raises capital and provides technical assistance to aid small businesses in creating jobs. The authority sells general and industrial revenue bonds.

The governor has designated a portion of block grant funds to provide loans and technical assistance for small business development. The emphasis is on businesses that will create new jobs in a community. Preference is given to less developed areas of the state.

Carolina Investment Corporation, a mirror corporation of the Jobs Economic Development Authority, is empowered to make loans or equity investments in South Carolina small businesses. The maximum amount per investment is $75,000.

Contact: Mr. Elliott Franks, Director, South Carolina Jobs — Economic Development Authority, 1201 Main Street, AT&T Capital Center, Suite 1750, Columbia, SC 29201. (803) 737-0079.

SBA 503/504 Certified Development Company

Certified Development Companies (CDCs) are local or statewide corporations or authorities — both for-profit and non-profit, depending on the situation — that package SBA, bank, state, and private money into a financial assistance package for existing business capital improvement. Each state has at least one CDC.

All areas of South Carolina have CDCs, either through various councils of governments or local CDCs that provide service to a specific area.

Contact: Mr. Luder Messervy, Loan Specialist, Finance Division, U.S. Small Business Administration, P.O. Box 2786, Columbia, SC 29202. (803) 253-3119.

SOUTH DAKOTA

The **Revolving Economic Development and Initiative Fund** (REDI Fund) was created in 1987 by the South Dakota legislature to encourage economic development and job creation. The fund was financed by a one-year, 1% sales tax. The legislation authorized the Board of Economic Development (BED), appointed by the governor, to develop and implement the criteria for making loans from the REDI Fund.

Loans are made to any for-profit firm or non-profit business cooperative that is either a start-up firm, an existing South Dakota business, or an existing business that will locate and create primary jobs in South Dakota. The basic requirements are a reasonable prospect of business success, loan repayment, job creation, and economic development impact.

Interest rates are set initially at 3%. The interest rate offered by the REDI Fund is determined by the Board of Economic Development on a semiannual basis; however, each loan has a fixed rate of interest. The loans are amortized over a period of time, up to 20 years, with a balloon after five years.

Contacts: Mr. Troy Jones, Jr., Director of Finance, Governor's Office of Economic Development, 711 Wells Avenue, Capitol Lake Plaza, Pierre, SD 57501. (605) 773-5032, (800) 952-3625 (toll-free, in-state), (800) 843-8000 (toll-free, out-of-state)

The **Enterprise Initiation Higher Education Program** was created to incorporate the state's higher education institutions into the state's overall economic development plan by encouraging research and development activities on the state's campuses.

Each eligible state-funded institution has a **Center for Innovation Technology and Enterprise** (CITE) responsible for collecting and analyzing applied research and service proposals for funding and submitting them to the director of Enterprise Initiation. Proposals are judged on how they relate to the overall economic development program for the state. If a proposal is accepted, a contract is drawn up to fund the work on a reimbursable basis.

Contact: Mr. Ken Schaack, Director, Enterprise Initiation, Governor's Office of Economic Development, 711 Wells Avenue, Capitol Lake Plaza, Pierre, SD 57501. (605) 773-5032, (800) 952-3625 (toll-free, in-state), (800) 843-8000 (toll-free, out-of-state).

Economic Development Finance Authority

In March 1986 the state legislature authorized the **Economic Development Finance Authority** to pool tax-exempt bonds for sale in secondary money markets. The authority's department reserve account was capitalized at $3 million.

Eligible project costs include building construction, land, financing charges, expenses incidental to determining the feasibility of each development project, and costs of machinery, equipment, and installation. Working capital and refinancing costs do not qualify. Fixed rate loans are available for a maximum of 20 years. The maximum loan amount is 80% of the market value of property and 75% of the market value of equipment.

Contact: Mr. Troy Jones, Jr., Director of Finance, Governor's Office of Economic Development, 711 Wells Avenue, Capitol Lake plaza, Pierre, SD 57501. (605) 773-5032, (800) 843-8000 (toll-free, out-of-state), (800) 952-3625 (toll-free, in-state).

Assistance for Rural Small Businesses

The **Agricultural Loan Participation Program** supplements existing credit. Loans are administered and serviced through local lenders, with the South Dakota **Department of Agriculture's Rural Development Office** providing up to 80% of the loan for an enterprise. Applicants must be at least 21 years of age and derive at least 60% of income in the past tax year from farming. Money may not be used to construct, purchase, or renovate a personal dwelling.

Contact: Mr. Randy Englund, Rural Development Officer, South Dakota Office of Rural Development, 445 East Capitol, Anderson Building, Pierre, SD 57501. (605) 773-3375.

TEXAS

Texas Department of Commerce

The **Finance Office** administers several programs that benefit small businesses, including those authorized under the **Industrial Development Corporation Act** of 1979 and the **Rural Development Act**, as well as the state industrial revenue bond program.

The **Industrial Development Corporation Act** of 1979 enables a political subdivision to create a nonprofit development corporation to act on its behalf in issuing revenue bonds. It provides financing for industrial and limited commercial projects.

The **Rural Development Act** empowers the Department of Commerce to provide direct loans to local nonprofit industrial foundations or corporations for up to 40% of the total cost of financing industrial expansion in designated rural areas. The funds may be used to finance manufacturing or industrial enterprise projects, excluding working capital and inventory. Funds for the program are limited; only projects of less than $1 million are considered.

The Department of Commerce also administers the state industrial revenue bond program. In addition, through a public-private cooperative effort, the Joint Economic Development Commission, banks, and local industrial foundation projects provide financing for land, buildings, and equipment.

Contact: Mr. Gary King, Deputy Director for Finance, Department of Commerce, 410 East

Fifth Street, P.O. Box 12728, Austin, TX 78711. (512) 472-5059.

Loans for Manufacturing and Industrial Enterprises

Eligible business are manufacturing or industrial enterprises located in a rural city with a pop. of 35,000 or less or a country with a pop. of 150,000 or less & predominantly rural in character. Preference given to food & fiber processing industries.

The funds may be used for land, buildings, equipment, facilities, and working capital. They cannot be used to refinance existing debt.

Contact: Armando Ruiz, Texas Department of Commerce, 410 East Fifth Street, P.O. Box 12728, Austin, TX 78711. (512) 320-9649

Texas Capital Fund

The project must be located in a rural area with a population of 50,000 or less & non-entitlement countries of less than 200,000. Ineligible counties: Dallas, Tarrant, Hidalgo, Bexar, & Harris.

Minimum loan is for $50,000, it may be used for land, buildings, equipment, and working capital.

Contact: Lina Dane, Department of Commerce, 410 East Fifth Street, P.O. Box 12728, Austin, TX 78711. (512) 320-9555.

Texas Loan Program

Loans are for manufactured products with at least 25% Texas source components, labor, or intellectual property, and the export preparation of agricultural product or livestock.

The minimum loan is $10,000 and may be used for raw materials, inventory, other manufacturing costs, marketing, and equipment.

Contact: Edward Sosa, Department of Commerce, 410 East Fifth Street, P.O. Box 12728, Austin, TX 78711. (512) 320-9443.

Product Commercialization Fund

Direct loans are available for commercialization of new products or processes. Preference for technology, SBBIR award winners, commercialization of university technology.

Contact: Mike Klonsinski, Department of Commerce, 410 East Fifth Street, P.O. Box 12728, Austin, TX 78711. (512) 320-9678.

Texas SBA 504 Certified Development Corporations

Certified Development Corporations provide long-term, fixed note loans for small and medium sized firms. There are a large number of these in Texas. For the ones that service your district, call your local Small Business Administration office or the Texas Department of Commerce at (800) 888-0511.

Texas Sources of Capital

The Texas Department of Commerce publishes an outstanding resource list, instructions for requesting funds, examples of financial states plus names and descriptions of federal, state, venture capital resources, plus others in Texas. To get a copy of *Texas Sources of Capital*, call The Small Business Division of the Texas Department of Commerce at (800) 888-0511.

UTAH

SBA 503/504 Certified Development Companies

Three Utah development companies, located in Salt Lake City, Ogden, and Provo, lend to small and medium-sized businesses at fixed rates for terms of 10 to 20 years. Companies must create one job for every $15,000 received in financing. A 504 loan is funded through the sale of a debenture that is guaranteed by the U.S. Small Business Administration up to $750,000 or 40% of the total cost of land, buildings, and equipment.

Contacts: Mr. Scott Davis, President, Deseret Certified Development Company, 4885 South 900 East, Suite 304, Salt Lake City, UT 84117. (801) 266-0443.

Mr. Mike Vanchiere, Director, Provo Central Utah Certified Development Company, 152 West Center, Provo, UT 84601. (801) 374-1025, (801) 375-1822.

Mr. George Whiting, Director, Historic 25th Street Certified Development Company, 2540 Washington Boulevard, 6th Floor, Ogden, UT 84401. (801) 629-8397.

Funds for Research Contracts and Program Grants

The purpose of the **Utah Technology Finance Corporation** is to encourage and assist the incubation and growth of new and emerging high technology businesses throughout Utah. The corporation, which concentrates on Utah's small businesses, provides funds for research contracts and program grants.

Contact: Mr. Grant Cannon, Executive Director, Utah Technology Finance Corporation, 419 Wakara Way, Suite 215, Salt Lake City, UT 84108. (801) 583-8832.

Utah Innovation Center

The **Utah Innovation Center** works to improve the economic viability of the state through the encouragement of technical innovation and entrepreneurship. The center assists in the creation of new companies based on promising technology and capable, innovative people. The center performs the following functions:

- Screens concepts to determine their technical and economic viability;

- Forms appropriate business entities for worthy projects, with the center as an equity partner;

- Provides legal, administrative, accounting, technical, and clerical support for the companies, together with adequate space for both incubation and growth in the center's facilities;

- Assists in securing both debt and equity financing at favorable terms to meet the expansion needs of the companies;

- Develops real estate to house the companies in close proximity to the center; and

- Supports the efforts of public and private organizations working to improve the high technology business climate in the region.

Introductions to Money Sources

The **Utah Innovation Foundation** is a non-profit educational organization that trains entrepreneurs on how to raise money and assists them with introductions to money sources. The foundation also sponsors international programs on technical innovation and entrepreneurship.

Contact: Mr. Bradley B. Bertoch, Executive Director, Utah Innovation Foundation, 417 Wakara Way, Suite 195, Salt Lake City, UT 84108. (801) 584-2520.

VERMONT

Vermont Job Start

Vermont Job Start is a state-funded economic opportunity program aimed at increasing self-employment by low-income Vermonters. The program lends up to $10,000 to start, strengthen, or expand a small business.

The interest rate is 8.5%, with a maximum term of four years.

To be eligible, applicants must be residents of Vermont, have insufficient access to other sources of credit, lack adequate personal financial resources for their businesses, and, depending on the size of their household, have a maximum annual income of between $14,000 and $24,000.

The program was established in 1978. Since that time, loans totalling over $1 million have been made. A recent study found that the state was spending approximately $3,500 to help create or sustain each full-time job under the program.

Contact: Mr. Thomas Schroeder, Job Start Coordinator, Office of Economic Opportunity, 103 South Main Street, Waterbury, VT 05676. (802) 241-2450.

Vermont Industrial Development Authority

The **Vermont Industrial Development Authority** has several financial programs to assist small and medium-sized manufacturing firms in the state. The authority can provide mortgage insurance up to 90% of principal and interest for a project, with the average guarantee between 80 and 90%. The guarantee is backed by the full faith and credit of the state, with the amount not to exceed $10 million.

The authority also provides direct loans for fixed-asset financing. Up to 40% of a project can be financed with an interest rate of 4%. Last year, the authority made approximately 27 direct loans totaling $3. 3 million.

Contact: Mr. Robert E. Fletcher, Manager, Vermont Industrial Development Authority, 58 East State Street, Montpelier, VT 05602. (802) 223-7226.

Small Business Development Agency

The **Small Business Development Agency** was created within the Department of Commerce in 1969. The Small Business Development Agency is charged to assist local small businessmen and women in establishing profitable operations through management counseling and financial and loan assistance. The agency is heading by an executive director appointed by the governor with the advice and consent of the legislature.

In order to be eligible for assistance, a person must own at least 50% legal or equitable interest in a small business either established or to be established in the Virgin Islands. The owner must be active in the management or operation of the small business on a full-time basis; the small business must be his or her principal means of support.

In addition, the owner must be a native-born or continuous resident of the Virgin Islands for at least 10 years. If one parent is native-born, the 10-year residency requirement is reduced to five years.

Contact: Mr. Jean D. Larsen, Director, Small Business Development Agency, P.O. Box 6400, St. Thomas, VI 00801. (809) 774-8784.

The **Fredriksted Small Business Revolving Loan Fund** provides financial assistance to small businesses located in the Fredriksted district of St. Croix. The maximum amount for loans is $20,000.

Contact: Mr. Jean D. Larsen, Director, Small Business Development Agency, P.O. Box 6400, St. Thomas, VI 00801. (809) 774-8784.

VIRGINIA

Virginia Department of Economic Development

The **Office of Small Business and Financial Services** was created in 1984 to provide information and assistance to Virginia's small businesses. Through this office, small business owners can receive information on business.

The **Financial Services Manager** identifies financial resources available to businesses and directs small firms to private and government capital sources available in Virginia.

Contact: Mr. David V. O'Donnell, Director, Office of Small business and Financial Services, Virginia Department of Economic Development, 1000 Washington Building, 9th Floor, Richmond, VA 23219. (804) 786-3791.

Virginia Small Business Financing Authority

The **Small Business Financing Authority** was created in 1984 to assist small businesses in obtaining financing for development and expansion. The authority currently has the following programs:

- **Industrial Development Bonds (IDBs): Tax-exempt revenue bonds are issued to** eligible small businesses to finance manufacturing projects. They can be used to finance land, buildings, and new capital equipment. The authority's umbrella program allows small businesses to take advantage of the public capital market's attractive rates and terms for tax-exempt bonds.

- **Taxable Bond Program:** Taxable revenue bonds are issued to provide long-term financing for the land, building, and capital equipment needs of small businesses not eligible for tax-exempt IDB financing. In certain circumstances, a portion of the taxable bond proceeds may be used to

refinance existing debt on fixed assets or for working capital.

- **Working Capital Loan Guaranty Program:** this program is designed to reduce the risk to banks in making working capital loans and thereby increase the working capital financing available to small firms for purchasing inventory, increasing marketing efforts, or otherwise improving and expanding their businesses.

The program provides a maximum guaranty of 50% of a bank loan, or $50,000, whichever is less, with terms up to 36 months.

Contact: Ms. Cathleen Mackey, Executive Director, Virginia Small business Financing Authority, 1000 Washington Building, 11th Floor, Richmond, VA 23219. (804) 786-3791.

The Rural Virginia Development Foundation

The **Rural Virginia Development Foundation** provides a system of unique and innovative financing alternatives for rural business starts. The foundation, designed to aid rural industries and enhance the growth of compatible industries, provides equity and loan financing, entrepreneurship development, and human capital development.

Contact: Mr. Berkwood M. Farmer, Executive Director, Rural Virginia Development Foundation, 223 Governor Street, Richmond, VA 23219. (804) 786-3978.

WASHINGTON

Industrial Revenue Bonds (IRBs) can be issued to finance the acquisition, construction, enlargement, or improvement of industrial development facilities. Interest paid to the buyer of the bonds is not subject to federal income tax. Beginning in 1987, eligible industrial development projects are limited to manufacturing facilities.

The **State Umbrella Bond Program** is available to firms whose borrowing needs are too small to warrant packaging a single-borrower bond issue or who are unable to find a purchaser for the bonds because of new federal tax code changes. Bond pooling allows the costs of issuing tax-exempt bonds to be divided among several borrowers, making bonds a more economical means of financing and enabling borrowers to benefit from lower rates.

Contact: Mr. Bryant Woods, Bond Program Administrator, Department of Trade and Economic Development, 101 General Administration Building, AX-13, Olympia, WA 98504-0613. (206) 586-1667.

Loan Programs

The department's **Finance Program** helps business and industry secure needed financing by combining private financial loans with federal and state "gap financing" loans. Existing businesses can secure loans that afford long-term financing, reasonable rates, and low down payments.

Contact: Mr. Bill Davidson, Acting Program Manager, Department of Community Development, 9th and Columbia Building, Olympia, WA 98504. (206) 753-4900.

Financial Assistance

The **Small Business Export Finance Assistance Center** is a non-profit corporation established by the state to encourage exports by small and medium-sized companies. The center provides assistance to prospective exporters statewide in the mechanics and financing of exports.

Contact: Mr. Robert Sebastian, President, Small Business Export Finance Assistance Center, 312 First Avenue North, Seattle, WA 98109. (206) 464-7123.

WEST VIRGINIA

The **International Development Division** provides a computerized trade lead referral service. The division identifies international bankers to help companies with financial problems, and participates in trade shows and trade missions.

Contact: Mr. Stephen Spence, Director, International Development Division, Governor's Office of Community and Industrial Development, M-146 State Capital, Charleston, WV 25305. (304) 348-0400.

Low Interest Loans

The West Virginia Economic Development Authority (WVEDA) provides low-interest loans for land or building acquisition, building construction, and equipment purchases. It may participate in up to 50% of the project cost for new or expansion projects. The loan programs are directed to manufacturing firms, with an emphasis on new job creation.

Contact: Mr. David Warner, Manager of Finance, West Virginia Economic Development Authority, Building 6, Room 525, State Capitol, Charleston, WV 25305. (304) 348-3650.

West Virginia SBA 504 Certified Development Corporation

The **Certified Development Corporation** provides long-term, fixed-rate loans for small and medium-sized firms. Interest rates are tied to U.S. Treasury bond rates of comparable maturity.

Contact: Mr. David Warner, Manager, West Virginia Certified Development Corporation, 1900 Washington Street E., Building 6, Room 525, Charleston, WV 25305. (304) 348-3650.

Treasurer's Economic Development Deposit Incentive

The **Treasurer's Economic Development Deposit Incentive** (TEDDI) program provides low-cost financing for businesses that operate exclusively in West Virginia with employment of fewer than 200 or with gross annual receipts of less than $4 million. Financing must be used for activities that create new jobs or preserve existing ones.

Contact: Mr. Dwight Smith, Director, TEDDI Program, Treasurer of State's Office, State Capitol Building, Room E147, Charleston, WV 25303. (304) 346-2623.

West Virginia Industrial and Trade Jobs Development Corporation

West Virginia's Industrial and Trade Jobs Development Corporation supplements other financial incentive programs to help create jobs. This program is not restricted to a specific job-creation level and has the flexibility to fund many types of projects.

Contact: Ms. E. Ann Shabb, Executive Director, West Virginia Industrial and Trade Jobs Development Corporation, Governor's Office, M146, State Capitol, Charleston, WV 25305. (304) 348-0400.

WISCONSIN

Wisconsin Department of Development

The **Bureau of Development Financing** administers the following economic development financing programs:

- **Wisconsin Development Fund-Economic Development Component.** This program is funded through the federal Small Cities Community Development Block Grant program. Its purpose is job creation and

retention with a special emphasis on creating job opportunities for persons of low and moderate income.

The applicant must be an eligible unit of local government making an application on behalf of a business. The assistance to the business is in the form of a loan with terms and conditions that may vary based on the business' demonstrated need.

- **Customized Labor Training Fund.** This fund was established in 1984 to meet the critical manpower needs of Wisconsin businesses when the training for their labor force is not available through existing Federal, state, or local resources. It works to stimulate expansion of existing businesses, the creation of new businesses, and the retooling of Wisconsin's industrial base through the introduction of new products and processes.

The fund can provide grants for up to 50% of the cost of training or retaining workers in emerging occupations for expanding or retooling firms.

- **Technology Development Fund.** This fund was created in 1984 to provide financial support through a consortia of businesses and institutions of higher education for research and development of new products and processes. The goals of the program are the promotion of business development in Wisconsin, the encouragement of business retooling and diversification, and the expansion of business access to the universities of the state.

A match provision limits total awards to a maximum of 40% of the total project's value and requires a 20-to 90-percent contribution, cash or in-kind, from the business.

- **Employee Ownership Assistance Loan Program.** Under this program, financial assistance is provided to a group of employees to determine the feasibility of employee ownership of a business. To qualify, the business must have experienced substantial layoffs or a closing not more than one year before the date of application.

- **Major Economic Development Projects Program.** The purpose of this program is to retain or increase employment in Wisconsin through the support of projects likely to have a substantial economic impact. Assistance can take the form of a grant or loan, depending on the circumstances. Applicants must commit to locate in Wisconsin and not displace workers or relocate out of state. A match is required.

Contact: Mr. James A. Gruentzel, Director, Bureau of Development Financing, Wisconsin Department of Development, 123 West Washington Avenue, P.O. Box 7970, Madison, WI 53707. (608) 266-3075.

The **Bureau of Expansion and Recruitment** coordinates and facilitates business creation, retention, and expansion efforts in Wisconsin. The bureau's business consultants assist communities in developing programs that will attract and retain businesses. They provide assistance to businesses opening new facilities, expanding operations, or recovering from business setbacks. Services include identifying financial resources, supplies, and sites and buildings. Information is also provided on taxes, utility services, available worker training, and labor availability.

Contact: Mr. Robert Fleming, Acting Director, Bureau of Expansion and Recruitment, Wisconsin Department of Development, 123 West Washington Avenue, P.O. Box 7970, Madison, WI 53707. (608) 266-0165.

Statewide SBA 504 Certified Development Corporation

The **Wisconsin Business Development Finance Corporation** is a private, nonprofit U.S. Small Business Administration Certified Development Corporation. Its program provides small business financing for the purchase of land, buildings, machinery, and equipment, and the construction and modernization of facilities. Businesses must obtain private financing for at least 50% of each project. The program offers long-term financing with maturities of 10 and 20 years.

Contact: Mr. John Giegel, Executive Director, Wisconsin Business Development Finance Corporation, 217 South Hamilton Street, P.O. Box 2717, Madison, WI 53701. (608) 258-8830.

Wisconsin Housing and Economic Development Authority

The **Wisconsin Housing and Economic Development Authority** (WHEDA) has several programs for financing small business development. These programs are available through participating lenders and financial institutions.

The **Business Development Bond** (BDB) program is an industrial revenue bond program that offers fixed-rate, 10-year loans of $200,000 to $4.2 million to manufacturing firms. The rates are set at the time of issue and are approximately 1% above prime. The loans are available to eligible manufacturers for fixed-asset financing only, which includes the purchase and/or rehabilitation of land, buildings, and equipment.

The **Linked Deposit Loan** (LiDL) program is a reduced-rate loan fund designed to assist small Wisconsin businesses that are more than 50-percent owned or controlled by women or minority group members.

The program, a $5 million revolving loan fund, can help reduce the costs of borrowing on new bank loans ranging from $10,000 to $99,000 for periods of two years or less. These bank loans may be used only for the purchase or rehabilitation of land, buildings, and business equipment. Loans for working capital or the purchase of inventory are not permitted under this program.

The **Business Energy Fund** (BEF) offers Wisconsin businesses loans at rates as low as 3% for energy-related improvements and equipment purchases.

Funded with monies from the Stripper Well Oil Overcharge Settlement Agreement, the program offers loans from $1,000 to $500,000 to eligible borrowers. The program also makes rebates for eligible cash purchases below $5,000. An energy audit is required for most improvements.

Through the **Venture Capital Fund**, WHEDA is authorized by the Wisconsin legislature in invest up to $1 million in new and existing businesses that are developing new products. Proposals must be sponsored by venture capital companies doing business in the state.

Contact: Mr. Christopher Swain, Director, Economic Development Group, Wisconsin Housing and Economic Development Authority, 1 South Pinckney Street, Suite 500, Madison, WI 53703. (608) 266-9991.

Wisconsin Community Capital, Inc.

Wisconsin Community Capital, Inc. (WCC) is a job creation and retention program for low-income communities of Wisconsin. WCC makes loans to and invests in expanding companies.

Contact: Mr. Paul Eble, President, Wisconsin Community Capital, Inc., 1 South Pinckney, Suite 500, Madison, WI 53703. (608) 256-3441.

WYOMING

Economic Development and Stabilization Board

Funds from the **Wyoming Economic Development Block Grant** (EDBG) program help communities attract or expand local industry by providing low interest loans to businesses for low- and moderate-income job creation and retention.

Contact: Mr. John Sedgwick, Block Grant Manager, Economic Development and Stabilization Board, 122 West 25th Street, 3rd Floor East, Cheyenne, WY 82002. (307) 777-7287, (800) 262-3425 (toll-free, out-of-state)

The **Economic Development Loan Program** provides direct loans and loan guarantees with flexible rates and terms to Wyoming businesses.

Contact: Mr. Dan Purdue, Acting Executive Director, Economic Development and Stabilization Board, 122 West 25th Street, 3rd Floor East, Cheyenne, WY 82002. (307) 777-7287, (800) 262-3425 (toll-free, out-of-state)

The **Governor's International Trade Program** assists Wyoming businesses with exporting to international markets. An international data base stores information about Wyoming exporters and allows quick access to pertinent international trade information. The data base helps define which overseas markets are being accessed from Wyoming.

This office also publishes the Wyoming International Trade Directory, which lists Wyoming exporters, export marketing consultants, freight forwarders, international banks, and foreign contacts.

An **Export Incentive Program** offers limited financial support to businesses to conduct research assessing the foreign market potential for specific Wyoming products and industries.

Contact: Mr. Peter Cunningham, Director of International Trade, Economic Development and Stabilization Board, 122 West 25th Street, 3rd Floor East Wing, Cheyenne, WY 82002. (307) 777-6412.

Loans/Capital Formation

The **Wyoming Retirement System** and the **Wyoming Industrial Development Corporation** (WIDC) have agreed to purchase from Wyoming financial institutions the guaranteed portion of U.S. Small Business Administration (SBA) and Farmers Home Administration loans to small businesses. These loans are then pooled into a common fund of the Wyoming Retirement System. The program enables small businesses to obtain loans at more reasonable rates and terms than would otherwise be available.

Contact: Mr. Scott Weaver, Executive Vice President, Wyoming Industrial Development Corporation, P.O. Box 3599, Casper, WY 82602. (307) 234-5351.

Small Business Assistance Act

Under **Wyoming's Small Business Assistance Act**, the state treasurer is authorized to buy the guaranteed portion of SBA loans, then pool, package, and sell them on the secondary money market to obtain a reduced interest rate for small business borrowers.

Contacts: Mr. Stan Smith, Wyoming State Treasurer, State Capitol Building, Cheyenne, WY 82002. (307) 777-7408.

State Linked Deposit Plan

The Wyoming state treasurer can contact for deposits with Wyoming financial institutions at a rate of up to 3% below market rates. This program provides businesses with a five-year fixed-rate interest subsidy. The buy-down rate under this program is a maximum of 3%. A maximum loan of $750,000 can be applied towards structures, equipment, land, livestock, and capital.

Contact: Mr. Earl Kabeiseman, Deputy State Treasurer, Office of the State Treasurer, Capital Building, Cheyenne, WY 82002. (307) 777-7408.

Job Training Administration

The **Job Training Administration** provides funds to Wyoming businesses to support worker training and retraining. Direct subsidies can reach 50% of an employee's wages during training. Funds can be used for on- or off-site classroom training, on-the-job training, or support services.

Contact: Mr. David Griffin, Wyoming Private Industry Council Officer, Job Training Administration, 2301 Central Avenue, Cheyenne, WY 82002. (307) 777-7671.

CHAPTER 4

HOW TO FIND VENTURE CAPITAL

A VENTURE CAPITAL PRIMER

This section was furnished courtesy of The Small Business Administration.

Summary

Small businesses never seem to have enough money. Bankers and suppliers, naturally, are important in financing small business growth through loans and credit, but an equally important source of long term growth capital is the venture capital firm. Venture capital financing may have an extra bonus, for if a small firm has an adequate equity base, banks are more willing to extend credit.

This section discusses what venture capital firms look for when they analyze a company and its proposal for investment, the kinds of conditions venture firms may require in financing agreements, and the various types of venture capital investors. It stresses the importance of formal financial planning as the first step to getting venture capital financing.

What Venture Capital Firms Look For

One way of explaining the different ways in which banks and venture capital firms evaluate a small business seeking funds, put simply, is: Banks look at its immediate future, but are most heavily influenced by its past. Venture capitalists look to its longer-run future.

To be sure, venture capital firms and individuals are interested in many of the same factors that influence bankers in their analysis of loan applications from smaller companies. All financial people want to know the results and ratios of past operations, the amount and intended use of the needed funds, and the earnings and financial condition of future projections. But venture capitalists look much more closely at the features of the product and the size of the market than do commercial banks.

Banks are creditors. They're interested in the product/market position of the company,' to the extent they look for assurance that this service or product can provide steady sales and generate sufficient cash flow to repay the loan. They look at projections to be certain that owner / managers have done their homework.

Venture capital firms are owners. They hold stock in the company, adding their invested capital to its equity base. Therefore, they examine existing or planned products or services and the potential markets for them with extreme care. They invest only in firms they believe can rapidly increase sales and generate substantial profits.

Why? Because venture capital firms invest for long- term capital, not for interest income. A common estimate is that they look for three to five times their investment in five or seven years. Of course venture capitalists don't realize capital gains on all their investments. Certainly they don't make capital gains of 300% to 500% except on a very limited portion of their total investments. But their intent is to find venture projects with this appreciation potential to make up for investments that aren't successful.

Venture capital is a risky business, because it's difficult to judge the worth of early stage companies. So most venture capital firms set rigorous policies for venture proposal size, maturity of the seeking company, requirements and evaluation procedures to reduce risks, since their investments are unprotected in the event of failure.

Size of the Venture Proposal

Most venture capital firms are interested in investment projects requiring an investment of $250,000 to $1,500,000. Projects requiring under $250,000 are of limited interest because of the high cost of investigation and administration; however, some venture firms will consider smaller proposals if the investment is intriguing enough.

The typical venture capital firm receives over 1,000 proposals a year. Probably 90% of these will be rejected quickly because they don't fit the established geographical, technical, or market area policies of the firm — or because they have been poorly prepared.

The remaining 10% are investigated with care. These investigations are expensive. Firms may hire consultants to evaluate the product, particularly when it's the result of innovation or is technologically complex. The market size and competitive position of the company are analyzed by contacts with present and potential customers, suppliers, and others. Production costs are reviewed. The financial condition of the company is confirmed by an auditor. The legal form and registration of the business are checked. Most importantly, the character and competence of the management are evaluated by the venture capital firm, normally via a thorough background check.

These preliminary investigations may cost a venture firm between $2,000 and $3,000 per company investigated. They result in perhaps ten to fifteen proposals of interest. Then, second investigations, more thorough and more expensive than the first, reduce the number of proposals under consideration to only three or four. Eventually the firm invests in one or two of these.

Maturity of the Firm Making the Proposal

Most venture capital firms' investment interest is limited to projects proposed by companies with some operating history, even though they may not yet have shown a profit. Companies that can expand into a new product line or a new market with additional funds are particularly interesting. The venture capital firm can provide funds to enable such companies to grow in a spurt rather than gradually, as they would on retained earnings.

Companies that are just starting or that have serious financial difficulties may interest some venture capitalists, if the potential for significant gain over the long run can be identified and assessed. If the venture firm has already extended its portfolio to a large risk concentration, they may be reluctant to invest in these areas because of increased risk of loss.

However, although most venture capital firms will not consider a great many proposals from start-up companies, there are a small number of venture firms that will do only "start-up" financing. The small firm that has a well thought-out plan and can demonstrate that its management group has an outstanding record (even if it is with other companies) has a decided edge in acquiring this kind of seed capital.

Management of the Proposing Firm

Most venture capital firms concentrate primarily on the competence and character of the proposing firm's management. They feel that even mediocre products can be successfully manufactured, promoted, and distributed by an experienced, energetic management group.

They look for a group that is able to work together easily and productively, especially under conditions of stress from temporary reversals and competitive problems. They know that even excellent products can be ruined by poor management. Many venture capital firms really invest in management capability, not in product or market potential.

Obviously, analysis of managerial skill is difficult. A partner or senior executive of a venture capital firm normally spends at least a week at the offices of a company being considered, talking with and observing the management, to estimate their competence and character.

Venture capital firms usually require that the company under consideration have a complete management group. Each of the important functional areas — product design, marketing, production, finance, and control — must be under the direction of a trained, experienced member of the group. Responsibilities must be clearly assigned. And, in addition to a thorough understanding of the industry, each member of

the management team must be firmly committed to the company and its future.

The "Something Special" in the Plan

Next in importance to the excellence of the proposing firms' management group, most venture capital firms seek a distinctive element in the strategy or product/market/process combination of the firm. this distinctive element may be a new feature of the product or process or a particular skill or technical competence of the management. But it must exist. It must provide a competitive advantage.

ELEMENTS OF A VENTURE PROPOSAL

Purpose and Objectives — a summary of the what and why of the project.

Proposed Financing — the amount of money you'll need from the beginning to the maturity of the project proposed, how the proceeds will be used, how you plan to structure the financing, and why the amount designated is required.

Marketing — a description of the market segment you've got or plan to get, the competition, the characteristics of the market, and your plans (with costs) for getting or holding the market segment you're aiming at.

History of the Firm — a summary of significant financial and organizational milestones, description of employees and employee relations, explanations of banking relationships, recounting of major services or products your firm has offered during its existence, and the like.

Description of the Product or Service — a full description of the product (process) or service offered by the firm and the costs associated with it in detail.

Financial Statements — both for the past few years and pro forma projections (balance sheets, income statements, and cash flows) for the next 3-5 years, showing the effect anticipated if the project is undertaken and if the financing is secured (This should include an analysis of key variables affecting financial performance, showing what could happen if the projected level of revenue is not attained).

Capitalization — a list of shareholders, how much is invested to date, and in what form (equity/debt).

Biographical Sketches — the work histories and qualifications of key owners/employees.

Principal Suppliers and Customers

Problems Anticipated and Other Pertinent Information — a candid discussion of any contingent liabilities, pending litigation, tax or patent difficulties, and any other contingencies that might affect the project you're proposing.

Advantages — a discussion of what's special about your product, service, marketing plans or channels that gives your project unique leverage.

Provisions of the Investment Proposal

What happens when, after the exhaustive investigation and analysis, the venture capital firm decides to invest in a company? Most venture firms prepare an equity financing proposal that details the amount of money to be provided, the percentage of common stock to be surrendered in exchange for these funds, the interim financing method to be used, and the protective covenants to be included.

This proposal will be discussed with the management of the company to be financed. The final financing agreement will be negotiated and generally represents a compromise between the management of the company and the partners or senior executives of the venture capital firm. The important elements of this compromise are: ownership, control, annual charges, and primary objectives.

Ownership

Venture capital financing is not inexpensive for the owners of a small business. The partners of the venture firm buy a portion of the business's equity in exchange for their investment.

This percentage of equity varies, of course, and depends upon the amount of money provided, the success and worth of the business, and the anticipated investment return. It can range from perhaps 10% in the case of an established, profitable company to as much as 80% or 90% for beginning or financially troubled firms.

Most venture firms, at least initially, don't want a position of more than 30% to 40% because they want the owner to have the incentive to keep building the business. If additional financing is required to support business growth, the outsiders' stake may exceed 50%, but investors realize that small business owner-managers can lose their entrepreneurial zeal under those circumstances.

In the final analysis, however, the venture firm, regardless of its percentage of ownership, really wants to leave control in the hands of the company's managers, because it is really investing in that management team in the first place.

Most venture firms determine the ratio of funds provided to equity requested by a comparison of the present financial worth of the contributions made by each of the parties to the agreement. The present value of the contribution by the owner of a starting or financially troubled company is obviously rated low. Often it is estimated as just the existing value of his or her idea and the competitive costs of the owner's time. The contribution by the owners of a thriving business is valued much higher. Generally, it is capitalized at a multiple of the current earnings and/or net worth.

Financial valuation is not an exact science. The final compromise on the owner's contribution's worth in the equity financing agreement is likely to be much lower than the owner thinks it should be and considerably higher than the partners of the capital firm think it might be.

In the ideal situation, of course, the two parties to the agreement are able to do together what neither could do separately: 1) the company is able to grow fast enough with the additional funds to do more than overcome the owner's loss of equity, and 2) the investment grows at a sufficient rate to compensate the venture capitalists for assuming the risk.

An equity financing agreement with an outcome in five to seven years which pleases both parties is ideal. Since, of course, the parties can't see this outcome in the present, neither will be perfectly satisfied with the compromise reached.

It is important, though, for the business owner to look at the future. He or she should carefully consider the impact of the ratio of funds invested to the ownership given up, not only for the present, but for the years to come.

Control

Control is a much simpler issue to resolve. Unlike the division of equity over which the parties are bound to disagree, control is an issue in which they have a common (though perhaps unapparent) interest. While it's understandable that the management of a small company will have some anxiety in this area, the partners of a venture firm have little interest in assuming control of the business. They have neither the technical expertise nor the managerial personnel to run a number of small companies in diverse industries. They much prefer to leave operating control to the existing management.

The venture capital firm does, however, want to participate in any strategic decisions that might change the basic product/market character of the company and in any major investment decisions that might divert or deplete the financial resources of the company. They will, therefore, generally ask that at least one partner be made a director of the company.

Venture capital firms also want to be able to assume control and attempt to rescue their investments, if severe financial, operating, or marketing problems develop. Thus, they will usually include protective covenants in their equity financing agreements to permit them to take control and appoint new officers if financial performance is very poor.

Annual Charges

The investment of the venture capital firm may be in the final form of direct stock ownership which does not impose fixed charges. More likely, it will be in an interim form — convertible subordinated debentures or preferred stock. Financing may also be straight loans with options or warrants that can be converted to a future equity position at a pre-established price.

The convertible debenture form of financing is like a loan. The debentures can be converted at an established ratio to the common stock of the company within a given period, so that the venture capital firm can prepare to realize their capital gains at their option in the future. These instruments are often subordinated to existing and planned debt to permit the company invested in to obtain additional bank financing.

Debentures also provide additional security and control for the venture firm and impose a fixed charge for interest (and sometimes for principal payment, too) upon the company. The owner-manager of a small company seeking equity financing should consider the burden of any fixed annual charges resulting from the financing agreement.

Final Objectives

Venture capital firms generally intend to realize capital gains on their investments by providing for a stock buy-back by the small firm, by arranging a public offering of stock of the company invested in, or by providing for a merger with a larger firm that has publicly traded stock. They usually hope to do this within five to seven years of their initial investment. (It should be noted that several additional stages of financing may be required over this period of time.)

Most equity financing agreements include provisions guaranteeing that the venture capital firm may participate in any stock sale or approve any merger, regardless of their percentage of stock ownership. Sometimes the agreement will require that the management work toward an eventual stock sale or merger.

Clearly, the owner-manager of a small company seeking equity financing must consider the future impact upon his or her own stock holdings and personal ambition of the venture firm's aims, since taking in a venture capitalist as a partner may be virtually a commitment to sell out or go public.

TYPES OF VENTURE CAPITAL FIRMS

There is quite a variety of types of venture capital firms. They include:

Traditional partnerships—which are often established by wealthy families to aggressively manage a portion of their funds by investing in small companies;

Professionally managed pools—which are made up of institutional money and which operate like the traditional partnerships;

Investment banking firms—which usually trade in more established securities, but occasionally form investor syndicates for venture proposals;

Insurance companies—which often have required a portion of equity as a condition of their loans to smaller companies as protection against inflation;

Manufacturing companies—which have sometimes looked upon investing in smaller companies as a means of supplementing their R & D programs (Some "Fortune 500" corporations have venture capital operations to help keep them abreast of technological innovations); and Small Business Investment Corporations (SBICs)—which are licensed by the Small Business Administration (SBA) and which may provide management assistance as well as venture capital. (When dealing with SBICs, the small business owner-manager should initially determine if the SBIC is primarily interested in an equity position, as venture capital, or merely in long-term lending on a fully-secured basis.)

In addition to these venture capital firms there are individual private investors and finders. Finders, which can be firms or individuals, often know the capital industry and may be able to help the small company seeking capital to locate it, though they are generally not sources of capital themselves.

Care should be exercised so that a small business owner deals with reputable, professional finders whose fees are in line with industry practice. Further, it should be noted that venture capitalists generally prefer working directly with principals in making investments, though finders may provide useful introductions.

The Importance of Formal Financial Planning

In case there is any doubt about the implications of the previous sections, it should be noted: It is extremely difficult for any small firm—especially the starting or struggling company—to get venture capital.

There is one thing, however, that owner-managers of small businesses can do to improve the chances of their venture proposals at least escaping the 90% which are almost immediately rejected. In a word—plan.

Having financial plans demonstrates to venture capital firms that you are a competent manager, that you may have that special managerial edge over other small business owners looking for equity money. You may gain a decided advantage through well-prepared plans and projections that include: cash budgets, pro forma statements, and capital investment analysis and capital source studies.

Cash budgets should be projected for one year and prepared monthly. They should combine expected sales revenues, cash receipts, material, labor and overhead expenses, and cash disbursements on a monthly basis. This permits anticipation of fluctuations in the level of cash and planning for short term borrowing and investment.

Pro forma statements should be prepared for planning up to 3 years ahead. They should include both income statements and balance sheets. Again, these should be prepared quarterly to combine expected sales revenues; production, marketing, and administrative expenses; profits; product, market, or process investments; and supplier, bank, or investment company borrowing. *Pro forma* statements permit you to anticipate the financial results of your operations and to plan intermediate term borrowing and investments.

Capital investment analyses and capital source studies should be prepared for planning up to 5 years ahead. The investment analyses should compare rates of return for product, market, or process investment, while the source alternatives should compare the cost and availability of debt and equity and the expected level of retained earnings, which together will support the selected investments. These analyses and source studies should be prepared quarterly so you may anticipate the financial consequences of changes in your company's strategy. They will allow you to plan long term borrowing, equity placements, and major investments.

There's a bonus in making such projections. They force you to consider the results of your actions. Your estimates must be explicit; you have to examine and evaluate your managerial records; disagreements have to be resolved—or at least discussed and understood. Financial planning may be burdensome, but it's one of the keys to business success.

Now, making these financial plans will not guarantee that you'll be able to get venture capital. Not making them, will virtually assure that you won't receive favorable consideration from venture capitalists.

We recommend use of *The Business Planning Guide* by Andy Bangs. Information on ordering is found at the back of this book.

HOW TO FIND AN ANGEL

This section was provided by the Office of Small Business Research and Development of the National Science Foundation.

Entrepreneurs trying to raise from $100,000 to $1,000,000 for ventures that are unlikely to be publicly held or acquired by a larger firm within five to ten years will seldom attract the interest of professional venture investors. These entrepreneurs should turn their attention to an invisible segment of the risk capital market - individual investors (business angels).

Business angels are a diverse and dispersed population of individuals of means, many of whom have created their own successful ventures. By providing seed capital for inventors and start-up firms, and equity financing for established small firms, angels fill a void in the institutional risk capital market.

The evidence suggests that angels finance as many as twenty-five thousand ventures per year, many of them high-tech start-ups.

Most angels make their own investment decision; therefore, they usually invest in technologies or markets with which they are familiar. Angels tend to invest close to home, typically within a day's drive. They like to stay in touch with ventures they finance, often providing invaluable guidance. Angels require rewards commensurate with the risks they take. Therefore even angel money is expensive. However, angels often look for psychic income (forms of non-financial rewards) from their risk capital investments. As a result, they often demand less equity than professional venture capitalists.

Angels are sophisticated investors. They look for competent management; they seldom invest in the absence of a documented business plan; and they want to know when and how they can cash in their chips.

Entrepreneurs looking for angels should put their proposals in writing and then look close to home for investors familiar with the technology and markets they plan to exploit. Finding the first angel is tough. The second and third come more easily. Angels tend to be linked by an informal network of friends and business associates, frequently sharing investment opportunities.

VENTURE CAPITAL CLUBS

Venture capital clubs are organizations with the purpose of providing a forum where entrepreneurs and investors can meet to discuss business opportunities.

Venture capital members are investors, accountants, attorneys, commercial and investment bankers, entrepreneurs, stockbrokers, management consultants, venture capitalists, and other business professionals who are interested in helping their local economy grow. While the clubs do not have pools of funds available to entrepreneurs and do not collectively invest in businesses, members may provide a business with direct financial support or non-financial support on an individual basis. The clubs do provide screening and referral services to local venture capital firms.

There are approximately 90 venture capital clubs throughout the world today. The first club, the Connecticut Venture Group, was formed 14 years ago by venture capitalist and Forbes magazine columnist, Thomas P. Murphy.

Typically the process is as follows; investors will be categorized by the characteristics of business ventures in which they are interested. Each month they will receive a listing of venture ideas that meet their criteria. In addition to the list, they will receive a copy of the executive summary of each company's business plan and pro forma statement. If an investor is interested in making contact with any of the entrepreneurs, then he or she must notify the venture capital club. The club notifies the entrepreneur and will furnish both parties with information about each other from the original application. At this point, the club is no longer a party to any subsequent transactions that occur between the two parties.

Clubs in the United States

The following is a partial list of clubs. Updated lists can be obtained from:

Mary Woita, Nebraska Venture Group, 1313 Farnam, Suite 132, Omaha, NE 68182-0248;

International Venture Capital Institute, P.O. Box 1333, Stamford, CT 06904.

U.S. Clubs are listed alphabetically by state.

Birmingham Venture Club
P.O. Box 10127
Birmingham, AL 35202
(205) 323-5461
  Don Newton

Montgomery Venture Group
P.O. Box 1013
Montgomery, AL 36192
  (205) 834-5100

Alaska Venture Capital Club
613 E. 22nd
Anchorage, AK 99503
(907) 277-7474
  Walt Fournier

Sacramento Valley
Venture Capital Forum
P.O. Box 15364
Sacramento, CA 95851
(916) 646-0068
  Richard C. Dorf

Orange County Venture Forum
P.O. Box 2011
Laguna Hills, CA 92654
(714) 855-9250
  Gregory Beck

Los Angeles Venture Association
c/o Greentree Capital
4605 Lankershim Blvd.
North Hollywood, CA 91602
(818) 508-0994
  Fonz VonBradsky

Northern California
Venture Capital Association
1470 Wild Rose Way
Mountain View, CA 94043
(808) 536-1827
  Darryl Morita

San Diego Venture Group
c/o Deloitte, Haskins, & Sells
701 B St., Ste. 1900
San Diego, CA 92101
(619) 457-2797
  F. David Hare

Community Entrepreneurs Organization
P.O. Box 2781
San Rafael, CA 94912
(415) 435-4461
  Robert Crandall, Ph.D.

Channel Islands Venture Association
500 Esplanade Dr., #810
Oxnard, CA 93030
(805) 988-1207
  Mark B. Shapee

Rockies Venture Club
1600 Broadway, Ste. 2125
Denver, CO 80202
(303) 832-2737
  Debbie Chavez

Connecticut Venture Group
71 East Ave., Ste. S
Norwalk, CT 06851
(203) 852-7168
  Eugene Pettinelli

Gold Coast Venture Capital Club
5820 N. Federal Highway
Boca Raton, FL 33487
(305) 782-1119
  Michael J. Donnelly

Acorn
302 N. Barcelona St.
Pensacola, FL 32501
(904) 433-5619
  Dan Horvath

Atlanta Venture Forum, Inc.
2100 Gaslight Tower
235 Peachtree St., N.E.
Atlanta, GA 30043
(404) 584-1364
  Mary King

Treasure Valley Venture
Capital Forum, Inc.
Idaho Small Business
Development Center
Boise State University
1910 University Dr.
Boise, ID 83725
(208) 385-3767
  Connie Charlton/Ron Hall

Southern Illinois Venture Capital Group
2120 Richview Rd.
Mount Vernon, IL 62864
(618) 242-1986
  Thomas M. Green

Venture Club of Indiana
c/o Business Development Concepts
8615 Algeciras Dr., #2A
Indianapolis, IN 46250-3628
(317) 875-7938
  Richard Lowe

Central Kentucky Venture
Capital Club
P.O. Box 508
Elizabethtown, KY 42701
  (502) 769-1410
  Ralph M. Mobley

Kentucky Venture Group
c/o Louisville Chamber of Commerce
One Riverfront Plaza
Louisville, KY 40202-2974
(502) 566-5000 or (502) 566-5067
  Mary Ann Cronan

Greater Baton Rouge
Venture Capital Forum
P.O. Box 3217
Baton Rouge, LA 70821
(504) 381-7133
  Skip Smart

Greater New Orleans
Venture Capital Club
c/o Center of Economic Development
Room BA 368
New Orleans, LA 70148
(504) 286-6663
  Oksana Kurowyckyj

128 Venture Group
Bedford Road
Lincoln, MA 01773
(617) 259-8776
  Michael Belanger

New Enterprise Forum
912 North Main St.
Ann Arbor, MI 48104
(313) 662-0550
  Thomas S. Porter

Missouri Venture Forum, Inc.
101 South Hanley, Ste. 1250
St. Louis, MO 63105
(314) 862-5475
  Lary R. Kirchenbauer

Montana Venture Capital Network
P.O. Box 916
Helena, MT 59624
(406) 442-3850
  Richard Bourke

Mid-Nebraska Venture Capital Club
Grand Island Industrial Foundation
P.O. Box 1486
Grand Island, NE 68802
(308) 382-9210
  Dick Good

Cornhusker Venture Exchange, Inc.
P.O. Box 80837
Lincoln, NE 68501
(402) 476-2811
  Ron Harris

Nebraska Venture Group
1313 Farnam-on-the-Mall, Ste. 132
Omaha, NE 68182-0248
(402) 554-8381
  Mary L. Woita

Mid Atlantic Venture
Capital Group, Inc.
1200 Campus Dr., R.R. #30
P.O. Box 3115
Mount Holly, NJ 08060
(609) 261-6000
  David Wiesen

Bergen County Venture Club
14 Bergen St.
Hackensack, NJ 07601
(201) 488-8445
  John R. Lieberman

Long Island Venture Group
Business Research Institute
Hofstra University
Hempstead, NY 11550
(516) 560-5175
  Russell Moore

Hudson Valley Venture Group
45 E. 25 St., Ste. 18B
New York, NY 10010
(914) 236-7118
  Scott Saland

New York Venture Group
605 Madison Ave., Ste. 300
New York, NY 10022-1901
  (212) 832-7300
  Donna Merer

Westchester Venture Capital Network
c/o Chamber of Commerce
222 Mamaroneck Ave.
White Plains, NY 10605
(914) 948-2110
  Harold E. Voght

Minndak Seed Capital Club
Center for Innovation and
Business Development
P.O. Box 8103
University Station
Grand Forks, ND 58202
(701) 777-3132
  Bruce Gjovig

Ohio Venture Association
P.O. Box 22618
Cleveland, OH 44122
(216) 831-2521
  Robert Donaldson

Columbus Investment
Interest Group
37 North High St.
Columbus, OH 43215
(614) 222-3901
  Mike Horn

Delaware Valley
Venture Group
1346 Chestnut St., Ste. 800
Philadelphia, PA 19107
(215) 875-6763
  Kathryn McCombs

Eastern South Dakota
Venture Capital Forum
University of South Dakota
414 East Clark St.
Vermillion, SD 57069
(605) 677-5272
  Don Greenfield

Western Tennessee Venture
Capital Club
P.O. Box 382012
Germantown, TN 38138
(901) 324-4040
  Ben Bewley

Tennessee Venture Group
27 Music Square East
Nashville, TN 37203
(615) 244-4622
  David Hinds

East Texas Venture Capital Group
P.O. Box 763
Beaumont, TX 77704
(409) 832-5901
  George A. Weller, Jr.

Southwest Venture Forum
SMU-External Affairs
Edwin L. Cox
School of Business
Dallas, TX 75275
(214) 692-3027
  Dan Wesgon

Houston Venture Club Association
c/o Texas Commerce Investment Co.
P.O. Box 2558
Houston, TX 77252-8082
(713) 236-4719
  Frederic Hamilton, Jr.

South Texas Venture Capital Club
c/o JMB Enterprises
3407 Buckhaven
San Antonio, TX 78230
(512) 496-7553
  John J. Krouser or Alan Mason

Mountain West Venture Group
P.O. Box 210, 50 South Main Street
Salt Lake City, UT 84144
(801) 533-0777
  Robert Springmeyer

Baltimore-Washington Venture Group
2022 Columbia Rd., N.W., Ste. 714
Washington, DC 20009
(202) 483-0297
  John C. Ver Steeg

Puget Sound Venture Club
14606 N.E. 51st., #C-1
Bellevue, WA 98007-3025
(206) 882-0605
  Gary R. Ritner

Northwest Venture Group
P.O. Box 21693
Seattle, WA 98111-3693
(206) 746-1973
  Kevin Collette

Wisconsin Venture Network
c/o Arthur Young
111 E. Kilbourn, 9th Floor
Milwaukee, WI 53202
(414) 453-1353
  Ralph Ells

Venture Capital Network

Venture Capital Network, Inc. (VCN), founded in 1984, is a not-for-profit corporation managed by the Center for Venture Research at the University of New Hampshire.

VCN provides entrepreneurs with a cost effective process for reaching wealthy individuals interested in investing in early-stage or high-growth private companies.

Entrepreneurs most likely to benefit from participation in VCN are those that: Require between $50,000-$1,000,000 of equity-type financing, are starting or managing ventures with the potential for generating substantial capital gains, need earlier stage financing or smaller amounts of financing than can typically be raised from traditional venture capital sources.

Entrepreneurs with promising ventures are often referred to VCN by venture capital funds and by accountants, attorneys, and bankers.

Most VCN investors are individuals of means, many of whom have created their own successful ventures. Typically, they are active investors (often referred to as "angels") who provide entrepreneurs with know-how as well as capital. They invest in products and services in markets with significant growth potential, require rewards commensurate with the risks they take, and seldom invest in the absence of a business plan. They will insist upon a management team with integrity, competence, and commitment. The investors will need to know-how and when they can cash in their investment.

How does VCN work?

VCN manages a confidential database of investors and entrepreneurs:

Investors submit Investment Interest Profile describing their investment criteria. Entrepreneurs submit Investment Opportunity Profiles, a business plan executive summary, and financial projections.

VCN uses a two-stage computerized matching process during which both parties remain anonymous.

VCN sends to investors only those opportunity Profiles which meet their investment criteria.

Entrepreneurs are introduced to investors interested in pursuing an investment opportunity.

VCN's role terminates with the introduction of an entrepreneur and investor. VCN provides no assurance that particular entrepreneurs will be matched with any prospective investors. VCN maintains a record of reasons reported by investors for rejecting an investment opportunity. This information is reported periodically to VCN entrepreneurs. VCN places no geographic restrictions on its services.

VCN charges a fee for each profile submitted. VCN receives no additional fees, commissions, or other remuneration related to the eventual outcome of any entrepreneur/investor negotiations. The fees are:

Entrepreneurs: Six month registration
U.S. $200
　Overseas distribution $300

Investors: One year registration
Individual Investor
U.S. $200
　Overseas distribution $500

Venture Capital Funds/Corporate Investors/Other Institutional Investors
U.S. $500
Overseas distribution $1000

Does VCN evaluate applications?

No. VCN is neither an investment advisor nor a broker-dealer of securities. VCN provides only an information service for entrepreneurs and investors. VCN neither evaluates nor endorses the merits of investment opportunities presented through its services. VCN conducts no investigations to verify either the accuracy or completeness of information provided by entrepreneurs and investors.

VCN is designed to provide investors with a pre-screened flow of investment opportunities. VCN is not designed as a source of clients for consultants, finders, or others providing fee services to entrepreneurs. VCN reserves the right to withhold its services from individuals and organizations who are not acting as principals investing on their own behalf.

For more information call (603) 743-3993, or write; Venture Capital Network, Inc., P.O. Box 882, Durham, NH 03824-0882.

Computerized Matching Services

For fees of about $150 there are matching services available to get you introduced to an Angel. Most of these limit their services to their immediate geographical area or state.

These services do not finance business themselves and do not evaluate the propositions. They simply match up a potential investor with an appropriate entrepreneur. (This keeps the potential investor from being flooded with irrelevant propositions.)

Who and Where

At the time of this writing, the organizations that link Angels with entrepreneurs via computer match-ups are as follows.

Matching Service Geographical Limits
Seed Capital Network, Inc.
Operations Center
8905 Kingston Pike, Suite 12493
Knoxville, TN 37923
   (615) 693-2091

Indiana Seed Capital Network Indiana
Institute of New Business Ventures, Inc.
One North Capital, Suite 420
Indianapolis, IN 46204
   (317) 634-8418

Upper Peninsula Venture Capital Network
   Inc. Michigan
206 Cohodas Administration Center
Northern Michigan University
Marquette, MI 49855
   (906) 227-2406

Heartland Venture Capital Network Illinois
Evanston Business Investment Corporation
1710 Orrington Avenue
Evanston, IL 60201
   (312) 864-7970

Texas Capital Network
8716 North Mopac Blvd Suite 200
Austin, TX 78759
   (512) 794-9398

The Computerized Ontario Investment Network Ontario
(COIN)
Ontario Chamber of Commerce
2323 Yonge Street
Toronto, Ontario
Canada M4P 2C9
   (416) 482-5222

Midwest Venture Capital Network Missouri
P.O. Box 4659
St. Louis, MO 63108
   (314) 534-7204

Venture Capital Network of New York, Inc.
   New York
TAC
State University College of Arts and Science
Plattsburgh, NY 12901
   (518) 564-2214

Investment Contact Network North Carolina
Institute for the Study of Private Enterprise
University of North Carolina
The Kenan Center 498A
Chapel Hill, NC 27514
  (919) 962-8201

Venture Capital Network, Inc.
P.O. Box 882
Durham, NH 03824
  (603) 862-3556

Casper College Wyoming
Small Business Development Center
125 College Drive
Casper, WY 82601
  (307) 235-4825

University of South Carolina at Aiken South
  Carolina
171 University Parkway
Aiken, SC 29801
  (803) 648-6851

Mississippi Venture Capital Clearinghouse
  Mississippi
Mississippi Research and Development Center
3825 Ridgewood Road
Jackson, MS 39211
  (601) 982-6425

Venture Capital Network of Atlanta, Inc
  Georgia
230 Peachtree Street, N.E., Suite 1810
Atlanta, GA 30303
  (404) 658-7000

Venture Capital Exchange
Enterprise Development Center
The University of Tulsa
Tulsa, OK 74104
  (918) 592-6000 Extension 3152 or 2684

VENTURE CAPITAL FIRMS

There are over 100 companies, including some that foreign-owned, that have venture capital programs in the U.S.

The amount loaned has more than tripled in the last ten years and as of 1990 is approximately four billion dollars a year. Of these loans about 15% are made to business start-ups, the remainder being established firms, second loans, et al.

Many of the firms will invest only within their own sphere of expertise, for example, Apple Computer is interested in early-stage personal computer related endeavors. As equity partners they not only make available funding but also give management assistance as appropriate. Some invest in a fairly broad range of businesses, for example Grace Ventures seeks early-stage opportunities in service businesses, consumer products ventures, specialty chemicals, computer software, biotechnology, waste management, and regional banks to name a few.

Some companies set part of their funds up to sponsor employees in new ventures. They benefit by increased employee creativity plus the opportunity to invest with people they know.

One Xerox employee had an idea for a compressed spelling dictionary microchip for a personal computer. It didn't fit in their product line so they invested $450,000 in a new company headed by the employee. Now Xerox buys the microchips for its typewriters.

To get further information on corporate investing you can contact the National Venture Capital Association at 1655 North Fort Myer Drive, Suite 700, Arlington, VA 22209. Phone (703) 528-4370.

Here are some corporations you may wish to contact; although all will consider seed/start-up deals, the ones with the * are specifically interested in business start-ups.

* Acorn Ventures, Inc.
520 Post Oak Blvd., Suite 130
Houston, TX 77027
(713) 622-9595

Adler & Company
375 Park Ave., Suite 3303
New York, NY 10152
(212) 759-2800

* Advanced Technology Ventures
10 Post Office Square, Suite 970
Boston, MA 02109
(617) 423-4050

Advent International Corp.
191 Federal Street
Boston, MA 02110
(617) 951-9400

* Aegis Funds
One Cranberry Hill
Lexington, MA 02173
(617) 862-0200

Allied Capital Corp.
1666 K Street, N.W., Suite 901
Washington, DC 20006-2803
(202) 331-1112

Allsop Venture Partners
2750 First Ave., N.E., Suite 210
Cedar Rapids, IA 52402

Allstate Venture Capital
Allstate Plaza North, E-2
Northbrook, IL 60062
(312) 402-5681

* Specifically interested in business start ups

* American Research & Development, Inc.
45 Milk Street
Boston, MA 02109
  (617) 423-7500

Ameritech Development Corp.
10 South Wacker Dr., Floor 21
Chicago, IL 60606
  (312) 609-6000

* Ampersand Ventures
55 William Street, Suite 240
Wellesley, MA 02181
  (617) 239-0700

Apple Computer, Inc.
20525 Mariani Avenue M/S, 38-G
Cupertino, CA 95014
  (408) 974-3143

Applied Technology
55 Wheeler Street
Cambridge, MA 02138
  (617) 354-4107

* Arete Ventures, Inc.
6110 Executive Blvd., Suite 1040
Rockville, MD 20852
  (301) 881-2555

* Asset Management Company
275 E. Bayshore Rd., Suite 150
Palo Alto, CA 94303
  (415) 494-7400

* Atlas Associates, Inc.
101 Federal Street, 4th Floor
Boston, MA 02110
  (617) 951-9420

BCM Technologies, Inc.
1709 Dryden, Suite 901
Houston, TX 88030
  (713) 795-0105

BMW Technologies, Inc.
800 South Street
Waltham, MA 02154
  (617) 894-8222

* BT Capital Corporation
280 Park Avenue, 9W
New York, NY 10017
  (212) 850-1903

BancBoston Ventures, Inc.
100 Federal Street
Boston, MA 02110
  (617) 434-2442

BankAmerica Ventures, Inc.
555 California Street
12th Floor, Dept. 3908
San Francisco, CA 94104
  (415) 622-2230

Batterson, Johnson & Wang
Venture Partners
3030 West Madison, Suite 1110
Chicago, IL 60606
  (312) 222-2660

* Battery Ventures, L.P.
200 Portland Street
Boston, MA 02114
  (617) 367-1011

Bellsouth Ventures Corp.
Room 5G06
1155 Peachtree Street, N.E.
Atlanta, GA 30367-6000
  (404) 249-4571

Bessemer Ventures Partners
630 Fifth Avenue, 38th Floor
New York, NY 10111
  (212) 708-9300

  * Specifically interested in business start ups

* William Blair Venture Partners
135 South LaSalle Street
Chicago, IL 60603
  (312) 853-8250

* Boston Capital Ventures
Old City Hall
45 School Street
Boston, MA 02108
  (617) 227-6550

* Bryan & Edwards
600 Montgomery St. 35th Floor
San Francisco, CA 94111
  (415) 421-9990

Burr, Egan, Deleage & Co.
One Post Office Square
Suite 3800
Boston, MA 02109
  (617) 482-8020

CW Group, Inc.
1041 Third Avenue
New York, NY 10021
  (212) 308- 5266

* Cable & Howse Ventures
777 108th Avenue, N.E.
Bellevue, WA 98004
  (206) 646-3030

* Canaan Venture Partners
105 Rowayton Avenue
Rowayton, CT 06853
  (203) 855-0400

Capital Southwest Corporation
12900 Preston Road, Suite 700
Dallas, TX 75230
  (214) 233-8242

The Centennial Funds
1999 Broadway, Suite 2100
Denver, CO 80202
  (303) 298-9066

Chase Manhattan Capital Corp.
One Chase Manhattan Plaza
13th Floor
New York, NY 10081
  (212) 552-6275

Chemical Venture Partners
885 Third Avenue, Suite 810
New York, NY 10022-4834
  (212) 230-2255

* Cherry Tree Ventures
3800 West 80th St., Suite 1400
Minneapolis, MN 55431
  (612) 893-9012

Cilcorp Ventures, Inc.
300 Liberty Street
Peoria, IL 61602
  (309) 672-5158

Citicorp Venture Capital, Ltd.
153 East 53rd Street
New York, NY 10043
  (212) 559-1117

The Columbine Venture Funds
6312 S. Fiddler's Green Circle
Suite 260N
Englewood, CO 80111
  (303) 694-3222

Concord Partners
535 Madison Avenue
New York, NY 10022
  (212) 906-7000

* Specifically interested in business start ups

Continental Illinois Venture Corp.
231 South LaSalle Street
Chicago, IL 60697
(312) 828-8021

* Copley Venture Partners
600 Atlantic Ave., 13th Floor
Boston, MA 02210-2214
(617) 722-6030

Criterion Venture Partners
1000 Louisiana, Suite 6200
Houston, TX 77002
(713) 751-2400

Crosspoint Venture Partners
One First Street
Los Altos, CA 94022
(415) 948-8300

Curtin & Co., Inc.
1200 Travis, Suite 2050
Houston, TX 77002-6062
(713) 658-9806

* DSV Partners
221 Nassau Street
Princeton, NJ 08542
(609) 924-6420

Delphi Bioventures, L.P.
3000 Sand Hill Road
Building 1, Suite 135
Menlo Park, CA 94025
(415) 854-9650

* Demuth, Folger & Terhune
One Exchange Plaza at 55 Broadway
New York, NY 10006
(212) 509-5580

* Dougery, Jones & Wilder
2003 Landings Drive
Mountain View, CA 94043
(415) 968-4820

Eastech Management Company, Inc.
260 Franklin Street, Suite 530
Boston, MA 02110
(617) 439-6130

Edelson Technology Partners
Park 80 West, Plaza Two
Saddle Brook, NJ 07662
(201) 843-4474

* Edison Venture Fund
Princeton Pike Corporate Center
997 Lenox Drive
Lawrenceville, NJ 08648
(609) 896-1900

* El Dorado Ventures
2 North Lake Avenue, Suite 480
Pasadena, CA 91101
(818) 793-1936

Elf Technologies, Inc.
P.O. Box 10037
High Ridge Park
Stamford, CT 06904-2037
(203) 968-5121

Euclid Partners Corp.
50 Rockefeller Plaza
Suite 1022
New York, NY 10020
(212) 489-1770

Fidelity Venture Associates
82 Devonshire St. - L7A
Boston, MA 02109
(617) 570-5200

* Specifically interested in business start ups

First Analysis Corporation
20 N. Wacker Dr., Suite 4220
Chicago, IL 60606-3103
  (312) 372-3111

First Boston Corporation
12 East 49th Street
New York, NY 10017
  (212) 909-4588

* Fostin Capital Corp.
681 Anderson Drive
Building 6, 3rd Floor
Pittsburgh, PA 15220
  (412) 928-1400

Frontenac Company
208 S. LaSalle St., Suite 1900
Chicago, IL 60604
  (312) 368-0044

* Glenwood Management
3000 Sand Hill Road
Building 4, Suite 230
Menlo Park, CA 94025
  (415) 854-8070

Golder, Thoma & Cressey
120 S. LaSalle St., Suite 630
Chicago, IL 60603
  (312) 853-3322

Grace Ventures Corp.
Horn Venture Partners
20300 Stevens Creek Blvd.
Suite 330
Cupertino, CA 95014
  (408) 725-0774

* Greater Washington Investors, Inc.
5454 Wisconsin Ave., Suite 1315
Chevy Chase, MD 20815
  (301) 656-0626

Greylock Management Corp.
One Federal Street
Boston, MA 02110
  (617) 423-5525

* Grotech Partners, L.P.
9690 Deereco Road
Timonium, MD 21093
  (301) 560-2000

Hambrecht & Quist Inc.
One Bush Street
18th Floor
San Francisco, CA 94104
  (415) 576-3300

Hancock Venture Partners
One Financial Center
39th Floor
Boston, MA 02111
  (617) 350-4002

Harriscorp Capital Corp.
111 W. Monroe
Chicago, IL 60690
  (312) 461-3262

Harvest Ventures, Inc.
767 Third Avenue
New York, NY 10017
  (212) 838-7776

Hewlett-Packard Co.
Corporate Investments
3000 Hanover Street
Palo Alto, CA 94304
  (415) 857-2314

* Hill, Carman, Kirby & Washing
885 Arapahoe
Boulder, CO 80302
  (303) 442-5151

* Specifically interested in business start ups

Hillman Ventures, Inc.
2200 Sand Hill Road, #240
Menlo Park, CA 94025
  (415) 854-4653

Howard, Lawson & Co.
Two Penn Center
Philadelphia, PA 19102
  (215) 988-0010

IEG Venture Management, Inc.
10 South Riverside Plaza
14th Floor
Chicago, IL 60606-3802
  (312) 644-0890

Inco Venture Capital Management
One New York Plaza, 37th Floor
New York, NY 10004
  (212) 612-5620

Innoven Group
Park 80 Plaza West-One
Saddle Brook, NJ 07662
  (201) 845-4900

Instoria, Inc. & Providentia, Ltd.
15 West 54th Street, 2nd Floor
New York, NY 10019
  (212) 957-3232

Integrated Health Care
Investments, Inc.
10 Union Square East-5th Floor
New York, NY 10003
  (212) 353-6427

International Technology
Ventures, Inc.
200 Park Ave., Suite 4501
New York, NY 10166
  (212) 972-5233

Jafco America Ventures, Inc.
The Continental Center
180 Maiden Lane, 21st Floor
New York, NY 10038-4939
  (212) 269-8900

Johnston Associates, Inc.
181 Cherry Valley Road
Princeton, NJ 08540
  (609) 924-3131

Kitty Hawk Capital
1640 Independence Center
Charlotte, NC 28246
  (704) 333-3777

Kleiner Perkins Caufield & Byers
Four Embarcadero Center, # 3520
San Francisco, CA 94111
  (415) 421-3110

The Lambda Funds
Drexel Burnham Lambert
60 Broad Street, 7th Floor
New York, NY 10004
  (212) 232-3965

Lawrence, Tyrrell, Ortale & Smith
515 Madison Avenue, 29th Floor
New York, NY 10022-5403

Lubar & Co.
777 E. Wisconsin Ave., Suite 3380
Milwaukee, WI 53202
  (414) 291-9000

Lubrizol Business Development Company
Venture Investment Division
(Formerly Lubrizole Enterprises, Inc.)
29400 Lakeland Blvd.
Wickliffe, OH 44092
  (216) 943-4200

* Specifically interested in business start ups

* M & I Ventures Corp.
770 North Water St., 11th Floor
Milwaukee, WI 53202
  (414) 765-7910

MBW Management, Inc.
365 South Street
Morristown, NJ 07960
  (201) 285-5533

MK Global Ventures
2471 East Bayshore Rd., Suite 520
Palo Alto, CA 94303
  (415) 424-0151

Marquette Venture Partners
1751 Lake Cook Rd., Suite 550
Deerfield, IL 60015
  (312) 940-1700

Matrix Partners
One Post Office Square, Ste. 3840
Boston, MA 02109
  (617) 482-7735

McCown De Leeuw & Co.
3000 Sand Hill Road
Building 3, Suite 290
Menlo Park, CA 94025
  (415) 854-6000

Medical Innovation Partners
Opus Center, Suite 421
9900 Bren Road East
Minneapolis, MN 55343
  (612) 931-0154

Menlo Ventures
3000 Sand Hill Road
Building 4, Suite 100
Menlo Park, CA 94025
  (415) 854-8540

* Meridian Venture Partners
Suite 220
The Fidelity Court Building
259 Radnor-Chester Rd.
Radnor, PA 19087
  (215) 254-2999

Morgan Investment Corporation
902 Market Street
Wilmington, DE 19801
  (302) 651-2551

Morgenthaler Ventures
700 National City Bank Building
629 Euclid Avenue
Cleveland, OH 44114
  (216) 621-3070

New England Capital Corporation
One Washington Mall
Boston, MA 02108
  (617) 573-6400

New Enterprise Associates
1119 St. Paul Street
Baltimore, MD 21202
  (301) 244-0115

Norstar Venture Partners
One Norstar Plaza
Albany, NY 12207
  (518) 447-4050

North Star Ventures, Inc.
150 South Fifth St., Suite 3400
Minneapolis, MN 55402
  (612) 333-1133

Norton Venture Partners
375 Forest Avenue
Palo Alto, CA 94301
  (415) 853-0766

* Specifically interested in business start ups

Norwest Venture Capital
Management, Inc.
2800 Piper Jaffray Tower
222 South Ninth Street
Minneapolis, MN 55402
  (612) 667-1650

Oak Investment Partners
One Gorham Island
Westport, CT 06880
  (203) 226-8346

Olympic Venture Partners II
2420 Carillon Point
Kirkland, WA 98033
  (206) 889-9192

Oxford Partners
1266 Main Street
Stamford, CT 06902
  (203) 964-0592

P.R. Venture Partners, L.P.
40 Rowes Wharf
Boston, MA 02110
  (617) 439-6700

* Palmer Partners L.P.
300 Unicorn Park Drive
Woburn, MA 01801
  (617) 933-5445

Paragon Venture Partners
3000 Sand Hill Road
Building 2, Suite 190
Menlo Park, CA 94025
  (415) 854-8000

Alan Patricof Associates, Inc.
545 Madison Avenue
New York, NY 10022
  (212) 753-6300

* Pierce Nordquist Associates, L.P.
4020 lake Washington Blvd. N.E.
#203
Kirkland, WA 98033
  (206) 624-9540

Piper Jaffray Ventures, Inc.
Piper Jaffray Tower
P.O. Box 28
Minneapolis, MN 55440
  (612) 342-6310

* Plant Resources Venture Funds
75 State Street
Boston, MA 02109
  (617) 492-3900

Premier Venture Capital Corp.
451 Florida Street
Baton Rouge, LA 70801
  (504) 389-4421

T. Rowe Price Threshold Partnerships
100 East Pratt Street
Baltimore, MD 21202
  (301) 547-2000

* Prince Ventures
10 South Wacker Dr., Suite 2575
Chicago, IL 60606
  (312) 454-1408

Prudential Venture Capital Management, Inc.
717 Fifth Avenue, Suite 1100
New York, NY 10022
  (212) 753-0901

Prudential-Bache Capital Partners
Two Embarcadero Center, Suite 1765
San Francisco, CA 94111
  (415) 788-1800

* Specifically interested in business start ups

* Quest Venture
(Formerly, Continental Capital Ventures)
555 California Street, Suite 5000
San Francisco, CA 94104
  (415) 989-2020

RFE Investment Partners
36 Grove Street
New Canaan, CT 06840
  (203) 966-2800

* Robertson, Stephens & Company
One Embarcadero Center, Suite 3100
San Francisco, CA 94111
  (415) 781-9700

Rothschild Ventures, Inc.
One Rockefeller Plaza
New York, NY 10020
  (212) 757-6000

SAS Associates
515 S. Figueroa Street, #600
Los Angeles, CA 90071
  (213) 624-4232

* S.R. One, Limited
259 Radnor-Chester Road, Ste. 190
Radnor, PA 19087
  (215) 254-2944

SRB Management Company
Two Calleria Tower
13455 Noel Rd., Suite 1670
Dallas, TX 75240
  (214) 702-1100

* Salomon Brothers Venture Capital
Two New York Plaza
New York, NY 10004
  (212) 747-7900

* Saugatuck Capital Company
One Canterbury Green
Stamford, CT 06901
  (203) 348-6669

Schroder Ventures
787 Seventh Avenue
New York, NY 10019
  (212) 841-3880 Ext. 886

Scientific Advances, Inc.
601 West Fifth Avenue
Columbus, OH 43201-3195
  (614) 424-7005

* Sears Investment Management Co.
Xerox Centre
55 W. Monroe, 32nd Floor
Chicago, IL 60603
  (312) 875-7343

Security Pacific Capital Corp.
650 Town Center Drive
17th Floor
Costa Mesa, CA 92626
  (714) 556-1964

Seidman Jackson Fisher & Co.
233 North Michigan Ave., Ste 1812
Chicago, IL 60601
  (312) 856-1812

* Sierra Ventures
3000 Sand Hill road
Building One, Suite 280
Menlo Park, CA 94025
  (415) 854-1000

* Sigma Partners, A California Limited
  Partnership
2099 Gateway Place, Suite 310
San Jose, CA 95110
  (408) 453-9300

* Specifically interested in business start ups

* South Atlantic Venture Fund
614 West Bay St., Suite 200
Tampa, FL 33606-2704
  (813) 253-2500

* Southern California Ventures
9920 La Cienega Blvd., Ste. 510
Inglewood, CA 90301
  (213) 216-0544

* Southwest Venture Partnerships
300 Convent, Suite 1400
San Antonio, TX 78205
  (512) 227-1010

Sprout Group
140 Broadway
New York, NY 10005
  (212) 504-3600

Stuart-James Venture Partners I
L.P.
805 Third Avenue
New York, NY 10022
  (212) 758-4665

* Sutter Hill Ventures
755 Page Mill Road, Suite A200
Palo Alto, CA 94304
  (415) 493-5600

TA Associates
45 Milk Street
Boston, MA 02109
  (617) 338-0800

Taylor & Turner
220 Montgomery St. Penthouse 10
San Francisco, CA 94104
  (415) 398-6821

* Technology Venture Investors
3000 Sand Hill Road
Building 4, Suite 210
Menlo Park, CA 94025
  (415) 854-7472

3i Ventures Corporation
99 High Street, Suite 1530
Boston, MA 02110
  (617) 542-8560

U.S. Venture Partners
2180 Sand Hill Road, Ste. 300
Menlo Park, CA 94025
  (415) 854-9080

* Union Venture Corporation
445 S. Figueroa Street
Los Angeles, CA 90071
  (213) 236-4092

* Utah Ventures
419 Wakara Way, Suite 206
Salt Lake City, UT 84108
  (801) 583-5922

* Ventana Growth Funds
1660 Hotel Circle North, Suite 730
San Diego, CA 92108
  (619) 291-2757

* The Venture Capital Fund of New England
160 Federal Street
23rd Floor
Boston, MA 02110
  (617) 439-4646

* Venture First Associates
1400 Lake Hearn Drive, Suite 205
Atlanta, GA 30319
  (404) 843-5545

* Specifically interested in business start ups

VIMAC Corporation
12 Arlington Street
Boston, MA 02116
   (617) 267-2785

The Vista Group
36 Grove Street
New Canaan, CT 06840
   (203) 972-3400

Volpe & Covington
One Maritime Plaza, 11th Floor
San Francisco, CA 94111
   (415) 956-8120

E. M. Warburg Pincus & Co., Inc.
466 Lexington Avenue
New York, NY 10017-3147
   (212) 878-0600

Washington Resources Group, Inc.
1300 New York Avenue, N.W., Suite 204E
Washington, DC 20005
   (202) 789-0808

Weiss, Peck & Greer Venture Partners, L.P.
555 California Street, Suite 4760
San Francisco, CA 94104
   (415) 622-6864

J. H. Whitney & Co.
630 5th Avenue, Suite 3200
New York, NY 10111-0302
   (212) 757-0500

Wind Point Partners
321 North Clark St., Suite 3010
Chicago, IL 60610
   (312) 245-4949

* Wolfensohn Associates, L.P.
599 Lexington Avenue, 40th Floor
New York, NY 10022
   (212) 909-8100

Xerox Venture Capital
800 Long Ridge Road
Stamford, CT 06904
   (203) 968-4155

Zero Stage Capital Company
One Broadway, Kendall Square
Cambridge, MA 02142
   (617) 876-5355

CHAPTER 5

SMALL BUSINESS INVESTMENT COMPANIES

The **National Association of Small Business Investment Companies** keeps up to date information on SBICs.

They will answer further questions, write: NASBIC, 1156 15th St. N.W., Suite 1101, Washington, DC 20005. They provided the following information for us.

WHAT IS AN SBIC?

Although individual investors have been providing venture capital for new and small businesses in the United States for many years, no institutional sources of such financing existed until 1958 when Congress passed the Small Business Investment Act.

Small Business Investment Companies (SBICs) and **Minority Enterprise Small Business Investment Companies (MESBICs)** are financial institutions created to make equity capital and long-term credit (with maturities of at least 5 years) available to small, independent businesses.

SBICs are licensed by the Federal Government's Small Business Administration, but they are privately-organized and privately-managed firms which set their own policies and make their own investment decisions. In return for pledging to finance any small businesses, SBICs may qualify for long-term loans from SBA. Although all SBICs will consider applications for funds from socially and economically disadvantaged entrepreneurs, MESBICs normally make all their investments in this area.

WHAT HAVE SBICs DONE?

To date, SBICs have disbursed over $6 billion by making some 70,000 loans and investments. The concerns they have financed have far outperformed all national averages as measured by increases in assets, sales, profits, and new employment.

Literally thousands of owners of profitable businesses can tell you how much they have benefited from the dollars and management counseling made available to them by SBICs for 27 years.

NEED MONEY? WHICH SBIC SHOULD YOU SEE?

This chapter lists almost 400 SBICs and MESBICs. They represent approximately 90% of the industry's resources and are located in all parts of the country.

In using this listing, you should consider the following factors:

A. Geography: Generally speaking, SBICs are more likely to make loans and investments near their offices, even though many of them operate regionally or even nationally. Therefore, it would probably be wise to contact first those SBICs closest to your business.

B. Investment Policy: Even though most SBICs have both equity investments and straight loans in their portfolios, each of them has a policy on which type of financing it prefers.

C. Industry Preferences: Here again, SBICs differ widely. Because of the expertise of its officers and directors, an SBIC often specializes in making loans and investments in certain industries.

D. Size of Financing: Because they differ in size and investment policies, SBICs establish different dollar limits on the financing they make. This Directory has a symbol showing the preferred maximum size of loan or investment for each SBIC.

It should be emphasized that the information given in the listing should be considered only as a general guide. Every SBIC departs from its usual policies in special cases. Furthermore, SBICs often work together in making loans or investments in greater amounts than any of them could make separately. No SBIC should be ruled out as a possible source of financing.

IS YOUR FIRM ELIGIBLE FOR SBIC FINANCING?

Probably so, since the overwhelming majority of all business firms qualify as small. As a general rule, companies are eligible if they have net worth under $6 million and average after-tax earning of less than $2 million during the past two years. In addition, your firm may qualify as small either under an employment standard or amount of annual sales. Both these standards vary from industry to industry.

A phone call or a note to any NASBIC member — or to its Washington office — will clear up the eligibility question quickly.

HOW DO YOU PRESENT YOUR CASE TO AN SBIC?

There is nothing mysterious about asking an SBIC for money. You should prepare a report on your operations, financial condition, and requirements. Specifically, the report should include detailed information on key personnel, products, proposed new product lines, patent positions, market data and competitive position, distribution and sales methods, and other pertinent materials.

HOW LONG WILL IT TAKE?

There are no hard and fast rules about the length of time it will take an SBIC to investigate and close a transaction. Ordinarily, an initial response, either positive or negative, is made quickly. On the other hand, the thorough study an SBIC must make before it can make a final decision could take several weeks.

Naturally, a well-documented presentation on your part will reduce the amount of time the SBIC will require.

HOW IS SBIC FINANCING STRUCTURED?

Every single SBIC financing is tailored individually to meet your needs and to make the best use of the SBIC's funds. You and the SBIC will negotiate the terms. The SBIC might buy shares of your stock or it might make a straight loan.

Usually, SBICs are interested in generating capital gains, so they will purchase stock in your company or advance funds through a note, or debenture, with conversion privileges or rights to buy stock at a predetermined later date.

HOW CAN SBIC MONEY PROVIDE ADDITIONAL CREDIT LINES?

If the SBIC money is provided to you in a subordinated position, it will often do double or triple duty. Industry averages show that for every SBIC dollar placed with a small business concern, two additional senior dollars become available from commercial banks or other sources.

ARE THERE UNIQUE ADVANTAGES TO SBIC FINANCING?

Yes, indeed! Before it receives its license, an SBIC must prove that its management and directors are experienced individuals with a broad range of business and professional talents.

This expertise will be applied to assist your business, supplementing the skills of your own management team. Here again, the actual pattern of management and financial counseling will be cut to fit each specific situation.

SBICs can make only long-term loans or equity investments; therefore, their interests and yours will coincide—both of you will want your firm to grow and prosper.

WILL I BE TREATED FAIRLY?

As mentioned above, SBICs are licensed by the Federal government only after their officers and directors have been carefully screened. Furthermore, all the SBICs listed in this directory are NASBIC members and all have voluntarily subscribed to the Association's Code of Ethics and Trade Practice Rules.

The Code provides, in part, that "the constant goal of each SBIC shall be to improve the welfare of the small business concerns which it serves. Each SBIC shall promote and maintain ethical standards of conduct and deal fairly and honestly with all small business concerns seeking its assistance."

WHAT IS NASBIC?

It is the national trade association which represents the over-whelming majority of all active SBICs and MESBICs. It was formed in 1958, soon after the passage of the Small Business Investment Act, and has worked on behalf of small business generally and the SBIC industry in particular for 28 years.

In addition to providing educational and informational services for its members, NASBIC presses for a rational legal and regulatory framework for the industry. It also cooperates closely with other independent business associations in advancing the interests of small business on the Federal level.

NEED MORE INFORMATION?

Contact any SBIC in this Directory. If we can be of assistance, write the National Association of Small Business Investment Companies (NASBIC), 1156 15th Street, N.W., Suite 1101, Washington, DC 20005.

SMALL BUSINESS INVESTMENT COMPANIES

Alabama

First SBIC of Alabama
David Delaney, President
16 Midtown Park East
Mobile, AL 36606
  (205) 476-0700

Hickory Venture Capital Corporation
J. Thomas Noojin, President
699 Gallatin Street, Suite A-2
Huntsville, AL 35801
  (205) 539-1931

Remington Fund, Inc. (The)
Lana Sellers, President
1927 First Avenue North
Birmingham, AL 35202
  (205) 324-7709

Alaska

Alaska Business Investment Corporation
James Cloud, Vice President
301 West Northern Lights Blvd.
Mail: P.O. Box 100600
Anchorage, AK 99510
  (907) 278-2071

Arizona

Northwest Venture Partners
(Main Office: Minneapolis, MN)
88777 E. Via de Ventura, Suite 335
Scottsdale, AZ 85258
  (602) 483-8940

Norwest Growth Fund, Inc.
(Main Office: Minneapolis, MN)
88777 E. Via de Ventura, Suite 335
Scottsdale, AZ 85258
  (602) 483-8940

Rocky Mountain Equity Corporation
Anthony J. Nicoli, President
4530 Central Avenue
Phoenix, AZ 85012
  (602) 274-7534

Valley National Investors, Inc.
John M. Holliman III, V.P. & Manager
201 North Central Avenue, Suite 900
Phoenix, AZ 85004
  (602) 261-1577

Wilbur Venture Capital Corporation
Jerry F. Wilbur, President
4575 South Palo Verde, Suite 305
Tucson, AZ 85714
  (602) 747-5999

Arkansas

Small Business Inv. Capital, Inc.
Charles E. Toland, President
10003 New Benton Hwy.
Mail: P.O. Box 3627
Little Rock, AR 72203
  (501) 455-6599

Southern Ventures, Inc.
Jeffrey A. Doose, President & Director
605 Main Street, Suite 202
Arkadelphia, AR 71923
  (501) 246-9627

California

AMF Financial, Inc.
William Temple, Vice President
4330 La Jolla Village Dr. Suite 110
San Diego, CA 92122
  (619) 546-0167

Atalanta Investment Company, Inc.
(Main Office: New York, NY)
141 El Camino Drive
Beverly Hills, CA 90212
  (213) 273-1730

BNP Venture Capital Corporation
Edgerton Scott II, President
3000 Sand Hill Road
Building 1, Suite 125
Menlo Park, CA 94025
  (415) 854-1084

Bancorp Venture Capital, Inc.
Arthur H. Bernstein, President
11812 San Vicente Boulevard
Los Angeles, CA 90049
  (213) 820-7222

BankAmerica Ventures, Inc.
Patrick Topolski, President
555 California Street
San Francisco, CA 94104
  (415) 953-3001

CFB Venture Capital Corporation
Richard J. Roncaglia, Vice President
530 B Street, Third Floor
San Diego, CA 92101
  (619) 230-3304

CFB Venture Capital Corporation
(Main Office: San Diego, CA)
350 California Street, Mezzanine
San Francisco, CA 94104
  (415) 445-0594

Citicorp Venture Capital, Ltd.
(Main Office: New York, NY)
2 Embarcadero Place
2200 Geny Road, Suite 203
Palo Alto, CA 94303
  (415) 424-8000

City Ventures, Inc.
Warner Heineman, Vice Chairman
400 N. Roxbury Drive
Beverly Hills, CA 90210
  (213) 550-5709

Crosspoint Investment Corporation
Max Simpson, Pres. & CFO
1951 Landings Drive
Mountain View, CA 94043
  (415) 968-0930

Developers Equity Capital Corporation
Larry Sade, Chairman of the Board
1880 Century Park East, Suite 311
Los Angeles, CA 90067
  (213) 277-0330

Draper Associates, A California LP
Bill Edwards, President
c/o Timothy C. Draper
3000 Sand Hill Road, Bldg. 4, #235
Menlo Park, CA 94025
  (415) 854-1712

First Interstate Capital, Inc.
Ronald J. Hall, Managing Director
5000 Birch Street, Suite 10100
Newport Beach, CA 92660
  (714) 253-4360

First SBIC of California
Tim Hay, President
650 Town Center Drive
17th Floor
Costa Mesa, CA 92626
  (714) 556-1964

First SBIC of California
(Main Office: Costa Mesa, CA)
5 Palo Alto Square, Suite 938
Palo Alto, CA 94306
  (415) 424-8011

First SBIC of California
(Main Office: Costa Mesa, CA)
155 North Lake Avenue, Suite 1010
Pasadena, CA 91109
  (818) 304-3451

G C & H Partners
James C. Gaither, General Partner
One Maritime Plaza, 20th Floor
San Francisco, CA 94110
  (415) 981-5252

Hamco Capital Corporation
William R. Hambrecht, President
235 Montgomery Street
San Francisco, CA 94104

Imperial Ventures, Inc.
H. Wayne Snavely, President
9920 South La Cienega Blvd.
Mail: P.O. Box 92991, LA 90009
Inglewood, CA 90301
  (213) 417-5888

Jupiter Partners
John M. Bryan, President
600 Montgomery Street, 35th Floor
San Francisco, CA 94111
  (415) 421-9990

Latigo Capital Partners, II
Robert A. Peterson, General Partner
1800 Century Park East, Suite 430
Los Angeles, CA 90067
  (213) 556-2666

Marwit Capital Corp.
Martin W. Witte, President
180 Newport Center Drive, Suite 200
Newport Beach, CA 92660
  (714) 640-6234

Merrill Pickard Anderson & Eyre I
Steven L. Merrill, President
Two Palo Alto Square, Suite 425
Palo Alto, CA 94306
  (415) 856-8880

Metropolitan Venture Company, Inc.
Rudolph J. Lowy, Chairman of the Board
5757 Wilshire Blvd., Suite 670
Los Angeles, CA 90036
  (213) 938-3488

New West Partners II
Timothy P. Haidinger, Manager
4350 Executive Drive, Suite 206
San Diego, CA 92121
  (619) 457-0723

New West Partners II
(Main Office: San Diego, CA)
4600 Campus Drive, Suite 103
Newport Beach, CA 92660
  (714) 756-8940

PBC Venture Capital, Inc.
Henry L. Wheeler, Manager
1408 18th Street
Mail: P.O. Box 6008, Bakersfield, CA 93386
Bakersfield, CA 93301
  (805) 395-3555

Peerless Capital Company, Inc.
Robert W. Lautz, Jr., President
675 South Arroyo Parkway, Suite 320
Pasadena, CA 91105
  (818) 577-9199

Ritter Partners
William C. Edwards, President
150 Isabella Avenue
Atherton, CA 94025
  (415) 854-1555

Round Table Capital Corporation
Richard Dumke, President
655 Montgomery Street, Suite 700
San Francisco, CA 94111
  (415) 392-7500

San Joaquin Capital Corporation
Chester Troudy, President
1415 18th Street, Suite 306
Mail: P.O. Box 2538
Bakersfield, CA 93301
  (805) 323-7581

Seaport Ventures, Inc.
Michael Stopler, President
525 B Street, Suite 630
San Diego, CA 92101
  (619) 232-4069

Union Venture Corp.
Jeffrey Watts, President
445 South Figueroa Street
Los Angeles, CA 90071
  (213) 236-4092

VK Capital Company
Franklin Van Kasper, General Partner
50 California Street, Suite 2350
San Francisco, CA 94111
  (415) 391-5600

Vista Capital Corporation
Frederick J. Howden, Jr., Chairman
5080 Shoreham Place, Suite 202
San Diego, CA 92122
  (619) 453-0780

Walden Capital Partners
Arthur S. Berliner, President
750 Battery Street, Seventh Floor
San Francisco, CA 94111
  (415) 391-7225

Wells Fargo Capital Corporation
Ms. Sandra J. Menichelli, VP & GM
420 Montgomery Street, 9th Floor
San Francisco, CA 94163
  (415) 396-2059

Westamco Investment Company
Leonard G. Muskin, President
8929 Wilshire Blvd., Suite 400
Beverly Hills, CA 90211
  (213) 652-8288

Colorado

Associated Capital Corporation
Rodney J. Love, President
4891 Independence Street, Suite 201
Colorado Small Business Investment
  CompaniesWheat Ridge, CO 80033
  (303) 420-8155

UBD Capital, Inc.
Allan R. Haworth, President
1700 Broadway
Denver, CO 80274
  (303) 863-6329

Connecticut

AB SBIC, Inc.
Adam J. Bozzuto, President
275 School House Road
Cheshire, CT 06410
  (203) 272-0203

All State Venture Capital Corp.
Caesar N. Anquillare, President
The Bishop House
32 Elm Street, P.O. Box 1629
New Haven, CT 06506
  (203) 787-5029

Capital Impact Corp.
William D. Starbuck, President
961 Main Street
Bridgeport, CT 06601
  (203) 384-5670

Capital Resource Co. of Connecticut
I. Martin Fierberg, Managing Partner
699 Bloomfield Avenue
Bloomfield, CT 06002
  (203) 243-1114

Dewey Investment Corp.
George E. Mrosek, President
101 Middle Turnpike West
Manchester, CT 06040
  (203) 649-0654

First Connecticut SBIC
David Engelson, President
177 State Street
Bridgeport, CT 06604
  (203) 366-4726

First New England Capital, LP
Richard C. Klaffky, President
255 Main Street
Hartford, CT 06106
  (203) 728-5200

Marcon Capital Corporation
Martin A. Cohen, President
49 Riverside Avenue
Westport, CT 06880
  (203) 226-6893

Northeastern Capital Corporation
Joseph V. Ciaburri, Chairman & CEO
209 Church Street
New Haven, CT 06510
  (203) 865-4500

Regional Financial Enterprises, L.P.
Robert M. Williams, Managing Partner
36 Grove Street
New Canaan, CT 06840
  (203) 966-2800

SBIC of Connecticut, Inc. (The)
Kenneth F. Zarrilli, President
1115 Main Street
Bridgeport, CT 06603
  (203) 367-3282

Delaware

Morgan Investment Corporation
William E. Pike, Chairman
902 Market Street
Wilmington, DE 19801
  (302) 651-2500

District of Columbia

Allied Investment Corporation
David J. Gladstone, President
1666 K Street, N.W., Suite 901
Washington, DC 20006
  (202) 331-1112

American Security Capital Corp., Inc.
William G. Tull, President
730 Fifteenth Street, N.W.
Washington, DC 20013
  (202) 624-4843

DC Bancorp Venture Capital Company
Allan A. Weissburg, President
1801 K Street, N.W.
Washington, DC 20006
  (202) 955-6970

Washington Ventures, Inc.
Kenneth A. Swain, President
1320 18th Street, N.W., Suite 300
Washington, DC 20036
  (202) 895-2560

Florida

Allied Investment Corporation
(Main Office: Washington, DC)
Executive Office Center, Suite 305
2770 N. Indian River Blvd.
Vero Beach, FL 32960
  (407) 778-5556

First North Florida SBIC
J.B. Higdon, President
1400 Gadsden Street
P.O. Box 1021
Quincy, FL 32351
  (904) 875-2600

Gold Coast Capital Corporation
William I. Gold, President
3550 Biscayne Blvd., Room 601
Miami, FL 33137
  (305) 576-2012

J & D Capital Corporation
Jack Carmel, President
12747 Biscayne Blvd.
North Miami, FL 33181
  (305) 893-0303

Market Capital Corporation
E. E. Eads, President
1102 North 28th Street
P.O. Box 22667
Tampa, FL 33630
  (813) 247-1357

Quantum Capital Partners, Ltd.
Michael E. Chaney, President
2400 East Commercial Blvd. Suite 814
Fort Lauderdale, FL 33308
  (305) 776-1133

Southeast Venture Capital Limited I
James R. Fitzsimons, Jr., President
3250 Miami Center, 100 Chopin Plaza
Miami, FL 33131
  (305) 379-2005

Western Financial Capital Corporation
(Main Office: Dallas, TX)
1380 N.E. Miami Gardens Dr., Suite 225
North Miami Beach, FL 33179
  (305) 949-5900

Georgia

Investor's Equity, Inc.
I. Walter Fisher, President
2629 First National Bank Tower
Atlanta, GA 30383
  (404) 523-3999

North Riverside Capital Corporation
Tom Barry, President
50 Technology Park/Atlanta
Norcross, GA 30092
  (404) 446-5556

Hawaii

Bancorp Hawaii SBIC
James D. Evans, Jr., President
111 South King St. Suite 1060
Honolulu, HI 96813
  (808) 521-6411

Illinois

ANB Venture Corporation
Kurt L. Liljedahl, EVP
33 North LaSalle Street
Chicago, IL 60690
  (312) 855-1554

Alpha Capital Venture Partners, LP
Andrew H. Kalnow, General Partner
Three First National Plaza, 14th Fl.
Chicago, IL 60602
(312) 372-1556

Business Ventures, Inc.
Milton Lefton, President
20 North Wacker Drive, Suite 550
Chicago, IL 60606
(312) 346-1580

Continental Illinois Venture Corp.
John L. Hines, President
209 South LaSalle Street
Mail: 231 South LaSalle Street
Chicago, IL 60693
(312) 828-8023

First Capital Corp. of Chicago
John A. Canning, Jr., President
Three First National Plaza, Ste. 1330
Chicago, IL 60670
(312) 732-5400

Frontenac Capital Corporation
David A. R. Dullum, President
208 South LaSalle St., Room 1900
Chicago, IL 60604
(312) 368-0047

Heller Equity Capital Corporation
Robert E. Koe, President
200 North LaSalle St., 10th Floor
Chicago, IL 60601
(312) 621-7200

Mesirow Capital Partners SBIC, Ltd.
James C. Tyree, President of C.G.P.
1355 LaSalle Street, Suite 3910
Chicago, IL 60603
(312) 443-5773

Walnut Capital Corporation
Burton W. Kanter, Chairman
208 South LaSalle Street
Chicago, IL 60604
(312) 346-2033

Indiana

1st Source Capital Corporation
Eugene L. Cavanaugh, Jr., V.P.
100 North Michigan Street
P.O. Box 1602
South Bend, IN 46634
(219) 236-2180

Circle Ventures, Inc.
Robert Salyers, President
2502 Roosevelt Avenue
Indianapolis, IN 46218
(317) 636-7242

Equity Resource Company, Inc.
Michael J. Hammes, V.P.
One Plaza Place
202 South Michigan Street
South Bend, IN 46601
(219) 237-5255

Raffensperger Hughes Venture Corp.
Samuel B. Sutphin, President
20 North Meridian Street
Indianapolis, IN 46204
(317) 635-4551

White River Capital Corporation
Thomas D. Washburn, President
500 Washington Street
Mail: P.O. Box 929
Columbus, IN 47201
(812) 372-0111

Iowa

MorAmerica Capital Corporation
David R. Schroder, VP
800 American Building
Cedar Rapids, IA 52401
 (319) 363-8249

Kansas

Kansas Venture Capital, Inc.
Larry J. High, President
First National Bank Tower, Ste. 825
One Townsite Plaza
Topeka, KS 66603
 (913) 233-1368

Kentucky

Financial Opportunities, Inc.
Gary Duerr, Manager
6060 Dutchman's Lane
Mail: P.O. Box 35710
Louisville, KY 40205
 (502) 451-3800

Mountain Ventures, Inc.
Jerry A. Rickett, EVP
London Bank & Trust Building
400 S. Main Street, Fourth Floor
London, KY 40741
 (606) 864-5175

Wilbur Venture Capital Corp.
(Main Office: Tucson, AZ)
400 Fincastle Building
3rd & Broadway
Louisville, KY 40202
 (502) 585-1214

Louisiana

Capital for Terrebonne, Inc.
Hartwell A. Lewis, President
27 Austin Drive
Houma, LA 70360
 (504) 868-3930

Louisiana Equity Capital Corp.
G. Lee Griffin, President
451 Florida Street
Baton Rouge, LA 70821
 (504) 389-4421

Maine

Maine Capital Corporation
David M. Coit, President
Seventy Center Street
Portland, ME 04101
 (207) 772-1001

Maryland

First Maryland Capital, Inc.
Joseph A. Kenary, President
107 West Jefferson Street
Rockville, MD 20850
 (301) 251-6630

Greater Washington Investment, Inc.
Don A. Christensen, President
5454 Wisconsin Avenue
Chevy Chase, MD 20815
 (301) 656-0626

Jiffy Lube Capital Corporation
Eleanor C. Harding, President
6000 Metro Drive
Mail: P.O. Box 17223
Baltimore, MD 21203-7223
Baltimore, MD 21215
  (301) 764-3234

Massachusetts

Advent Atlantic Capital Company, LP
David D. Croll, Managing Partner
45 Milk Street
Boston, MA 02109
  (617) 338-0800

Advent IV Capital Company
David D. Croll, Managing Partner
45 Milk Street
Boston, MA 02109
  (617) 338-0800

Atlas II Capital Corporation
Joost E. Tjaden, President
101 Federal Street, 4th Floor
Boston, MA 02110
  (617) 951-9420

BancBoston Ventures, Inc.
Paul F. Hogan, President
100 Federal Street
Mail: P.O. Box 2016
Boston, MA 02110
  (617) 434-2441

Bever Capital Corp.
Joost E. Tjaden, President
101 Federal Street, 4th Floor
Boston, MA 02110
  (617) 951-9420

Boston Hambro Capital Company
Edwin Goodman, President
160 State Street, 9th Floor
Boston, MA 02109
  (617) 523-7767

Business Achievement Corporation
Michael L. Katzeff, President
1172 Beacon Street, Suite 202
Newton, MA 02161
  (617) 965-0550

Chestnut Street Partners, Inc.
David D. Croll, President
45 Milk Street
Boston, MA 02109
  (617) 574-6763

First Capital Corp. of Chicago
(Main Office: Chicago, IL)
133 Federal Street, 6th Floor
Boston, MA 02110
  (617) 542-9185

First United SBIC, Inc.
Alfred W. Ferrara, Vice President
135 Will Drive
Canton, MA 02021
  (617) 828-6150

Fleet Venture Resources, Inc.
(Main Office: Providence, RI)
Carlton V. Klein, Vice-President
60 State Street
Boston, MA 02109
  (617) 367-6700

Mezzanine Capital Corporation
David D. Croll, President
45 Milk Street
Boston, MA 02109
  (617) 574-6752

Milk Street Partners, Inc.
Richard H. Churchill, Jr. President
45 Milk Street
Boston, MA 02109
  (617) 574-6723

Monarch-Narragansett Ventures, Inc.
George W. Siguler, President
One Financial Plaza
Springfield, MA 01102
  (413) 781-3000

New England Capital Corporation
Z. David Patterson, Vice President
One Washington Mall, 7th Floor
Boston, MA 02108
  (617) 573-6400

Northeast SBI Corp.
Joseph Mindick, Treasurer
16 Cumberland Street
Boston, MA 02115
  (617) 267-3983

Orange Nassau Capital Corporation
Joost E. Tjaden, President
101 Federal Street, 4th Floor
Boston, MA 02110
  (617) 951-9420

Pioneer Ventures Limited Partnership
Christopher W. Lynch, Managing Partner
60 State Street
Boston, MA 02109
  (617) 742-7825

Shawmut National Capital Corporation
Steven James Lee, President
One Federal Street, 30th Floor
Boston, MA 02211
  (617) 556-4700

Stevens Capital Corporation
Edward Capuano, President
168 Stevens Street
Fall River, MA 02721
  (617) 679-0044

UST Capital Corporation
Walter Dick, President
40 Court Street
Boston, MA 02108
  (617) 726-7137

Vadus Capital Corporation
Joost E. Tjaden, President
101 Federal Street, 4th Floor
Boston, MA 02110
  (617) 951-9420

Michigan

Michigan Tech Capital Corporation
Clark L. Pellegrini, President
Technology Park
601 West Sharon Avenue
P.O. Box 364
Houghton, MI 49931
  (906) 487-2970

Minnesota

FBS SBIC, Limited Partnership
John M. Murphy, Jr., Managing Agent
1100 First Bank Place East
Minneapolis, MN 55480
  (612) 370-4764

North Star Ventures II, Inc.
Terrence W. Glarner, President
150 South Fifth Street, Ste 3400
Minneapolis, MN 55402
  (612) 333-1133

Northland Capital Venture Partnership
George G. Barnum, Jr., President
613 Missabe Building
Duluth, MN 55802
  (218) 722-0545

Northwest Venture Partners
Robert F. Zicarelli, Managing G.P.
2800 Piper Jaffray Tower
222 South Ninth Street
Minneapolis, MN 55402
  (612) 372-8770

Norwest Growth Fund, Inc.
Daniel J. Haggerty, President
2800 Piper Jaffray Tower
222 South Ninth Street
Minneapolis, MN 55402
  (612) 372-8770

Shared Ventures, Inc.
Howard W. Weiner, President
6550 York Ave. South, Suite 419
Edina, MN 55435
  (612) 925-3411

Missouri

Bankers Capital Corporation
Raymond E. Glasnapp, President
3100 Gillham Road
Kansas City, MO 64109
  (816) 531-1600

Capital for Business, Inc.
James B. Hebenstreit, President
1000 Walnut, 18th Floor
Kansas City, MO 64106
  (816) 234-2357

Capital for Business, Inc.
(Main Office: Kansas City, MO)
11 South Meramec, Suite 804
St. Louis, MO 63105
  (314) 854-7427

MBI Venture Capital Investors, Inc.
Anthony Sommers, President
850 Main Street
Kansas City, MO 64105
  (816) 471-1700

MorAmerica Capital Corporation
(Main Office: Cedar Rapids, IA)
911 Main Street, Suite 2724A
Commerce Tower Building
Kansas City, MO 64105
  (816) 842-0114

United Missouri Capital Corp.
Joe Kessinger, Manager
1010 Grand Avenue
Kansas City, MO 64106
  (816) 556-7333

Nebraska

First of Nebraska Investment Corp.
Dennis O'Neal, Managing Officer
One First National Ctr., Suite 701
Omaha, NE 68102
  (401) 633-3585

United Financial Resources Corp.
Dennis L. Schulte, Manager
6211 L Street
Mail: P.O. Box 1131
Omaha, NE 68101
  (402) 734-1250

Nevada

Enterprise Finance Cap Develop. Corp.
Robert S. Russell, Sr., President
First Interstate Bank of Nevada Bldg.
One East First Street, Suite 1100
Reno, NV 89501
  (702) 329-7797

New Hampshire

VenCap, Inc.
Richard J. Ash, President
1155 Elm Street
Manchester, NH 03101
  (603) 644-6100

New Jersey

Bishop Capital, L.P.
Charles J. Irish
58 Park Place
Newark, NJ 07102
  (201) 623-0171

ESLO Capital Corp.
Leo Katz, President
212 Wright Street
Newark, NJ 07114
  (201) 242-4488

First Princeton Capital Corp.
Michael D. Feinstein, President
Five Garret Mountain Plaza
West Paterson, NJ 07424
  (201) 278-8111

Monmouth Capital Corp.
Eugene W. Landy, President
125 Wycoff Road
Midland National Bank Bldg.
P.O. Box 335
Eatontown, NJ 07724
  (201) 542-4927

Tappan Zee Capital Corporation
Karl Kirschner, President
201 Lower Notch Road
Little Falls, NJ 07424
  (201) 256-8280

Unicorn Ventures II, L.P.
Frank P. Diassi, General Partner
6 Commerce Drive
Cranford, NJ 07016
  (201) 276-7880

Unicorn Ventures, Ltd.
Frank P. Diassi, President
6 Commerce Drive
Cranford, NJ 07016
  (201) 276-7880

United Jersey Venture Capital, Inc.
Stephen H. Paneyko, President
301 Carnegie Center
P.O. Box 2066
Princeton, NJ 08540
  (609) 987-3490

New Mexico

Albuquerque SBIC
Albert T. Ussery, President
501 Tijeras Avenue, N.W.
P.O. Box 487
Albuquerque, NM 87103
  (505) 247-0145

Equity Capital Corp.
Jerry A. Henson, President
119 East Marcy Street, Suite 101
Santa Fe, NM 87501
  (505) 988-4273

Southwest Capital Investments, Inc.
Martin J. Roe, President
The Southwest Building
3500-E Comanche Road, N.E.
Albuquerque, NM 87107
  (505) 884-7161

United Mercantile Capital Corp.
Joe Justice, General Manager
2400 Louisiana Blvd., Bldg 4, Ste 101
Albuquerque, NM 87110
  (505) 883-8201

New York

767 Limited Partnership
H. Wertheim and H. Mallement, G.P.
767 Third Avenue
New York, NY 10017
  (212) 838-7776

ASEA- Harvest Partners II
Harvey Wertheim, General Partner
767 Third Avenue
New York, NY 10017
  (212) 838-7776

American Commercial Capital Corp.
Gerald J. Grossman, President
310 Madison Avenue, Suite 1304
New York, NY 10017
  (212) 986-3305

American Energy Investment Corp.
John J. Hoey, Chairman
645 Fifth Avenue, Suite 1900
New York, NY 10022
  (212) 688-7307

Amev Capital Corp.
Martin Orland, President
One World Trade Center 50th Floor
New York, NY 10048
  (212) 775-9100

Atalanta Investment Company, Inc.
L. Mark Newman, Chairman
450 Park Avenue
New York, NY 10022
  (212) 832-1104

BT Capital Corporation
James G. Hellmuth, Deputy Chairman
280 Park Avenue, 10 West
New York, NY 10017
  (212) 850-1916

Boston Hambro Capital Company
(Main Office: Boston, MA)
17 East 71st Street
New York, NY 10021
  (212) 288-9106

Bridger Capital Corporation
Seymour L. Wane, President
645 Madison Avenue, Suite 810
New York, NY 10022
  (212) 888-4004

CMNY Capital L.P.
Robert Davidoff, General Partner
77 Water Street
New York, NY 10005
  (212) 437-7078

Central New York SBIC (The)
Albert Wertheimer, President
351 South Warren Street
Syracuse, NY 13202
  (315) 478-5026

Chase Manhattan Capital Corporation
Custav H. Koven, President
1 Chase Manhattan Plaza, 23rd Floor
New York, NY 10081
  (212) 552-6275

Chemical Venture Capital Associates
Jeffrey C. Walker, Managing Gen. Partner
277 Park Avenue, 10th Floor
New York, NY 10172
  (212) 310-7578

Citicorp Venture Capital, Ltd.
William Comfort, Chairman
399 Park Avenue, 6th Floor
New York, NY 10043
  (212) 559-1127

Clinton Capital Corporation
Mark Scharfman, President
79 Madison Avenue, Suite 800
New York, NY 10016
  (212) 696-4334

Croyden Capital Corporation
Lawrence D. Gorfinkle, President
45 Rockefeller Plaza, Suite 2165
New York, NY 10111
  (212) 974-0184

Diamond Capital Corporation
Steven B. Kravitz, President
805 Third Avenue, Suite 1100
New York, NY 10017
  (212) 838-1255

Edwards Capital Company
Edward H. Teitlebaum, President
215 Lexington Avenue, Suite 805
New York, NY 10016
  (212) 686-2568

F/N Capital Limited Partnership
Raymond A. Lancaster, President
One Norstar Plaza
Albany, NY 12207
  (518) 447-4050

Fairfield Equity Corporation
Matthew A. Berdon, President
200 East 42nd Street
New York, NY 10017
  (212) 867-0150

Ferranti High Technology, Inc
Sandford R. Simon, Pres. & Dir.
515 Madison Avenue
New York, NY 10022
  (212) 688-9828

Fifty-Third Street Ventures, L.P.
Patricia Cloherty & Dan Tessler, G.P.
155 Main Street
Cold Spring, NY 10516
  (914) 265-5167

Franklin Corporation SBIC (The)
Norman S. Strobel, President
767 Fifth Avenue
G.M. Building, 23rd Floor
New York, NY 10153
  (212) 486-2323

Fundex Capital Corporation
Howard Sommer, President
525 Northern Blvd.
Great Neck, NY 11021
  (516) 466-8551

GHW Capital Corp.
Philip Worlitzer, Vice President
25 West 45th Street, Suite 707
New York, NY 10036
  (212) 869-4584

Genesee Funding, Inc.
A. Keene Bolton, President, GEO
100 Corporate Woods
Rochester, NY 14623
  (716) 272-2332

Hanover Capital Corp. (The)
Geoffrey T. Selzer, President
150 East 58th Street, Suite 2710
New York, NY 10155
  (212) 980-9670

Intergroup Venture Capital Corp.
Ben Hauben, President
230 Park Avenue
New York, NY 10017
  (212) 661-5428

Interstate Capital Company, Inc.
David Scharf, President
380 Lexington Avenue
New York, NY 10017
  (212) 986-7333

Irving Capital Corp.
Andrew McWethy, President
1290 Avenue of the Americas
New York, NY 10104
  (212) 408-4800

Kwiat Capital Corp.
Sheldon F. Kwiat, President
576 Fifth Avenue
New York, NY 10036
  (212) 391-2461

M & T Capital Corp.
William Randon, President
One M & T Plaza
Buffalo, NY 14240
  (716) 842-5881

MH Capital Investors, Inc.
Edward L. Kock III, President
270 Park Avenue
New York, NY 10017
  (212) 286-3222

Multi-Purpose Capital Corp.
Eli B. Fine, President
5 West Main Street, Room 207
Elmsford, NY 10523
  (914) 347-2733

NYBDC Capital Corporation
Robert W. Lazar, President
41 State Street
Albany, NY 12207
  (518) 463-2268

NYSTRS/NV Capital Limited Partnership
Raymond A. Lancaster, President
One Norstar Plaza
Albany, NY 12207
  (518) 447-4050

NatWest USA Capital Corporation
Orville G. Aarons, General Manager
175 Water Street
New York, NY 10038
  (212) 602-1200

Norstar Capital, Inc.
Raymond A. Lancaster, President
One Norstar Plaza
Albany, NY 12207
  (518) 447-4043

Norwood Venture Corporation
Mark R. Littell, President
145 West 45th Street, Suite 1211
New York, NY 10036
  (212) 869-5075

Onondaga Venture Capital Fund, Inc.
Irving W. Schwartz, Exec. V.P.
327 State Tower Building
Syracuse, NY 13202
  (315) 478-0157

Preferential Capital Corporation
Bruce Bayroff, Secretary-Treasurer
16 Court Street
Brooklyn, NY 11241
  (718) 855-2728

Pyramid Ventures, Inc.
John Popovitch, Treasurer
280 Park Avenue — 10 West
New York, NY 10015
  (212) 850-1934

Questech Capital Corp.
John E. Koonce, President
320 Park Avenue, 3rd Floor
New York, NY 10022
  (212) 891-7500

R & R Financial Corp.
Imre Rosenthal, President
1451 Broadway
New York, NY 10036
  (212) 790-1441

Rand SBIC, Inc.
Donald Ross, President
1300 Rand Building
Buffalo, NY 14203
  (716) 853-0802

Realty Growth Capital Corp.
Alan Leavit, President
271 Madison Avenue
New York, NY 10016
  (212) 983-6880

Republic SBI Corporation
Robert V. Treanor, Senior VP
452 Fifth Avenue
New York, NY 10018
  (212) 930-8639

SLK Capital Corporation
Edward A. Kerbs, President
115 Broadway, 20th Floor
New York, NY 10006
  (212) 587-8800

Small Bus. Elec. Investment Corp.
Stanley Meisels, President
1220 Peninsula Blvd.
Hewlett, NY 11557
  (516) 374-0743

Southern Tier Capital Corporation
Harold Gold, Secretary-Treasurer
55 South Main Street
Liberty, NY 12754
  (914) 292-3030

Sterling Commercial Capital, Inc.
Harvey L. Granat, President
175 Great Neck Road — Suite 404
Great Neck, NY 11021
  (516) 482-7374

TLC Funding Corporation
Philip G. Kass, President
141 South Central Avenue
Hartsdale, NY 10530
  (914) 683-1144

Tappan Zee Capital Corporation
(Main Office: Little Falls, NJ)
120 North Main Street
New City, NY 10956
  (914) 634-8890

Telesciences Capital Corporation
Mike A. Petrozzo, Contact
26 Broadway, Suite 841
New York, NY 10004
  (212) 425-0320

Vega Capital Corp.
Victor Harz, President
720 White Plains Road
Scarsdale, NY 10583
  (914) 472-8550

Ventura SBIC, Inc.
Arnold Feldman, President
249-12 Jericho Turnpike
Floral Park, NY 11001
  (516) 352-0068

WFG-Harvest Partners, Ltd.
Harvey J. Wertheim, General Partner
767 Third Avenue
New York, NY 10017
  (212) 838-7776

Winfield Capital Corporation
Stanley M. Pechman, President
237 Mamaroneck Avenue
White Plains, NY 10605
  (914) 949-2600

Wood River Capital Corporation
Thomas A. Barron, President
667 Madison Avenue
New York, NY 10022
  (212) 750-9420

North Carolina

Delta Capital, Inc.
Alex B. Wilkins, Jr. President
227 North Tryon Street, Suite 201
Charlotte, NC 28202
  (704) 372-1410

Falcon Capital Corporation
P.S. Prasad, President
400 West Fifth Street
Greenville, NC 27834
  (919) 752-5918

Heritage Capital Corporation
William R. Starnes, President
2095 Two First Union Center
Charlotte, NC 28282
  (704) 334-2867

Kitty Hawk Capital, Limited Partnership
Walter H. Wilkinson, President
Independence Center, Suite 1640
Charlotte, NC 28246
  (704) 333-3777

NCNB SBIC Corporation
Troy S. McCrory, Jr., President
One NCNB Plaza — T05 — 2
Charlotte, NC 28255
  (704) 374-5583

NCNB Venture Company, L.P.
S. Epes Robinson, General Partner
One NCNB Plaza, T-39
Charlotte, NC 28255
  (704) 374-5723

Ohio

A.T. Capital Corporation
Robert C. Salipante, President
900 Euclid Avenue, T-18
Mail: P.O. Box 5937
Cleveland, OH 44101
  (216) 687-4970

Capital Funds Corporation
Carl G. Nelson, Chief Inv. Officer
800 Superior Avenue
Cleveland, OH 44114
  (216) 344-5775

Clarion Capital Corporation
Morton A. Cohen, President
35555 Curtis Blvd.
Eastlake, OH 44094
  (216) 953-0555

First Ohio Capital Corporation
David J. McMacken, General Manager
606 Madison Avenue
Mail: P.O. Box 2061; Toledo, OH 43603
Toledo, OH 43604
  (419) 259-7146

Gries Investment Company
Robert D. Gries, President
1500 Statler Office Tower
Cleveland, OH 44115
  (216) 861-1146

JRM Capital Corporation
H. F. Meyer, President
110 West Streetsboro Street
Hudson, OH 44236
  (216) 656-4010

National City Capital Corporation
Michael Sherwin, President
629 Euclid Avenue
Cleveland, OH 44114
  (216) 575-2491

SeaGate Venture Management, Inc.
Charles A. Brown, Vice-President
245 Summit Street, Suite 1403
Toledo, OH 43603
  (419) 259-8605

Tamco Investors (SBIC), Inc.
Nathan H. Monus, President
375 Victoria Road
Youngstown, OH 44515
  (216) 792-3811

Oklahoma

Alliance Business Investment Co.
Barry Davis, President
17 East Second Street
One Williams Center, Suite 2000
Tulsa, OK 74172
  (918) 584-3581

Western Venture Capital Corporation
William B. Baker, Chief Op. Officer
4880 South Lewis
Tulsa, OK 74105
  (918) 749-7981

Oregon

First Interstate Capital, Inc.
(Main Office: Newport Beach, CA)
227 S.W. Pine Street, Suite 200
Portland, OR 97204
  (503) 223-4334

Northern Pacific Capital Corp.
John J. Tennant, Jr., President
1201 S.W. 12th Avenue, Suite 608
Mail: P.O. Box 1658, Portland 97207
Portland, OR 97205
  (503) 241-1255

Norwest Growth Fund, Inc.
(Main Office: Minneapolis, MN)
1300 S.W. 5th Street, Suite 3108
Portland, OR 97201
  (503) 223-6622

U.S. Bancorp Capital Corporation
Stephen D. Fekety, President
111 S.W. Fifth Ave., Suite 1570
Portland, OR 97204
  (503) 275-5860

Pennsylvania

Capital Corporation of America
Martin M. Newman, President
225 South 15th Street, Suite 920
Philadelphia, PA 19102
  (215) 732-1666

Enterprise Venture Capital
Corporation of Pennsylvania
Don Cowie, CEO
227 Franklin Street, Suite 215
Johnstown, PA 15901
  (814) 535-7597

Erie SBIC
George R. Heaton, President
32 West 8th St., Suite 615
Erie, PA 16501
  (814) 453-7964

Fidelcor Capital Corporation
Bruce H. Luehrs, President
123 S. Broad Street
Philadelphia, PA 19109
  (215) 985-7287

First SBIC of California
(Main Office: Costa Mesa, CA)
Daniel A. Dye, Contact
P.O. Box 512
Washington, PA 15301
  (412) 223-0707

First Valley Capital Corp.
Matthew W. Thomas, President
640 Hamilton Mall, 8th Floor
Allentown, PA 18101
  (215) 776-6760

Franklin Corporation SBIC (The)
(Main Office: New York, NY)
Phymouth Meeting Executive Congress
Suite 461-610 W. Germantown Pike
Plymouth Meeting, PA 19462

Meridian Capital Corporation
Joseph E. Laky, President
Suite 222, Blue Bell West
650 Skippack Pike
Blue Bell, PA 19422
  (215) 278-8907

Meridian Venture Partners
Raymond R. Rafferty, Gen. Partner
The Fidelity Court Building
259 Radnor-Chester Road
Radnor, PA 19087
  (215) 293-0210

PNC Capital Corporation
Gary J. Zentner, President
Pittsburgh National Building
Fifth Avenue and Wood Street
Pittsburgh, PA 15222
  (412) 355-2245

Rhode Island

Domestic Capital Corporation
Nathaniel B. Baker, President
815 Reservoir Avenue
Cranston, RI 02910
  (401) 946-3310

Fleet Venture Resources, Inc.
Robert M. Van Degna, President
111 Westminster Street
Providence, RI 02903
  (401) 278-6770

Moneta Capital Corporate
Arnold Kilberg, President
285 Governor Street
Providence, RI 02906
  (401) 861-4600

Old Stone Capital Corporation
Arthur C. Barton, President
One Old Stone Square, 11th Floor
Providence, RI 02903
  (401) 278-2559

Wallace Capital Corporation
Lloyd W. Granoff, President
170 Westminister St. Suite 300
Providence, RI 02903
  (401) 273-9191

South Carolina

Carolina Venture Capital Corp.
Thomas H. Harvey III, President
14 Archer Road
Hilton Head Island, SC 29928
  (803) 842-3101

Charleston Capital Corporation
Henry Yaschik, President
111 Church Street
P.O. Box 328
Charleston, SC 29402
  (803) 723-6464

Floco Investment Company, Inc. (The)
William H. Johnson, Sr., President
Highway 52 North
Mail: P.O. Box 919, Lake City, SC 29560
Scranton, SC 29561
  (803) 389-2731

Lowcountry Investment Corporation
Joseph T. Newton, Jr., President
4444 Daley Street
P.O. Box 10447
Charleston, SC 29411
  (803) 554-9880

Reedy River Ventures
John M. Sterling, President
233 East Main Street, Suite 202
Mail: P.O. Box 17526
Greenville, SC 29606
  (803) 232-6198

Tennessee

Financial Resources, Inc.
Milton Picard, Chairman
2800 Sterick Building
Memphis, TN 38103
  (901) 527-9411

Leader Capital Corporation
James E. Pruitt, Jr., President
158 Madison Avenue
P.O. Box 708, Memphis, 38101-0708
Memphis, TN 38101
  (901) 578-2405

Texas

Alliance Business Investment Co.
(Main Office: Tulsa, OK)
911 Louisiana
One Shell Plaza, Suite 3990
Houston, TX 77002
  (713) 224-8224

Brittany Capital Company
Steve Peden, Partner
1525 Elm Street
2424 LTV Tower
Dallas, TX 75201
  (214) 954-1515

Business Capital Corp.
James E. Sowell, Chairman
4809 Cole Avenue, Suite 250
Dallas, TX 75205
  (214) 522-3739

Capital Marketing Corporation
Ray Ballard, Manager
100 Nat Gibbs Drive
P.O. Box 1000
Keller, TX 76248
  (817) 656-7309

Capital Southwest Venture Corp.
William R. Thomas, President
12900 Preston Road, Suite 700
Dallas, TX 75230
  (214) 233-8242

Central Texas SBI Corp.
David G. Horner, President
P.O. Box 2600
Waco, TX 76702
  (817) 753-6461

Charter Venture Group, Inc.
Winston C. Davis, President
2600 Citadel Plaza Drive, Ste. 600
Houston, TX 77008
  (713) 863-0704

Citicorp Venture Capital, Ltd.
(Main Office: New York, NY)
717 N. Harwood, Suite 2920-LB87
Dallas, TX 75201
  (214) 880-9670

Energy Assets, Inc.
Laurence E. Simmons, Exec. V.P.
4900 Republic Bank Center
700 Louisiana
Houston, TX 77002
  (713) 236-9999

Enterprise Capital Corporation
Fred Zeidman, President
4543 Post Oak Place, #130
Houston, TX 77027
  (713) 621-9444

FCA Investment Company
Robert S. Baker, Chairman
3000 Post Oak, Suite 1790
Houston, TX 77056
  (713) 965-0061

First Interstate Cap. Corp.
Richard S. Smith, President
1000 Louisiana, 7th Floor
Mail: P.O. Box 3326, Houston, 77253
Houston, TX 77002
  (713) 224-6611

Ford Capital, Ltd.
C. Jeff Pan, President
1525 Elm Street
Mail: P.O. Box 2140, Dallas, 75221
Dallas, TX 75201
  (214) 954-0688

Houston Partners, SBIP
Harvard Hill, President, CGP
Capital Center Penthouse
401 Louisiana
Houston, TX 77002
  (713) 222-8600

MCap Corporation
J. Wayne Gaylord, Manager
1717 Main Street, 6th Floor
Momentum Place
Dallas, TX 75201
  (214) 939-3131

MVenture Corporation
Wayne Gaylord, President
1717 Main Street, 6th Fl.
Momentum Pl.
Mail: P.O. Box 662090, Dallas, 75266
Dallas, TX 75201
  (214) 939-3131

Mapleleaf Capital Ltd.
Edward Fink, President
55 Waugh, Suite 710
Houston, TX 77007
  (713) 880-4494

Mid-State Capital Corp.
Smith E. Thomasson, President
510 North valley Mills Drive
Waco, TX 76710
  (817) 772-9220

Neptune Capital Corporation
Richard C. Strauss, President
5956 Sherry Lane, Suite 800
Dallas, TX 75225
  (214) 739-1414

Omega Capital Corporation
Theodric E. Moor, Jr. President
755 South 11th Street, Suite 250
Mail: P.O. Box 2173
Beaumont, TX 77704
  (409) 832-0221

Republic Venture Group, Inc.
Robert H. Wellborn, CEO
325 N. St. Paul 2829 Tower II
Mail: P.O. Box 655961, Dallas 75265
Dallas, TX 75201
  (214) 922-3500

Revelation Resources, Ltd.
Mr. Chris J. Mathews, Manager
2929 Allen Parkway, Suite 1705
Houston, TX 77019
  (713) 526-5623

Rust Capital Limited
Jack A. Morgan, Partner
114 West 7th Street, Suite 500
Austin, TX 78701
  (512) 482-0806

SBI Capital Corporation
William E. Wright, President
6305 Beverly Hill Lane
Mail: P.O. Box 570368, Houston 77257
Houston, TX 77057
  (713) 975-1188

San Antonio Venture Group, Inc.
Domingo Bueno, President
2300 West Commerce Street
San Antonio, TX 78207
  (512) 223-3633

South Texas SBIC
Kenneth L. Vickers, President
120 South Main Street
P.O. Box 1698
Victoria, TX 77902
  (512) 573-5151

Southwestern Venture Cap. Texas, Inc.
James A. Bettersworth, President
1336 East Court Street
P.O. Box 1719
Seguin, TX 78155
  (512) 379-0380

Southwestern Venture Cap. Texas, Inc.
(Main Office: Seguin, TX)
1250 N.E. Loop 410, Suite 300
San Antonio, TX 78209
  (512) 822-9949

Sunwestern Capital Corporation
Thomas W. Wright, President
3 Forest Plaza
12221 Merit Drive, Suite 1300
Dallas, TX 75251
  (214) 239-5650

Texas Commerce Investment Company
Fred Lummis, Vice President
Texas Commerce Bank Bldg., 30th Floor
712 Main Street
Houston, TX 77002
  (713) 236-4719

UNCO Ventures, Inc.
John Gatti, President
909 Fannin Street, 7th Floor
Houston, TX 77010
  (713) 853-2422

Wesbanc Ventures, Ltd.
Stuart Schube, General Partner
520 Post Oak Blvd., Suite 130
Houston, TX 77027
  (713) 622-9595

Western Financial Capital Corp.
Mrs. Marion Rosemore, President
17772 Preston Rd. Suite 101
Dallas, TX 75252
  (214) 380-0044

Vermont

Queneska Capital Corporation
Albert W. Coffrin, III, President
123 Church Street
Burlington, VT 05401
  (802) 865-1806

Virginia

Crestar Capital
A. Hugh Ewing, III, Managing G.P.
9 South 12th Street, Third Floor
Richmond, VA 23219
  (804) 643-7358

James River Capital Assoc.
A. Hugh Ewing, Managing Partner
9 South 12th Street
Mail: P.O. Box 1776, Richmond 23219
Richmond, VA 23214
  (804) 643-7323

Metropolitan Capital Corporation
John B. Toomey, President
2550 Huntington Avenue
Alexandria, VA 22303
  (703) 960-4698

Sovran Funding Corporation
David A. King, Jr., President
Sovran Center, 6th Floor
One Commercial Plaza
Mail: P.O. Box 600
Norfolk, VA 23510
  (804) 441-4041

Tidewater SBI Corporation
Gregory H. Wingfield, President
1214 First Virginia Bank Tower
101 St. Paul's Blvd.
Norfolk, VA 23510
  (804) 627-2315

Washington

Capital Resource Corporation
T. Evans Wyckoff, President
1001 Logan Building
Seattle, WA 98101
  (206) 623-6550

Northwest Business Investment Corp.
C. Paul Sandifur, President
929 West Sprague Avenue
Spokane, WA 99204
  (509) 838-3111

Seafirst Capital Corporation
David R. West, EVP
Columbia Seafirst Center
701 Fifth Avenue
P.O. Box 34103
Seattle, WA 98124
  (206) 358-7441

U.S. Bancorp Capital Corporation
(Main Office: Portland, OR)
1415 Fifth Avenue
Seattle, WA 98171
  (206) 344-8105

Washington Trust Equity Corp.
John M. Snead, President
Washington Trust Financial Ctr.
P.O. Box 2127
Spokane, WA 99210
  (509) 455-3821

Wisconsin

BancOne Venture Corporation
H. Wayne Foreman, President
111 East Wisconsin Avenue
Milwaukee, WI 53202
  (414) 765-2274

Bando-McGlocklin Capital Corp.
George Schonath, Invest. Advisor
13555 Bishops Court, Suite 225
Brookfield, WI 53005
  (414) 784-9010

Capital Investments, Inc.
Robert L. Banner, Vice President
Commerce Building, Suite 400
744 North Fourth Street
Milwaukee, WI 53203
  (414) 273-6560

M & I Ventures Corp.
John T. Byrnes, President
770 North Water Street
Milwaukee, WI 53202
  (414) 765-7910

MorAmerica Capital Corporation
(Main Office: Cedar Rapids, IA)
600 East Mason Street
Milwaukee, WI 53202
  (414) 276-3839

Super Market Investors, Inc.
David H. Maass, President
23000 Roundy Drive
Mail: P.O. Box 473, Milwaukee 53202
Pewaukee, WI 53072
  (414) 547-7999

Wisconsin Community Capital, Inc.
Paul J. Eble, President
1 South Pinckney St. Suite 500
Madison, WI 53703
  (608) 256-3441

CHAPTER 6

MINORITY ENTERPRISE INVESTMENT COMPANIES
(MESBICS)

All Small Business Investment Companies (SBICs) listed in Chapter 6 will consider applications from socially and economically disadvantaged entrepreneurs. MESBICs, however, make all their investments in this area. MESBICs are licensed by the Small Business Administration and obtain long-term loans from the government. They make equity capital and long-term credit loans of 5 years or more to small independent businesses.

MESBICs may specialize in loans to certain industries. You may contact the National Association of Small Business Investment Companies at (202) 833-8230 to see which ones near you specialize in your business.

Alabama

Alabama Capital Corporation
David C. Delaney, President
16 Midtown Park East
Mobile, AL 36606
  (205) 476-0700

Alabama Small Business Investment Co.
Harold Gilchrist, Manager
206 North 24th Street
Birmingham, AL 35203
  (205) 324-5234

Tuskegee Capital Corporation
A. G. Bartholomew, President
4453 Richardson Road
Hampton Hall Building
Montgomery, AL 36108
  (205) 281-8059

Alaska

Calista Business Investment Corp.
Alex Raider, President
503 East Sixth Avenue
Anchorage, AK 99501
  (907) 281-8059

Arkansas

Capital Management Services, Inc.
David L. Hale, President
1910 North Grant Street Suite 200
Little Rock, AR 72207
  (501) 664-8613

Power Ventures, Inc.
Dorsey D. Glover, President
829 Highway 270 North
Malvern, AR 72104
  (501) 332-3695

California

ABC Capital Corporation
Anne B. Cheng, President
610 East Live Oak Avenue
Arcadia, CA 91006
  (818) 570-0653

Allied Business Investors, Inc.
Jack Hong, President
428 South Atlantic Blvd.
Monterey Park, CA 91754
  (818) 289-0186

Ally Finance Corporation
Percy P. Lin, President
9100 Wilshire Blvd., Suite 408
Beverly Hills, CA 90212
  (213) 550-8100

Asian American Capital Corporation
David Der, President
1251 West Tennyson Road, Suite #4
Hayward, CA 94544
  (415) 887-6888

Astar Capital Corporation
George Hsu, President
7282 Orangethorpe Ave., Suite 8
Buena Park, CA 90621
  (714) 739-2218

Bentley Capital
John Hung, President
592 Vallejo Street, Suite #2
San Francisco, CA 94133
  (415) 362-2868

Best Finance Corporation
Vincent Lee, General Manager
1814 W. Washington Blvd.
Los Angeles, CA 90007
  (213) 731-2268

Business Equity & Development Corp.
Leon M.N. Garcia, President/CEO
767 North Hill Street, Suite 401
Los Angeles, CA 90012
  (213) 613-0916

Calsafe Capital Corporation
Bob T. C. Chang, Chairman
240 South Atlantic Blvd.
Alhambra, CA 91801
  (818) 289-4080

Charterway Investment Corp.
Harold H. M. Chuang, President
222 South Hill Street, Suite 800
Los Angeles, CA 90012
  (213) 687-8539

Continental Investors, Inc.
Lac Thantrong, President
8781 Seaspray Drive
Huntington Beach, CA 92646
  (714) 964-5207

Equitable Capital Corporation
John C. Lee, President
855 Sansome Street
San Francisco, CA 94111
  (415) 434-4114

First American Capital Funding, Inc.
Luu TranKiem, Chairman
38 Corporate Park, Suite B
Irvine, CA 92714
  (714) 660-9288

Helio Capital, Inc.
Chester Koo, President
5900 South Eastern Ave. Suite 136
Commerce, CA 90040
  (213) 721-8053

LaiLai Capital Corporation
Hsing-Jong Duan, President
223 E. Garvey Avenue, Suite 228
Monterey, CA 91754
  (818) 288-0704

Magna Pacific Investments
David Wong, President
700 North Central Ave., Suite 245
Glendale, CA 91203
  (818) 547-0809

Myriad Capital, Inc.
Felix Chen, President
328 S. Atlantic Blvd., Ste 200 A
Monterey Park, CA 91754
  (818) 570-4548

New Kukje Investment Company
George Su Chey, President
3670 Wilshire Blvd. Suite 418
Los Angeles, CA 90010
  (213) 389-8679

Opportunity Capital Corporation
J. Peter Thompson, President
One Fremont Place
39650 Liberty Street, Suite 425
Fremont, CA 94538
  (415) 651-4412

Positive Enterprises, Inc.
Kwok Szeto, President
399 Arguello Street
San Francisco, CA 94118
  (415) 386-6606

RSC Financial Corporation
Frederick K. Bae, President
323 E. Matilija Road, #208
Ojai, CA 93023
  (805) 646-2925

San Joaquin Business Investment Group, Inc.
Joe Williams, President
2310 Tulare Street, Suite 140
Fresno, CA 93721
  (209) 233-3580

Colorado

Colorado Invesco, Inc.
1999 Broadway, Suite 2100
Denver, CO 80202
  (303) 293-2431

District of Columbia

Allied Financial Corporation
David J. Gladstone, President
1666 K Street, N.W., Suite 901
Washington, DC 20006
  (212) 331-1112

Broadcast Capital, Inc.
John E. Oxendine, President
1771 N Street, N.W. Suite 421
Washington, DC 20036
  (202) 429-5393

Consumers United Capital Corp.
Ester M. Carr-Davis, President
2100 M Street, N.W.
Washington, DC 20037
  (202) 872-5274

Fulcrum Venture Capital Corp.
C. Robert Kemp, Chairman
1030 15th Street, N.W., Suite 203
Washington, DC 20005
  (202) 785-4253

Minority Broadcast Investment Corp.
Walter L. Threadgill, President
1200 18th St. N.W., Suite 705
Washington, DC 20036
  (202) 293-1166

Syncom Capital Corp.
Herbert P. Wilkins, President
1030 - 15th Street, N.W., Ste 203
Washington, DC 20005
  (202) 293-9428

Florida

Allied Financial Corporation
(Main Office: Washington, DC)
Executive Office Center, Suite 305
2770 N. Indian River Blvd.
Vero Beach, FL 32960
  (407) 778-5556

First American Lending Corp. (The)
Roy W. Talmo, Chairman
1926 10th Avenue North
Mail: P.O. Box 24660
West Palm Beach, 33416
Lake Worth, FL 33461
  (305) 533-1511

Ideal Financial Corporation
Ectore T. Reynaldo, General Manager
780 N.W. 42nd Avenue, Suite 303
Miami, FL 33126
  (305) 442-4665

Pro-Med Investment Corporation
(Main Office: Dallas, TX)
1380 N.E. Miami Gardens Dr., Ste 225
N. Miami Beach, FL 33179
  (305) 949-5900

Venture Group, Inc.
Ellis W. Hitzing, President
5433 Buffalo Avenue
Jacksonville, FL 32208
  (904) 353-7313

Georgia

Renaissance Capital Corporation
Samuel B. Florence, President
161 Spring St., N.W., Suite 610
Atlanta, GA 30303
  (404) 658-9061

Hawaii

Pacific Venture Capital, Ltd.
Dexter J. Taniguchi, President
222 South Vineyard Street, PH.1
Honolulu, HI 96813
  (808) 521-6502

Illinois

Amoco Venture Capital Company
Gordon E. Stone, President
200 E. Randolph Drive
Chicago, IL 60601
  (312) 856-6523

Chicago Community Ventures, Inc.
Phyllis George, President
104 S. Michigan Ave. Ste 215-218
Chicago, IL 60603
  (312) 726-6084

Combined Fund, Inc.
E. Patrick Jones, President
1525 East 53rd Street
Chicago, IL 60615
  (312) 753-9650

Neighborhood Fund, Inc. (The)
James Fletcher, President
1950 East 71st Street
Chicago, IL 60649
  (312) 684-8074

Peterson Finance & Investment Co.
James S. Rhee, President
3300 W. Peterson Ave., Suite A
Chicago, IL 60659
  (312) 583-6300

Tower Ventures, Inc.
Robert T. Smith, President
Sears Tower, BSC 43-50
Chicago, IL 60684
  (312) 875-0571

Kentucky

Equal Opportunity Finance, Inc.
Franklin Justice, Jr., V.P./Manager
420 Hurstbourne Lane, Suite 201
Louisville, KY 40222
  (502) 423-1943

Louisiana

SCDF Investment Corporation
Martial Mirabeau, Manager
1006 Surrey Street
P.O. Box 3885
Lafayette, LA 70502
  (318) 232-3769

Maryland

Albright Venture Capital, Inc.
William A. Albright, President
1355 Piccard Drive, Suite 380
Rockville, MD 20850
  (301) 921-9090

Security Financial & Invest Corp.
Han Y. Cho, President
7720 Wisconsin Avenue, Ste 207
Bethesda, MD 20814
  (301) 951-4288

Massachusetts

Argonauts MESBIC Corporation (The)
Mr. Chi Fu Yeh, President
2 Vernon Street
P.O. Box 2411
Framingham, MA 01701
  (508) 820-3430

New England MESBIC, Inc.
Etang Chen, President
530 Turnpike Street
North Andover, MA 01845
  (617) 688-4326

Transportation Capital Corp.
(Main Office: New York, NY)
45 Newbury Street, Suite 207
Boston, MA 02116
  (617) 536-0344

Michigan

Dearborn Capital Corporation
Michael LaManes, President
P.O. Box 1729
Dearborn, MI 48121
  (313) 337-8577

Metro-Detroit Investment Co.
William J. Fowler, President
30777 Northwestern Hwy, Suite 300
Farmington Hill, MI 48018
  (313) 851-6300

Motor Enterprises, Inc.
James Kobus, Manager
3044 West Grand Blvd.
Detroit, MI 48202
  (313) 556-4273

Mutual Investment Company, Inc.
Jack Najor, President
21415 Civic Center Drive
Mark Plaza Building, Ste 217
Southfield, MI 48076
  (313) 557-2020

Minnesota

Capital Dimensions Ventures Fund, Inc.
Dean R. Pickerell, President
Two Appletree Square, Suite 244
Minneapolis, MN 55425
  (612) 854-3007

Mississippi

Sun-Delta Capital Access Center, Inc.
Howard Boutte, Jr., Vice President
819 Main Street
Greenville, MS 38701
  (601) 335-5291

New Jersey

Capital Circulation Corporation
Judy Kao, Manager
208 Main Street
Fort Lee, NJ 07024
  (201) 947-8637

Formosa Capital Corporation
Philip Chen, President
1037 Route 46 East, Unit C-208
Clifton, NJ 07013
  (201) 916-0016

Rutgers Minority Investment Company
Oscar Figueroa, President
92 New Street
Newark, NJ 07102
  (201) 648-5287

Transpac Capital Corporation
Tsuey Tang Wang, President
1037 Route 46 East
Clifton, NJ 07013
  (201) 470-0706

Zaitech Capital Corporation
Mr. Fu-Tong Hsu, President
1037 Route 46 East, Unit C-201
Clifton, NJ 07013
  (201) 365-0047

New Mexico

Assoc. Southwest Investors, Inc.
John R. Rice, General Manager
2400 Louisiana NE, Bldg #4, Ste 225
Albuquerque, NM 87110
  (505) 881-0066

New York

American Asian Capital Corp.
Howard H. Lin, President
130 Water Street, Suite 6-L
New York, NY 10005
  (212) 422-6880

Avdon Capital Corporation
A.M. Donner, President
1413 Avenue J
Brooklyn, NY 11230
  (718) 692-0950

CVC Capital Corporation
Jeorg G. Klebe, President
131 East 62nd Street
New York, NY 10021
  (212) 319-7210

Capital Invest & Management Corp.
Rose Chao, Manager
210 Canal Street, Suite 607
New York, NY 10013
  (212) 964-2480

Cohen Capital Corporation
Edward H. Cohen, President
8 Freer Street, Suite 185
Lynbrook, NY 11563
  (516) 887-3434

Columbia Capital Corporation
Mark Scharfman, President
79 Madison Avenue, Suite 800
New York, NY 10016
  (212) 696-4334

East Coast Venture Capital, Inc.
Zindel Zelmanovitch, President
313 West 53rd St., Third Floor
New York, NY 10019
  (212) 245-6460

Elk Associates Funding Corp.
Gary C. Granoff, President
600 Third Avenue, 38th Floor
New York, NY 10016
  (212) 972-8550

Equico Capital Corporation
Duane Hill, President
135 West 50th St. 11th Floor
New York, NY 10020
  (212) 641-7650

Everlast Capital Corporation
Frank J. Segreto, GM/VP
350 Fifth Avenue, Suite 2805
New York, NY 10118
  (212) 695-3910

Exim Capital Corporation
Victor K. Chun, President
290 Madison Avenue
New York, NY 10017
  (212) 683-3375

Fair Capital Corporation
Robert Yet Sen Chen, President
c/o Summit Associates
3 Pell Street, 2nd Floor
New York, NY 10013
  (212) 608-5866

Freshstart Venture Capital Corp.
Zindel Zelmanovich, President
313 West 53rd St., 3rd Floor
New York, NY 10019
  (212) 265-2249

Hanam Capital Corporation
Dr. Yul Chang, President
One Penn Plaza, Ground Floor
New York, NY 10119
  (212) 714-9830

Hop Chung Capital Investors, Inc.
Yon Hon Lee, President
185 Canal Street, Room 303
New York, NY 10013
  (212) 219-1777

Horn & Hardart Capital Corporation
Gerald Zarin, Vice President
730 Fifth Avenue
New York, NY 10019
  (212) 484-9600

Ibero American Investors Corp.
Emilio Serrano, President
38 Scio Street
Rochester, NY 14604
  (716) 262-3440

Intercontinental Capital Funding Corp.
James S. Yu, President
60 East 42nd Street, Suite 740
New York, NY 10165
  (212) 286-9642

International Paper Cap. Formation, Inc.
(Main Office: Memphis, TN)
Frank Polney, Manager
Two Manhattanville Road
Purchase, NY 10577
  (914) 397-1578

Japanese American Capital Corp.
Stephen C. Huang, President
19 Rector Street
New York, NY 10006
  (212) 964-4077

Jardine Capital Corporation
Evelyn Sy Dy, President
109 Lafayette Street, Unit 204
New York, NY 10038
  (212) 941-0966

Manhattan Central Capital Corp.
David Choi, President
1255 Broadway, Room 405
New York, NY 10001
  (212) 684-6411

Medallion Funding Corporation
Alvin Murstein, President
205 E. 42nd Street, Suite 2020
New York, NY 10017
  (212) 682-3300

Minority Equity Cap. Company, Inc.
Donald F. Greene, President
275 Madison Avenue
New York, NY 10016
  (212) 686-9710

Monsey Capital Corporation
Shamuel Myski, President
125 Route 59
Monsey, NY 10952
  (914) 425-2229

New Oasis Capital Corporation
James Huang, President
114 Liberty Street, Suite 304
New York, NY 10006
  (212) 349-2804

North American Funding Corp.
Franklin F. Y. Wong, VP/GM
177 Canal Street
New York, NY 10013
  (212) 226-0080

Pan Pac Capital Corporation
Dr. In Ping Jack Lee, President
121 East Industry Court
Deer Park, NY 11729
  (516) 585-7653

Pierre Funding Corporation
Elias Debbas, President
605 Third Avenue
New York, NY 10016
  (212) 490-9540

Situation Venture Corporation
Sam Hollander, President
502 Flushing Avenue
Brooklyn, NY 11205
  (718) 855-1835

Square Deal Venture Capital Corp.
Mordechai Z. Feldman, President
805 Avenue L
Brooklyn, NY 11230
  (718) 692-2924

Taroco Capital Corporation
David R. C. Chang, President
19 Rector Street, 35th Floor
New York, NY 10006
(212) 344-6690

Transportation Capital Corporation
Melvin L. Hirsch, President
60 East 42nd Street, Suite 3115
New York, NY 10165
(212) 697-4885

Triad Capital Corp. of New York
Lorenzo J. Barrera, President
960 Southern Blvd.
Bronx, NY 10459
(212) 589-6541

Trico Venture, Inc.
Avruhum Donner, President
1413 Avenue J
Brooklyn, NY 11230
(718) 692-0950

United Capital Investment Corp.
Paul Lee, President
60 East 42nd Street, Suite 1515
New York, NY 10165
(212) 682-7210

Venture Opportunities Corporation
A. Fred March, President
110 East 59th Street, 29th Floor
New York, NY 10022
(212) 832-3737

Watchung Capital Corporation
S. T. Jeng, President
431 Fifth Avenue, Fifth Floor
New York, NY 10016
(212) 889-3466

Yang Capital Corporation
Maysing Yang, President
41-40 Kissena Blvd.
Flushing, NY 11355
(516) 482-1578

Yusa Capital Corporation
Christopher Yeung, Chairman
622 Broadway
New York, NY 10012
(212) 420-1350

North Carolina

Business Capital Inv. Co., Inc.
Christopher S. Liu, Manager
327 South Road
High Point, NC 27260
(919) 889-8334

Ohio

Center City MESBIC, Inc.
Michael A. Robinson, President
Centre City Office Bldg., Suite 762
40 South Main Street
Dayton, OH 45402
(513) 461-6164

Rubber City Capital Corporation
Jesse T. Williams, President
1144 East Market Street
Akron, OH 44316
(216) 796-9167

Pennsylvania

Alliance Enterprise Corporation
W. B. Priestley, President
1801 Market Street, 3rd Floor
Philadelphia, PA 19103
(215) 977-3925

Greater Philadelphia Venture Capital Corp., Inc.
Martin Newman, Manager
920 Lewis Tower Bldg.
225 South Fifteenth Street
Philadelphia, PA 19102
(215) 732-3415

Salween Financial Services, Inc.
Dr. Ramarao Naidu, President
228 North Pottstown Pike
Exton, PA 19341
(215) 524-1880

Puerto Rico

North America Inv. Corporation
Santigo Ruz Betacourt, President
Banco CTR #1710, M Rivera Ave. Stop 34
Mail: P.O. Box 1831 Hato Rey Sta., PR 00919
Hato Rey, PR 00936
(809) 751-6178

Tennessee

Chickasaw Capital Corporation
Tom Moore, President
67 Madison Avenue
Memphis, TN 38147
(901) 523-6404

International Paper Cap. Formation, Inc.
John G. Herman, VP/Controller
International Place I
6400 Poplar Avenue, 10-74
Memphis, TN 38197
(901) 763-6282

Tennessee Equity Capital Corp.
Walter S. Cohen, President
1102 Stonewall Jackson Court
Nashville, TN 37220
(615) 373-4502

Tennessee Venture Capital Corp.
Wendell P. Knox, President
162 Fourth Ave. North, Suite 125
Mail: P.O. Box 2567
Nashville, TN 37219
(615) 244-6935

Valley Capital Corp.
Lamar J. Partridge, President
8th Floor Krystal Building
100 W. Martin Luther King Blvd.
Chattanooga, TN 37402
(615) 265-1557

West Tennessee Venture Capital Corp.
Osbie L. Howard, President
152 Beale Street, Suite 401
Mail: P.O. Box 300, Memphis 38101
Memphis, TN 38101
(901) 527-6091

Texas

Chen's Financial Group, Inc.
Samuel S. C. Chen, President
1616 West Loop South, Suite 200
Houston, TX 77027
(713) 850-0879

Evergreen Capital Company, Inc.
Shen-Lim Lin, Chairman & President
8502 Tybor Drive, Suite 201
Houston, TX 77074
(713) 778-9770

MESBIC Financial Corp. of Dallas
Donald R. Lawhorne, President
12655 N. Central Expressway
Suite 814
Dallas, TX 75243
(214) 991-1597

MESBIC Financial Corp. of Houston
Lynn H. Miller, President
811 Rusk, Suite 201
Houston, TX 77002
  (713) 228-8321

Minority Enterprise Funding, Inc.
Frederick C. Chang, President
17300 El Camino Real, Suite 107-B
Houston, TX 77058
  (713) 488-4919

Pro-Med Investment Corporation
Mrs. Marion Rosemore, President
17772 Preston Road, Suite 101
Dallas, TX 75252
  (214) 380-0044

Southern Orient Capital Corp.
Min H. Liang, President
2419 Fannin, Suite 200
Houston, TX 77002
  (713) 225-3369

United Oriental Capital Corp.
Don J. Wang, President
908 Town & Country Blvd., Suite 310
Houston, TX 77024
  (713) 461-3909

Virginia

East West United Investment Company
Bui Dung, President
815 West Broad Street
Falls Church, VA 22046
  (703) 237-7200

Washington Finance & Invest. Corp.
Chang H. Lie, President
100 E. Broad Street
Falls Church, VA 22046
  (703) 534-7200

Wisconsin

Future Value Ventures, Inc.
William P. Beckett, President
622 North Water St., Suite 500
Milwaukee, WI 53202
  (414) 278-0377

CHAPTER 7

OTHER SOURCES

1. For Women Only

The **National Association for Female Executives (NAFE)** will invest $5,000 to $50,000 in business where all principals are women. This is not a loan. If the business fails you owe nothing. If it succeeds you give NAFE a percentage of the profits. A good business plan is required.

For information write; NAFE, 127 West 24th Street, New York, NY 10011 or call (212) 645-0770.

2. Suppliers

Companies that can benefit from your success often make special arrangements that, in effect, will finance your business. For example extended credit is equal to cash. After you've done the preliminary steps in establishing a relationship with a supplier, ask to pay 30 to 90 days longer than normal. If, at the same time, you can accelerate receivables you've got it made.

Other techniques;

- Ask for inventory on consignment.

- Ask if he'll buy your accounts receivable

- Ask for loan of equipment if you buy supplies exclusively from him.

- Ask for favorable long-term leases of equipment.

- Offer an equity investment in return for equipment and supplies.

- Tell the owner of the supply company you need "working capital" (NEVER say you want to borrow the down payment.

3. Classified Ads

Place an ad in your local paper and the Thursday *Wall Street Journal* under Business Opportunities, New Business Offerings, or Capital Wanted.

4. Astute Investor

Approach an astute investor (Your parents, relatives, or doctor). The drawback to this is the potential for squabbles.

5. Home Equity Loan

Use a home equity loan on your house. You can borrow up to 75% of the appraised value of your house.

6. Credit cards

It is fairly simple to get multiple credit cards. Pay promptly and request higher limits. Note although you can borrow a considerable amount this way you MUST be able to pay these loans off quickly. You cannot afford to pay 19% interest.

7. Offer shares

Making an offering to sell shares to the general public involves the state and federal securities commission. Unless you're big time this is not for you. However within an organization you belong to, e.g. Plumbers, Union, Elks Club, etc., you can sell shares to a few people. Talk to your lawyer first.

8. Savings

If you have some cash available for a business, instead of putting it directly in the business, put it in a certificate of deposit and then use the CD as collateral to borrow money. Savings account loans such as these preserve capital while you establish credit.

9. Compensating Balances

This works best when the prime rate is high and the bank is short of cash. If you are buying an established successful business but the bank has no money, find someone with savings in a different bank. Offer him 2% interest to transfer it to the bank you want the loan from (this increases their yield about 35% assuming both banks pay equal interest on savings. The bank can now lend the money. **Note: the savings account is not the security against the loan—the successful business is.**

The agreement with the owner of the money in savings is simple (1) You will pay him 2% a year as long as the money stays in the bank (2) he can pull it out at any time providing he gives you 30 days notice.

APPENDIX A

BUSINESS INCUBATORS

Thanks to the **National Business Incubation Association** for helping us compile this list. This is a rapidly expanding phenomenon. For updates contact; NBIA, One President St., Athens, OH 45701. Phone (614) 593-4331.

Business Incubators offer low rent and lots of advice to help business start-ups. They usually provide low-cost accounting and legal services. Some incubators will get involved with financing your business but essentially all of them have consultants that will help you create a viable business plan that can open the doors to financing.

In addition, secretaries, copiers, fax machines are available on a pay-for-your-share basis.

There is a higher rate of success for businesses that start up in incubators. There is a sharing of information, contacts, and comradery that enhances one's chances of making it.

ALABAMA

Atmore Incubator Center
315 East Ridgley Street
Atmore, AL 36502
　(205) 368-5404

Alabama Incubator Center
Auburn University
306-C Tichenor Hall
Auburn University, AL 36849-5250
　(205) 826-5328

Auburn Incubator
P.O. Box 511
Auburn, AL 36831
(205) 887-4960

Birmingham Business Assistance Network
Midtown Center
1801 1st Avenue South, Suite 333
Birmingham, AL 35233
　(205) 250-8000

Center for the Advancement of Developing Industries
University of Alabama at Birmingham
1075 South 13th Street
Birmingham, AL 35205
　(205) 934-2190

Decatur Incubator System
305 Bank Street
Decatur, AL 35601
　(205) 355-4515

Business Innovative Center
2000 Old Bay Front Drive
Mobile, AL 36615
　(205) 433-2224

ARIZONA

Center for Innovation
1020 West 1st Street, No. 52
Tempe, AZ 85281
　(602) 965-2809

Innovative Research Center
2700 East Bilby
Tucson, AZ 85706
　(602) 889-8811

ARKANSAS

Genesis Project
Engineering Experiment Station
University of Arkansas
Fayetteville, AR 72701
　(501) 575-7227

East Arkansas Business Incubator System
Arkansas State University
5501 Kruger Drive
Jonesboro, AR 72401
　(501) 935-8365

Arkansas Science & Technology Authority
100 Main Street, Suite 450
Little Rock, AR 72201
　(501) 371-3554

The Technology Enterprise Center
University of Arkansas at Little Rock
100 Main Street, Suite 400
Little Rock, AR 72201
　(501) 371-5492

The Business Center
Southern Arkansas University
P.O. Box 1239
Magnolia, AR 71753
　(501) 235-4375

North Arkansas Business Incubator System
North Arkansas Community College
P.O. Box 739
Salem, AR 72576
　(501) 895-4050

CALIFORNIA

Alameda Incubator
1350 South Loop Road
Alameda, CA 94501
　(415) 769-5778

South Bay Development and Construction
511 Division Street
Campbell, CA 94008
　(408) 379-0400

The Business Center
1001 Willow Street
Chico, CA 95927
　(916) 345-3027

Southern California Innovation Centre
Suite H, 225 Yale Street
Claremont, CA 91711
　(714) 624-7161

City Training Institute
4513 East Compton Boulevard
Compton, CA 90221
  (213) 603-0380

Hub City Economic Development
Alameda Auto Plaza
Compton, CA
  (714) 383-1549/2945

Creative Systems Business Development
Room 232, 6410 Green Valley Circle
Culver City, CA 90230
  (213) 649-6623

City of Fresno
2326 Fresno Street
Fresno, CA 93721
  (209) 488-4591

Enterprise
Suite #100, 1900 Mariposa Mall
Fresno, CA 93721
  (209) 233-4260

NEDA San Joaquin Valley
Suite 103, 2010 North Fine Street
Fresno, CA 93727
  (209) 252-7551

Alameda Private Industry Council
26249 Industrial Boulevard
Hayward, CA 94545
  (415) 881-6400

Lancaster Economic Development Corp.
104 East Avenue, K4
Lancaster, CA 93534
  (805) 945-2741

Chancellor's Office, Research Programs
University of California, Los Angeles
Rm 3130-Murphy Hall, 405 Hilgard Ave.
Los Angeles, CA 90024

United Community Housing Development
128 South La Brea
Los Angeles, CA 90036
  (213) 936-8143

Urban University Center Incubator
USC Western Research Applications Center
3716 South Hope Street
Los Angeles, CA 90007
  (213) 743-2371

Pacific Import Mall
1800 Prescott Street
Modesto, CA 95350
  (209) 522-2233

Golden State Business League, Inc.
Wells Fargo Bank Building
333 Hegenberger Road
Oakland, CA 94621
  (415) 635-5900

Pryde Roberts & Carr, Inc.
Suite 915, 508 16th Street
Oakland, CA 94612
  (415) 452-0232

Security West Insurance and Financial Services, Inc.
528 Grand Avenue
Oakland, CA 94610
  (415) 893-3616

Selwyn Whitehead, Enterprises
4650 Scotia Avenue
Oakland, CA 94605
  (415) 635-8898

Tidewater Business Park
Suite 111, 519 17th Street
Oakland, CA 94621
  (415) 763-4297

Ontario Comm. Center
3535 Inland Empire Boulevard
Ontario, CA 91761
  (714) 944-7996

West End Investments
334 North Euclid Avenue
Ontario, CA 91762
  (714) 983-9601

Pasadena Development Corporation
586 North Lake Avenue
Pasadena, CA 91101
  (818) 792-5764

McDowell Industrial Business Center
921 Transportation Way
Petaluma, CA 90731
  (707) 762-6341

MHR Department
Cal Poly University, Pomona
3801 West Temple
Pomona, CA 91768
  (714) 869-2425

G.E. Industrial Park
Suite 455, 10681 Foothill Boulevard
Rancho Cucamonga, CA 91730
  (714) 980-1880

Business Incubator, Inc.
4311 Airport Road
Redding, CA 96002
  (916) 221-1377

Hilltop Comm. Center
3150 Hilltop Mall Road
Richmond, CA 94806
  (415) 222-0968

Superior Valley Small Bus. Dev. Corp.
926 J Street
Sacramento, CA 95814
  (916) 442-1729

California Coastal Rural Develop. Corp.
P.O. Box 2103
Salinas, CA 93902
  (408) 424-1099

Office of Community Development
San Bernardino County
474 West Fifth Street
San Bernardino, CA 92145

Innovative Partners, Inc.
P.O. Box 91255
San Diego, CA 92109
  (619) 453-8681

Southeast Economic Development Corp.
930 Gateway Center Way
San Diego, CA 92101
  (619) 236-7345

Washington Enterprises
Suite 900, 225 Broadway
San Diego, CA 92101
  (619) 237-0559

First California Business & Industrial
  Development Corporation
130 Montgomery Street
San Francisco, CA 94104
  (415) 392-2541

Hampton Roberts Properties
330 Townsend Street
San Francisco, CA 94017
  (415) 777-4247

Mission Economic Development Association
987 Valencia Street
San Francisco, CA
  (415) 282-3334

San Francisco Renaissance Entrepreneurship
  Center
5th Floor, 1453 Mission Street
San Francisco, CA 94103
  (415) 863-5337

City Council
City of San Jose
801 North First, Annex, Room 600
San Jose, CA 95110
  (408) 277-4000

San Pedro Venture Center
1951 North Gaffey Street
San Pedro, CA 90731
  (312) 855-8393

Santa Ana Business Enterprise Center
901 East Santa Ana Boulevard
Santa Ana, CA 92701
  (714) 647-1134

Santa Cruz Business Incubator
Suite B, 501 Cedar Street
Santa Cruz, CA 95060
  (408) 462-6113

California Business Centers
Suite 402, 1223 Wilshire Boulevard
Santa Monica, CA 90403
  (213) 394-1160

Lands Management
Stanford University
857 Serra Street
Stanford, CA 94305
  (415) 725-6886

COLORADO

Fremont County Business Develop. Center
402 Valley Road
Canon City, CO 81212
  (719) 275-8601

Fremont County Business Incubator
P.O. Box 510
Canon City, CO 81212
  (303) 275-8350

Denver Growth Center
3003 Arapahoe
Denver, CO 80205
  (303) 296-9400

Denver Partnership's Lower Downtown Business Support Office
1512 17th Street
Denver, CO 80202
  (303) 893-1144

Nucleus Capital, Inc.
6667 Dorado Avenue
Englewood, CO 80111
  (303) 721-8504

Food Research & Development Center
Colorado State University
Fort Collins, CO 80523
  (303) 491-6705

Business Innovation Center
Suite 400, Bldg. 19, 1667 Cole Blvd.
Golden, CO 80401
  (303) 238-0913

Western Colorado Bus. Development Corp.
304 West Main St., P.O. Box 3080
Grand Junction, CO 81502
  (303) 243-5242

Eastern Colorado Bus. Development Corp.
304 West Main, P.O. Box 3080
Grand Junction, CO 81502
  (303) 243-5242

Boulder County Bus. Development Center
2150 Miller Drive
Longmont, CO 80501
  (303) 772-6969

The Catalyst Project
717 Main Street, P.O. Box 385
Louisville, CO 80017
  (303) 665-6144

Business and Technology Center
301 North Main Street
Pueblo, CO 81002
  (303) 546-1133

Logan County Business Incubator Center
322 Poplar
Sterling, CO 80751
  (303) 522-4862

CONNECTICUT

Bridgeport Innovation Center
955 Connecticut Avenue
Bridgeport, CT 06607
  (203) 336-8864

Naugatuck Industrial Park
235 Meadows Street
Naugatuck, CT 06770
  (203) 729-4511

Constructive Workshop, Inc.
102 Washington Street
New Britain, CT 06051
  (203) 229-7700

Science Park Development Association
Five Science Park
New Haven, CT 06511
  (203) 786-5000

NERAC, Inc.
One Technology Drive
Tolland, CT 06084
  (203) 872-7000

Waterbury Industrial Commons Project
1875 Thomas Avenue
Waterbury, CT 06704
  (203) 574-7704

DELAWARE

Business Open Incubator Project
New Castle County Econ. Develop. Corp.
12th & Market Streets
Wilmington, DE 19801
  (302) 636-5050

Silverside Carr Executive Center
1501 Silverside Road
Wilmington, DE 19809
  (302) 792-1100

Woodmill Office Center
Suite 9, 5171 West Woodmill Drive
Wilmington, DE 19808
  (302) 998-0929

DISTRICT OF COLUMBIA

Georgetown Business Center
Suite 400 - East Lobby
1025 Thomas Jefferson Street, N.W.
Washington, DC 20007
  (202) 944-3600

FLORIDA

Florida Atlantic Innovation Center
Florida Atlantic University
500 N.W. 20th Street
Boca Raton, FL 33431
  (305) 776-1257

Entrepreneur & Bus. Development Center
Suite 19, 853 East Semoran Boulevard
Casselberry, FL 32707
  (407) 332-9600

"The Heritage House"
DeLand Housing Authority
300 Sunflower Circle
DeLand, FL 32724
  (904) 736-1696

Lake County Small Business Incubators
307 Magnolia Avenue
Bustis, FL 32726
  (904) 589-0644

Dunbar Business Incubator
3901 Anderson Avenue
Ft. Myers, FL 33901
  (813) 337-4141

Atkins Industrial Area
3401 S.W. 40th Boulevard
Gainesville, FL 32608-2399
  (904) 378-5555

Biomedical Research & Innovation Center
#650, 444 Brickell Avenue
Miami, FL 33131
  (305) 373-3606

Florida Trade and Exhibition Center
1417 West Flagler
Miami, FL 33135
  (305) 642-3870

The Business Assistance Center
P.O. Box 470830
Miami, FL 33247-0830
  (305) 693-3550

Southeastern Innovation Centers
Suite 400, 933 Lee Road
Orlando, FL 32810
  (407) 855-6524

Sumter County Small Business Incubator
103 North Webster Street
Wildwood, FL 32785
  (904) 748-5083

GEORGIA

City of Albany, GA
P.O. Box 447
Albany, GA 31703

Advanced Technology Development Center
Georgia Institute of Technology
Suite N116, 430 10th Street, N.W.
Atlanta, GA 30318
  (404) 894-3575

Sun/South Development
1705 Mount Vernon Road
Atlanta, GA 30338
  (404) 393-9993

Macon-Bibb County Industrial Authority
P.O. Box 207
Macon, GA 31202
  (912) 741-8014

Rome/Floyd County Center for Industry
100 East Callahan St., P.O. Box 5591
Rome, GA 30161
  (404) 295-3141

HAWAII

Kaimuki Technology Enterprises; Maui Res. &
    Tech., & Manoa Innovation Center
c/o High Technology Development Corp.
#35, 300 Kahelu Avenue
Mililani, HI 96789
  (808) 625-5293

IDAHO

Business Innovation Center
11100 Airport Drive
Hayden Lake, ID 83835
  (208) 772-0584

Idaho Innovation Center
2300 North Yellowstone
Idaho Falls, ID 83401
  (208) 523-1026

Business Technology Incubator
University of Idaho
Financial Affairs and Development
Moscow, ID 83843
  (208) 885-6174

Eastern Idaho Development Corporation
1651 Alvin Ricken Drive
Pocatello, ID 83201
  (208) 234-7541

Research and Business Park
Idaho State University
Campus Box 8044
Pocatello, ID 83209-8044
  (208) 236-2430

Southern Idaho Development Center
P.O. Box 1844
Twin Falls, ID 83303
  (208) 734-6586

ILLINOIS

Area Jobs Development Association
231 East Broadway
Bradley, IL 60915
  (815) 933-2537

The Bradley Industrial Site
180 East North Street
Bradley, IL 60915
  (815) 933-2537

Office of Economic Development
Southern Illinois University-Carbondale
SIU - Carbondale
Carbondale, IL 62901
  (618) 536-4451

Business and Technology Center
701 Devonshire Drive
Champaign, IL 61820
  (217) 398-5759

Control Data Bus. & Technology Center
701 Devonshire Drive
Champaign, IL 61820
  (217) 398-5759

CEDCO Business Enterprise Center
1812 South Kilborn
Chicago, IL 61623
  (312) 984-5950

Chicago Park Technology Corporation
2201 West Campbell Park Drive
Chicago, IL 60612
  (312) 829-7252

Enterprise Place
William D. Markle & Associates
355 North Ashland
Chicago, IL 60607
  (312) 633-4200

Evanston Research Park
Northwestern University
Suite 2200, 676 St. Clare
Chicago, IL 60611
  (312) 943-8800

Industrial Council of Northwest Chicago
2023 West Carroll Avenue
Chicago, IL 60612
  (312) 421-3941

Shetland Properties Incubator
County Limited Partnership
5400 West Roosevelt
Chicago, IL 61650
  (312) 921-5400

South Shore Enterprise Center
1750 East 71st Street
Chicago, IL 60649
  (312) 933-0200

Job Creation Services
Control Data Corporation
800 South Wells Street
Chicago, IL 60607

Decatur Industry & Tech. Center
2121 U.S. Route 51 South
Decatur, IL 62521
  (217) 423-2832

East St. Louis Small Business Center
1405 State Street
East St. Louis, IL 62205
  (618) 271-0303

Small Bus. Incubator, Tech. Innov. Cntr.
Northwestern University
906 University
Evanston, IL 60201
  (312) 491-3740

Highland Community College
Small Business Incubator
2998 West Pearl City Road
Freeport, IL 61032
  (815) 235-6121

Galesburg Business & Technology Center
2101 Windish Drive
Galesburg, IL 61401
  (309) 344-2233

Technical Enterprise Center
Suburban S. Business Campus
400 East Sibley, P.O. Box 1452
Harvey, IL 60473
  (312) 333-3900

S. Suburban Regional Economic
Development Coord. Council
1154 Ridge Road
Homewood, IL 60430
  (312) 957-6960

Des Plaines River Valley Enterprise Zone Incubator
912 East Washington
Joliet, IL 60433
  (815) 726-0028

Macomb Business and Technology Center
Seal Hall, Western Illinois
University
P.O. Box 6070
Macomb, IL 61455
  (309) 837-4684

Moline Incubator
Suite 830, 1630 Fifth Avenue
Moline, IL 61265
  (309) 762-0690

Maple City Bus. and Technology Center
620 South Main
Monmouth, IL 61462
  (309) 734-8544

Lovelace Tech. Center
Bradley University
1501 Wet Bradley Avenue
Peoria, IL 61625
  (309) 677-2852

Quincy Business and Technology Center
301 Oak Street
Quincy, IL 62301
  (217) 228-5500

Community and Economic Development
  Dept.
City of Rock Island
1528 Third Avenue
Rock Island, IL 61201
  (309) 793-3350

Reed-Chatwood Business Center for New
  Technology
1220 Rock Street
Rockford, IL 61101
  (815) 968-6833

Springfield Technology Enterprise Center
410 South Ninth Street
Springfield, IL 62701
  (217) 789-2377

Sterling Industrial Development Comm.
1741 Industrial Drive
Sterling, IL 61081
  (815) 625-5255

Sponsored Research Incubator Building
2004 South Wright
Urbana, IL 61801
  (217) 244-7742

University Micro-Electronics Center
1776 East Washington Street
Urbana, IL 61801
  (217) 367-2600

INDIANA

Business Innovation Center
c/o Regional Growth Enterprises, Inc.
1821 West Third Street
Bloomington, IN 47403
  (812) 332-1111

Columbus Enterprise Dev. Corp.
4920 North Warren Drive
Columbus, In 47203
  (812) 379-4041

Fort Wayne Enterprise Center
1830 Wayne Trace
Fort Wayne, IN 46803
  (219) 426-5700

Ferree Transportation, Inc.
Ferree Moving and Storage, Inc.
262 Wildwood Road
Hammond, IN 46324-1043
  (219) 932-6262

H.M. Childrey Enterprises
1036 North Capitol Avenue
Indianapolis, IN 46204
  (317) 634-8427

Indianapolis Center for Adv. Research
611 North Capitol Avenue
Indianapolis, IN 46204
  (317) 262-5000

Control Data Bus. & Technology Center
300 North Michigan Street
South Bend, IN 46601
  (219) 282-4340

Rose-Hulman Institute of Technology
5500 Wabash Avenue
Terre Haute, IN 47803
  (812) 877-1511

Inventure
1291 East Cumberland Ave. P.O. Box 2378
West Lafayette, IN 47906
  (317) 497-1108

IOWA

Iowa State Innovation System
Iowa State University
2501 North Loop Drive
Ames, IA 50010
  (515) 296-9900

Golden Circle Incubator
DMACC
200 South Ankeny Boulevard
Ankeny, IA 50021
  (515) 964-6700

Circle West Incubator
Lot 3, Industrial Park
Audubon, IA 50025
  (712) 563-2623

Charles City Area Development Corp.
610 South Grand Avenue
Charles City, IA 50616
  (515) 228-4238

Iowa Lakes Community College
19 South 7th Street
Estherville, IA 51334
  (712) 362-2601

Technology Innovation Center
University of Iowa
#109 Oakdale Campus
Iowa City, IA 52242
  (319) 335-4063

New Business Center
2945 10th Avenue
Marion, IA 52302
  (319) 377-7965

Sioux City Chamber Foundation
101 Pierce Street
Sioux City, IA 51101
  (712) 255-7903

Black Hawk County Economic Development
  Committee, Inc.
Eight West 4th Street
Waterloo, IA 50701
  (319) 232-1156

Waverly Economic Development Company
201 First Street SE, P.O. Box 616
Waverly, IA 50677
  (319) 352-5861

KANSAS

Mid-States Mall
21 South Main
Fort Scott, KS 66701

Southwestern Bell Telephone
407 North 7th, P.O. Box 1078
Garden City, KS 67846

Hutchinson Chamber of Commerce
P.O. Box 519
Hutchinson, KS 67501
  (316) 663-1921

Quest Center for Entrepreneurs
One East Ninth
Hutchinson, KS 67501
  (316) 665-8468

First Kansas Group
P.O. Box 203
Junction City, KS 66441

Riverfront Square
733 Massachusetts Street
Lawrence, KS 66044
  (913) 841-1265

University Corporation and Research Park
1611 St. Andrews Drive, P.O. Box 3726
Lawrence, KS 66046
  (913) 843-2842

Kansas Entrepreneurial Center
1640 Fairchild Avenue
Manhattan, KS 66502
  (913) 537-0110

KSU Foundation
Tecnipark
1408 Denison Street
Manhattan, KS 66502
  (913) 532-6266

Business Industrial Center
1901 South Boulevard
Parsons, KS 67351
  (316) 421-3613

Enterprise Place
1330 East First
Wichita, KS 67214

Wichita Area Chamber of Commerce
350 Douglas Avenue
Wichita, KS 67202

KENTUCKY

Ashland Business Center, Inc.
1325 Greenup Avenue
Ashland, KY 41101
  (606) 324-3690

The Innovation Center
225 Third Street
Bowling Green, KY 42101-1250
  (502) 782-5511

Northern Kentucky University
One Nunn Drive
Highland Heights, KY 41076
  (606) 572-5126

Small business Incubator of N. KY, Inc.
University Drive
Highland Heights, KY 41076

LOUISIANA

Louisiana BTC
Louisiana State University
South Stadium Drive
Baton Rouge, LA 70803-6110
  (504) 334-5555

NW Louisiana Business Incubation Center
Louisiana Technical University
635 Barksdale Boulevard
Bossier City, LA 71111
  (318) 741- 8306

Louisiana Productivity Center
University of Southwest Louisiana
P.O. Box 44172
Lafayette, LA 70504
  (318) 231-6767

NE Louisiana Business Incubation Center
Route 3, Box 182-12
Monroe, LA 71203
  (318) 343-2262

Northeast LA Incubation Center
Route 3, Box 182
Monroe, LA 71203
  (318) 343-2262

MAINE

Bangor Internat'l Enterprise Dev. Center
73 Harlow Street
Bangor, ME 04401
  (207) 947-0341

Lewiston Auburn
95 Park Street
Lewiston, ME 04240
  (207) 784-0161

Dyke Associates
309 Cumberland Avenue
Portland, ME 04101
  (207) 772-4996

MARYLAND

Baltimore Medical Incubator
Baltimore Economic Development Corp.
Suite 24, 36 South Charles Street
Baltimore, MD 21201
  (301) 837-9305

Bayview Biotech
4940 Eastern Avenue
Baltimore, MD 21224
  (301) 955-7724

Business and Technology Center
2901 Druid Park Drive
Baltimore, MD 21215
  (301) 367-1600

Technology Development Center
Three East 25th Street
Baltimore, MD 21218

University of Maryland — Baltimore County
Administrative Building, Room 925
Baltimore, MD 21228
  (301) 455-2274

Watson & Taylor Business Center
9244 East Hampton Drive
Capital Heights, MD 20743
  (301) 336-6456

Technology Advancement Program
University of Maryland
Wind Tunnel Building
College Park, MD 20742
  (301) 454-8827

Crossroads Venture Center
Suite 100, Three Commerce Drive
Cumberland, MD 21502

ABCO Enterprises
Suite 203, 3450 Ellicott Center Drive
Ellicott City, MD 21043
  (301) 992-9292

Capitol Executive Suite, Inc.
1232 Pickering Circle
Upper Marlboro, MD 20772
  (301) 336-8778

MASSACHUSETTS

Chicopee Business Development Corp.
165 First Street
Chicopee, MA 01019
  (413) 594-2684

Wadsworth Village
130 Centre Street
Danvers, MA 01923
  (617) 777-4602

Venture Center
324 Wells Street
Greenfield, MA 01302
  (412) 774-7204

J.B. Blood Building
Lynn Office of Economic Development
Suite 4, One Market Street
Lynn, MA 01901
  (617) 581-9399

128 Entrepreneurs' Center
100 Fifth Avenue
Waltham, MA 02154
  (617) 890-2834

Massachusetts Innovation Center
365 Plantation Street
Worcester, MA 01613
  (617) 797-0500

MICHIGAN

Albion Business Center
1104 Industrial Boulevard
Albion, MI 49224
  (517) 629-3926

Ann Arbor Innovation Center
912 North Main
Ann Arbor, MI 48104
  (313) 662-0550

Atlanta Industrial Incubator
P.O. Box 415
Atlanta, MI 49709
  (517) 785-4762

Ferris State College
School of Technology
Big Rapids, MI 48307
  (616) 796-3100

Metropolitan Center for High Technology
2727 Second Avenue
Detroit, MI 48201
  (313) 963-0616

Tower Executive Suites
3200 Cadillac Tower Building
Detroit, MI 48206
  (313) 961-2525

Flint Industrial Village for Enterprise
2712 North Saginaw
Flint, MI 48505
  (313) 235-5555

Delta Properties Industrial Leasing Co.
1300 Four Mile Road, N.W.
Grand Rapids, MI 49504
  (616) 451-2561

Delta Properties
Muskegon Center
1300 Four Mile Road, N.W.
Grand Rapids, MI 49504
  (616) 451-2561

Madison Square Co-Operative, Inc.
1155 Madison, SE
Grand Rapids, MI 49507
  (616) 245-2563

Research and Technical Institute
Suite 718, 301 West Fulton
Grand Rapids, MI 49504
  (616) 771-6800

Center for Small Business
Suite 654, One Jackson Square
Jackson, MI 49201
  (517) 787-0442

Kalamazoo Enterprise Center
225 Parsons
Kalamazoo, MI 49007
  (616) 345-3311

Lapeer Development Corporation
449 McCormick Drive
Lapeer, MI 48446
  (313) 667-0080

Northern Michigan University
Marquette, MI 49855
  (906) 227-2335

Skill Center Incubator
Northern Michigan University
Marquette, MI 49855
  (906) 227-2195

Center for Business Development
1105 North Front Street
Niles, MI 49120
  (616) 683-1833

Openings
40 West Howard
Pontiac, MI 48058
  (313) 335-7380

Consumers Power Center
4600 Coolidge Highway
Royal Oak, MI 48068
  (313) 335-7425

Soo Industrial Incubator
1301 Easterday Drive
Sault Ste. Marie, MI 49783
  (906) 635-9131

Southfield Chamber of Commerce
1877 West Ten Mile Road
Southfield, MI 48075

DCC Venture Center
15100 Northline
Southgate, MI 48195
  (313) 281-0700

MINNESOTA

Business and Technology Center
1270 Nielsen Ave., SE., P.O. Box 428
Bemidji, MN 56601
  (218) 751-6480

Joint Economic Development Commission
P.O. Box 602
Bemidji, MN 56601
  (218) 751-6529

Breckenridge Business Opportunities
420 Nebraska Avenue
Breckenridge, MN 56520
  (218) 643-1173

College of St. Thomas Enterprise Center
1007 Hazeltine Boulevard
Chaska, MN 55318
  (612) 448-8800

Business and Technology Center
301 First Avenue, N.W.
Grand Rapids, MN 55744
  (218) 327-2241

Science and Technology Resource Center
Southwest State University
Marshall, MN 56258
  (507) 537-7441

Business and Technology Center
511 11th Avenue, South
Minneapolis, MN 55415
  (612) 375-8066

Minneapolis Technology Enterprise Center
1313 Fifth Street, SE
Minneapolis, MN 55414
  (612) 623-7774

St. Cloud Business Center
14 North 7th Avenue
St. Cloud, MN 56301
  (612) 259-4000

Control Data Energy Park
1450 Energy Park Drive
St. Paul, MN 55108
  (612) 642-3030

Empire Builder Bus. Development Center
23 Blair Drive
St. Paul, MN 55103
  (612) 292-0451

Lowertown Business Center
245 East Sixth Street
St. Paul, MN 55101
  (612) 291-8995

Small Business Incubator
25 West Fourth Street
St. Paul, MN 55102
  (612) 228-3301

MISSISSIPPI

Biloxi Economic Development Foundation
1028 Fred Haise Boulevard
Biloxi, MS 39530
  (601) 374-3190

New Building Workspace for Women
MACE
119 South Theobald Street
Greenville, MS 38701
  (601) 335-3523

Jackson Enterprise Center
931 Highway 80 West
Jackson, MS 39204
  (601) 352-0957

Meridian Junior College
5500 Highway 19 North
Meridian, MS 39301
  (601) 483-8241

Mississippi Research and Technology Park
P.O. Box 2740
Starkville, MS 39759
  (601) 324-3219

MISSOURI

Missouri Ingenuity, Inc.
T-16 Research Park
Columbia, MO 65211
(3114) 882-2822

Business Resource Center
3128 Prospect Avenue
Kansas city, MO 64128
(816) 561-8567

Kansas City Business Center for Entrepreneurial Development
2208 East 18th Street
Kansas City, MO 64127
(816) 483-5100

Missouri IncuTech Foundation
Suite 111, 800 West 14th Street
Rolla, MO 65401
(314) 364-8570
Southwestern Bell Telephone
Steve Begshaw
1010 Pine
St. Louis, MO 63101

St. Louis County Enterprise Center
6510 Page Avenue
St. Louis, MO 63102
(314) 889-7663

St. Louis Technology Center
10143 Paget Drive
St. Louis, MO 63132
(314) 432-4204

MONTANA

Butte Development Center
305 West Mercury
Butte, MT 59701
(406) 723-4061

NEBRASKA

D & D Investments
240 North Main
Fremont, NE 68025
(402) 721-4124

Phoenix Industries
906 Juniata Avenue, P.O. Box 308
Juniata, NE 68955
(402) 751-2135

Business and Technology Centre
2505 North 24th Street
Omaha, NE 68110
(402) 346-8262

Railway Office Plaza
115 Railway Street
Scotts Bluff, NE 96361
(308) 632-7834

NEW HAMPSHIRE

New Ventures North
148 Pleasant Street
Berlin, NH 03570
(603) 752-2541

Thayer Innovation Incubator
Dartmouth College
Hanover, NH 03755
(603) 646-2851

The Incubator to Launch Your Innovation
Roan Ventures, Inc.
1155 Elm Street
Manchester, NH 03101
(603) 644-6110

NEW JERSEY

Entrepreneur's Mall
1414-16-18 Atlantic Avenue
Atlantic City, NJ 08401
  (609) 345-0099

Camden Business and Technology Center
Camden Department of Policy and Planning
Poet's Row Industrial Park
Camden, NJ 08101
  (609) 757-7200

Camden Economic Development Corp.
Suite 103, 800 Hudson Square
Camden, NJ 08102

The Incubator
130 North Broadway
Camden, NJ 08101
  (609) 757-7979

Professional Resources Center
190 Highway 18
East Brunswick, NJ 08816
  (201) 246-8181

Hi-Tech
Stevens Institute of Technology
Castle Point, Stevens Center, 13th Fl.
Hoboken, NJ 07030
  (201) 420-5246

Hoboken Business Incubator
City of Hoboken
Hoboken, NJ 07030

Incutech Corporation
#300, 120 Wood Avenue, South
Iselin, NJ 08830
  (201) 548-4410

DKM Properties & Tech Centers Internat'l
John A. Roebling Complex
Lawrenceville, NJ 08690
  (609) 586-4800, Ext. 602

Gates Equipment Corporation
208 Gates Road
Little Ferry, NJ 07643
  (201) 342-4660

Princeton Dynamics
17 Stratford Drive
Livingston, NJ 07039
  (201) 992-3213

Cumberland Technology Enterprise Center
1600 Mallon Street
Millville, NJ 08332
  (609) 825-2020

Nova International
1200 Campus Drive, RD 1
Mount Holly, NJ 08060
  (609) 261-6000

Enterprise Development Center of the New
  Jersey Institute of Technology
240 King Boulevard
Newark, NJ 07102
  (201) 643-5740

The Newark Collaboration Group
303-9 Washington Street
Newark, NJ 07102
  (201) 624-1007

Pemberton Farms Research Campus
North Pemberton Rd. & Route 206
Pemberton, NJ 08060
  (609) 261-6000

Expressway Technology Enterprise Center
100 Deadon Road, Suite 100
Pleasantville, NJ 08232
  (609) 641-1008

Harry Brenner
U.S. Route 1
Princeton, NJ 08540
  (609) 924-0808

Princeton Capital Corporation
P.O. Box 384
Princeton, NJ 08540
  (609) 924-7614

Thompson Executive Services
251 Park Street
Upper Montclair, NJ 07043
  (201) 744-1553

NEW MEXICO

New Mexico Business Innovation Center
3825 Academy Parkway South, NE
Albuquerque, NM 87109
  (505) 345-8668

Hobbs Business Incubator
P.O. Box 1376
Hobbs, NM 88240
  (505) 397-2039

Economic Development, NM State Univ.
P.O. Box 30001, Dept. 3RED
Las Cruces, NM 88003
  (505) 646-2022

Los Alamos Small Business Center
P.O. Box 715
Los Alamos, NM 87544
  (505) 662-0001

VIP Incubator
134 Rio Rancho Drive
Rio Rancho, NM 87124

NEW YORK

Orange St. Small Business Incubator
253 Orange Street
Albany, NY 12210
  (518) 434-5192

Batavia Industrial Center
56 Harvester Avenue
Batavia, NY 14020
  (716) 343-2800

Genesee County Indust. Develop. Agency
216 East Main Street
Batavia, NY 14020
  (716) 343-4866

Broome County Industrial Incubator
19 Chenango Street, P.O. Box 1026
Binghamton, NY 13902
  (607) 772-8212

South Bronx Development Organization
529 Courtland Avenue
Bronx, NY 10451
  (212) 402-1300

Building 131
Brooklyn Navy Yard Development Corp.
Flushing Avenue & Cumberland Street
Brooklyn, NY 11205
  (718) 852-1441

Local Development Corporation of East NY
116 Williams Avenue
Brooklyn, NY 11207
  (718) 385-6700

Erie County Industrial Land Development
Liberty Building
Suite 300, 424 Main Street
Buffalo, NY 14202
  (716) 856-6525

Industrial Growth Complex of Lackawanna/Erie, Erie County IDA
Suite 300, 424 Main Street
Buffalo, NY 14202
  (716) 856-6526

Industrial Incubator
Buffalo Urban Renewal Agency
920 City Hall
Buffalo, NY 14202
  (716) 855-5056

University at Buffalo
Foundation Incubator, Inc.
2211 Main Street, Building C
Buffalo, NY 14214
  (716) 636-3015

Western NY Technology Development Center
2211 Main Street, Building C
Buffalo, NY 14214
  (716) 831-3472

Technology Development Center
St. Lawrence County IDA
Canton Court House
Canton, NY 13617
  (315) 379-2283

New Enterprises Incubator
15 West Courtney Street
Dunkirk, NY 14048
  (716) 636-0084

Rochester Entrepreneurial Center
80 O'Connor Road
Fairport, NY 14450
  (716) 377-7590

Seneca Nation of Indians Bus. Incubator
1490 Route 438
Irving, NY 14081
  (716) 532-4900

Cornell Univ. Industry Research Park
P.O. Box DH - Real Estate
Ithaca, NY 14853-2801
  (607) 255-5341

Research Start Facility
61 Brown Road
Ithica, NY 14850
  (607) 273-0005

Chautauqua County Incubator
Jamestown Industrial Mall
200 Harrison Street
Jamestown, NY 14701
  (716) 664-3262

Jamestown Industrial Mall Incubator
200 Harrison Street
Jamestown, NY 14701
  (716) 661-3336

190 Willow Avenue Industrial Incubator
Public Development Corporation
161 Willow Avenue
New York, NY 10038
  (212) 619-5000

Audobon Research Park
Columbia University
402 How
New York, NY 10027
  (212) 280-8223

Business Centres International
150 East 58th Street
New York, NY 10155
  (212) 832-7500

NY-NJ Minority Purchasing Council
11th Floor, 1412 Broadway
New York, NY 10018

Rainbow Industrial Centre
3305 Haseley Drive
Niagara Falls, NY 14304-1460
  (716) 693-2333

Keuka Enterprise Center
100 West Lake Road
Penn Yan, NY 14527
  (315) 536-2388

Northern Advanced Technologies Corp.
Potsdam College
P.O. Box 72
Potsdam, NY 13676
  (315) 265-2194

New Opportunity Development
Eastman Kodak
343 State Street
Rochester, NY 14650
  (716) 781-1020

Rochester Institute of Technology
One Lomb Memorial Drive
Rochester, NY 14623
  (716) 475-2380

Rome Business Incubator
Rome Industrial Development Corporation
200 Liberty Plaza
Rome, NY 13440

Schenectady Bus. and Technology Center
Schenectady County Development Corp.
242 Canal Square
Schenectady, NY 12305
  (518) 393-7252

Stony Brook High Tech Incubator
SUNY at Stony Brook
Office of Research Administration
Stony Brook, NY 11794-4466

Central NY Regional Hi-Tech Dev. Council
Knowledge Systems and Research, Inc.
Room 826, 500 South Salina Street
Syracuse, NY 13202
  (315) 470-1350

Greater Syracuse Business Center
1201 East Fayette Street
Syracuse, NY 13201
  (315) 475-8456

Technology Businesses Associated, Inc.
719 East Genessee Street
Syracuse, NY 13202
  (315) 4224-1135

RPI Incubator Program
Rensselaer Polytechnic Institute
1223 Peoples Avenue
Troy, NY 12180
  (518) 266-6658

Central New York Bus. Incubator Group
Charlestown Factory Outlet Center
311 Turner Street
Utica, NY 13501
  (315) 793-8050

Providence Services
325 Central Avenue
White Plains, NY 10606
  (914) 682-7767

NORTH CAROLINA

Small Business Incubator
Roanoke-Chowan Technical College
Route 2
Ahoskie, NC 27910
  (919) 332-4042

The Ben Craig Center
5736 North Tryon Street
Charlotte, NC 27213
  (704) 597-9851

Haywood Small Business & Indus. Center
Western Carolina University Center
Improved Mountain Living
Cullowhee, NC 28723
  (704) 227-7492

Triangle South Enterprise Center
Dunn Area Committee of 200, Inc.
107 West Broad Street
Dunn, NC 28334
  (919) 774-6442

Dillard Business and Technical Center
P.O. Box 1543
Goldsboro, NC 27533
  (919) 735-0505

Greensboro Business Center, Inc.
P.O. Box 16287
Greensboro, NC 27416-0287
  (919) 275-8675

Hillsborough Business Center
P.O. Box 1418
Hillsborough, NC 27278
  (919) 732-6956

McDowell County Incubator
McDowell Committee of 100, Inc.
P.O. Box 1289
Marion, NC 28752
  (704) 652-9391

West Ridge Properties, Inc.
West Ridge Center, Highway 70W
Morehead City, NC 28557
  (919) 726-8070

Bus. Innov. & Tech. Advancement Center
P.O. Box 33489
Raleigh, NC 27636
  (919) 832-7105

Small business and Industry Center
100 Industrial Park
Waynesville, NC 28786
  (704) 456-3737

Business and Technology Corporation
P.O. Box 45, 1001 South Marshall Street
Winston-Salem, NC 27101
  (919) 777-3600

NORTH DAKOTA

Lake Agassiz Regional Council
321 North 4th
Fargo, ND 58102
  (701) 235-7885

OHIO

Akron-Summit Industrial Incubator
100 Lincoln Street
Akron, OH 44308
  (216) 253-7918

Office of Planning
City of Akron
166 South High Street
Akron, OH 44308

Innovation Center
Ohio University
One President Street
Athens, OH 45701
  (617) 593-1818

Institute of Local Government Administration
  and Rural Development
Bentley Hall, Ohio University
Athens, OH 45701-2979

Research and Graduate Programs
Ohio University
306 Cutter Hall
Athens, OH 45701
  (614) 593-2581

Barberton Incubator
576 West Park Avenue
Barberton, OH 44203
  (216) 745-3141

WSOS Economic Development
118 East Oak Street
Bowling Green, OH 43402

Stark County Incubator
Stark Development Board
800 Savannah Avenue, NE
Canton, OH 44704
  (216) 453-5900

Greater Cincinnati Chamber of Commerce
120 West Fifth Street
Cincinnati, OH 45202

Hamilton County Business Incubator
Xavier University
Room 307, 3800 Victory Parkway
Cincinnati, OH 45207
  (513) 745-3394

Hamilton County Development Company
Suite 108, 10921 Reed-Hartman Highway
Cincinnati, OH 45242

Center for Venture Development
Enterprise Development, Inc.
11000 Cedar Avenue
Cleveland, OH 44106
  (216) 229-9445

Cleveland Centre
3100 Chester Avenue
Cleveland, OH 44114

Cleveland Small Business Incubator
1145 Galewood Drive, P.O. Box 10440
Cleveland, OH 44110
  (216) 451-4747

Cleveland Youngstown Redevelopment Corp.
3866 Carnegie Avenue
Cleveland, OH 44115
  (216) 229-9445

Business and Technology Center
1445 Summit Street
Columbus, OH 43201
  (614) 294-0206

Office of Local Government Services
Ohio Department of Development
P.O. Box 1001
  Columbus, OH 43216

Small Business Development Center
23rd Floor, 30 East Broad Street
Columbus, OH 43216

The Thomas Edison Program
77 South High Street, 26th Floor
Columbus, OH 43266
  (614) 466-5867

City-Wide Development Corporation
2080 Miami Valley Tower
40 West 4th St.
Dayton, OH 45402

Dayton Technology Center
35 South St. Clair
Dayton, OH 45402

First Incorporation
1116 Stort Street
P.O. Box 801, Mid City Station
Dayton, OH 45402
  (513) 443-0316

Columbiana County Commd. Action Agency
93 James Street
East Palestine, OH 44413
  (216) 426-4311

Community Development Department
City of Hamilton
20 High Street
Hamilton, OH 45011

Mansfield-Richland Industrial Incubator
193 North Main Street
Mansfield, OH 44902
  (419) 525-1614

Lake County Economic Development Center
Camelot Building, Lakeland Comm. College
Mentor, OH 44060

Greater Lawrence Econ. Development Corp.
P.O. Box 488
South Point, OH 45680

Springfield Incubator
76 East High Street
Springfield, OH 45502
  (513) 324-7744

Springfield Technology Center
300 East Auburn Avenue
Springfield, OH 45505
  (513) 322-7821

Phil Weisberger
P.O. Box 1804
Steubenville, OH 43952

Business and Technology Center
1946 North 13th Street
Toledo, OH 43624
  (419) 255-6700

North River Development Corporation
725 LaGrange Street
Toledo, OH 43604

River East Corporation
615 Front Street
Toledo, OH 43605
  (419) 698-2310

Toledo Area Small Business Association
Toledo Area Chamber of Commerce
218 Huron Street
Toledo, OH 43604

Jim Converse
P.O. Box 100
Winona, OH 44493

Miami Valley Incubator
800 Livermore Street
Yellow Springs, OH 45387
  (513) 765-1424

Commonwealth
P.O. Box 6212
Youngstown, OH 44503

Edison Office of Entrepreneurship, Inc.
Jeff Hallett
Youngstown State University
Youngstown, OH 44555

Office for Entrepreneurial Advocacy
Cntr Urban Stud., Youngstown State Univ.
410 Wick Avenue
Youngstown, OH 44555
  (216) 742-3355

OKLAHOMA

Pontotoc County Skills Devel. Center
1830 Arlington
Ada, OK 74820

Delaware Tribe of Western Oklahoma
P.O. Box 825
Anadarko, OK 73005

Atoka Chamber of Commerce
P.O. Box 709
Atoka, OK 74525
  (405) 889-2410

Stifel and Nicolaus Company
209 East Main
Cordell, OK 73632

Industrial Incubator
Kiamichi Area Vo-Tech / Atoka Campus
P.O. Box 220
Atoka, OK 74525
  (405) 889-7321

Industrial Incubator
Bryan County Skill Center
810 Waldron Drive
Durant, OK 74701
  (405) 924-7081

Industrial Incubator
Rural Enterprises Incubator
10 Waldron Drive
Durant, OK 74701
  (405) 924-5094

Oklahoma Small Business Development
517 West University
Durant, OK 74701

Canadian County Incubator Program
3901 Valley Park Drive
El Reno, OK 73036

Hugo Chamber of Commerce
200 South Broadway
Hugo, OK 74743
  (405) 326-7511

Industrial Incubator
Kiamichi Area Vo-Tech School
107 South 15th
Hugo, OK 74743
  (918) 426-0940

REDARK
P.O. Box 1650
McAlester, OK 74502
  (918) 426-1879

Investment Financial Services
Suite 630, 1601 N.W. Expressway
Oklahoma City, OK 73119

Noble Center for Advancing Technology
External Educational Linkages
Oklahoma State Univ., Technical Branch
Okmulgee, OK 74447
  (918) 756-6211, Ext. 204

Seminole Chamber of Commerce
P.O. Box 1190
Seminole, OK 74868
  (405) 382-3640

Tulsa Innovation Center, Inc.
Suite D, 1216 North Lansing Avenue
Tulsa, OK 74106
  (918) 583-4115

OREGON

High Tech Sales, Inc.
North 10th Street
Baker, OR 97814
  (503) 523-4458

Oregon Graduate Center Science Park
Suite 300, 1600 N.W. Compton Drive
Beaverton, OR 97006
  (503) 690-1112

Coyote Business Incubator
P.O. Box 70
Corbett, OR 97019
  (503) 695-2296

Business Enterprise Center of Benton County
1325 N.W. Ninth Street
Corvallis, OR 97330
  (503) 758-4009

Oregon Technology Center Incubator
c/o KCEDA
P.O. Box 1777
Klamath Falls, OR 97601
  (503) 882-9600

Cascade Business Center Corp.
4134 North Vancouver
Portland, OR 97217
  (503) 284-3830

Parkrose Business Development Center
10700 NE Sandy Boulevard
Portland, OR 97220
  (503) 256-3573

PENNSYLVANIA

Bridgeworks
South Tenth Street
Allentown, PA 18105
  (215) 435-8890

Altoona Area Incubator
6th Avenue & 45th Street
Altoona, PA 16602
  (814) 949-2030

Homer Research Lab
South Mountain Drive
Bethlehem, PA 18015
  (215) 861-0584

Lehigh Valley Bank Incubator Center
4th & Broadway
Bethlehem, PA 18015
  (215) 861-0584

North East Tier Ben Franklin Tech. Cntr.
Lehigh University
Bethlehem, PA 18015

Bradford Incubator
20 Russell Boulevard
Bradford, PA 16701
  (814) 368-7170

Clarion Incubator
Clarion University of Pennsylvania
100 Haskell House
Clarion, PA 16214
  (814) 226-2060

South First Avenue
800 South First Street
Coatesville, PA 19320
  (215) 383-9800

Business Innovation Center
Development Corp. of Southwest Pennsylvania
One Library Place
Duquesne, PA 15110
  (412) 471-3939

Emporium Trade Center
Suite 700, 116 West Second Street
Emporium, PA 15834
  (814) 486-1707

Enterprise Development Center
East 33rd Street
Erie, PA 16510
  (814) 899-6022

Venango Area Industrial Complex
191 Howard Street
Franklin, PA 16323
  (814) 432-3466

Model Works Industrial Commons
Girard Area Industrial Development Corp.
227 Hathaway Street, East
Girard, PA 16417
  (814) 774-9339

Three Allegheny Court Partnership
Three Allegheny Court
Glassport, PA 15042
  (412) 672-3270

Greenville Business Incubator
12 North Diamond Street
Greenville, PA 16125
  (412) 588-1161

Robertshaw Center, Inc.
Indiana University of Pennsylvania
13th Street Extension
Indiana, PA 15705
  (412) 357-2179

Liberty Street Market Place
1733 Market Street Ext.,
P.O. Box 547
Warren, PA 16365
  (814) 726-2400

Opportunities Without Limits, Inc.
301 Academy Street
Johnstown, PA 15906
  (814) 535-7891

Pennsylvania State Tech. Dev. Center
650 South Henderson Road
King of Prussia, PA 19406
  (215) 265-7640

Lansdale Business Center
650 North Cannon Avenue
Lansdale, PA 19446
  (215) 855-6700

The Penn Center
110 East Bald Eagle Street
Lock Haven, PA 17745
  (717) 893-4130

Executive Office Link, Inc.
Rouse & Associates
Suite 210, 7 Great Valley Parkway
Malvern, PA 19350
  (215) 251-6850

Technology Business Incubator
30 East Swedesford Road
Malvern, PA 19355
  (215) 889-1300

McKeesport Innovation Center
201 Lysle Boulevard
McKeesport, PA 15132
  (412) 679-5049

Meadville Industrial Condominium
628 Arch Street
Meadville, PA 16335
  (814) 336-4290

Montgomeryville Tech. Enterprise Center
Technology Centers International, Inc.
1060 Route 309
Montgomeryville, PA 18936
  (215) 646-7800

Management Development Center
201 Power Street
New Castle, PA 16102
  (412) 658-5755

Paoli Technology Enterprise Center, Inc.
19 East Central Avenue
Paoli, PA 19301
  (215) 251-0505

Business and Technology Center
5070 Parkside Avenue
Philadelphia, PA 19131
  (215) 877-1404

Hunting Park West
S.W. Germantown Comm. Development
  Group
502 Wayne Avenue
Philadelphia, PA 19144
  (215) 843-2000

University City Science Center (West Philadelphia)
3624 Market Street
Philadelphia, PA 19104
  (215) 387-2255

Moshannon Valley Incubator
220 North Third Street
Philipsburg, PA 16866
  (814) 342-2260

Brewery Innovation Center
800 Vinial Street
Pittsburgh, PA 15212
  (412) 322-5300

Center for Entrepreneurial Development
120 South Whitfield Street
Pittsburgh, PA 15206
  (412) 361-5000

East Liberty Incubator
120 South Whitfield Street
Pittsburgh, PA 15206
  (412) 361-5000

Glasport Industrial Center
S.W. PA Economic Development Corp.
355 Fifth Avenue
Pittsburgh, PA 15222
  (412) 391-1240

Boulevard Buildings
South Sixth & Bingham Streets
Pittsburgh, PA 15203
  (412) 431-8200

South Side Development Center
401 Bingham Street
Pittsburgh, PA 15203
 (412) 431-8200

University of Pittsburgh Applied Res. Center
1000 Gulf Lab Road
Pittsburgh, PA 15204
 (412) 826-5019

University Technology Development Center
4516 Henry Street
Pittsburgh, PA 15213
 (412) 471-3939

University Technology Development Center
Regional Industrial Development Corp.
3400 Forbes Avenue
Pittsburgh, PA 15213
 (412) 471-3939

Pottstown Technology Development Center
191 South Kiem Street
Pottstown, PA 19461
 (215) 970-0222

North Central Pennsylvania Regional Planning
 and Development Commission
P.O. Box 488
Ridgeway, PA 15853
 (814) 772-6901

Business Advancement Center
415 North Washington Avenue
Scranton, PA 18503
 (717) 961-6181

Shippensburg Area Manufacturing Center
24 East Burd Street
Shippensburg, PA 17257
 (717) 532-6800

Crozer Mills Enterprise Center
600 Upland Avenue
Upland, PA 19015
 (215) 499-7400

W. Aliquippa Bus. & Technology Center
Aliquippa Alliance for Unity & Develop.
300 Main Street
West Aliquippa, PA 15001
 (412) 378-7422

Beaver Incubator
12330 Perry Highway, P.O. Box 216
Wexford, PA 15090
 (412) 931-8444

New Kensington Incubator
12330 Perry Highway, P.O. Box 216
Wexford, PA 15090
 (412) 931-8444

Southwest PA Business Development Center
P.O. Box 216
Wexford, PA 15090
 (412) 931-8444

SPEDD Incubator Network
12300 Perry Highway
Wexford, PA 15097
 (412) 935-6122

Luzerne County Business Incubator
421 North Pennsylvania Avenue
Wilkes-Barre, PA 18701
 (717) 823-7728

Coop. Resources Improving Business
1307 Park Avenue
Williamsport, PA 17701
 (717) 327-1857

CYBER Center
Thomas E. Ulmer, Manager
1600 Pennsylvania Avenue
York, PA 17404
 (717) 846-2927

RHODE ISLAND

East Bay Executive Centre
Suite 102, 1275 Wampanoag Trail
East Providence, RI 02915
  (401) 433-5583

Ecco Place Bus. Incubator & Mtg. Center
645 Elmwood Avenue
Providence, RI 02907
  (401) 461-4321

Providence Executive Center
1900 Hospital Trust Tower
Providence, RI 02903
  (401) 421-7200

Richmond Square Business & Tech. Center
One Richmond Square
Providence, RI 02906
  (401) 521-3000

SOUTH CAROLINA

Retail Incubator
P.O. Box 2827
Anderson, SC 29622
  (803) 231-2222

Sullivan Business Center
206 South Main Street
Anderson, SC 29622
  (803) 231-2223

Control Data Bus. & Technology Center
Jerome Clemons
701 East Bay Street
Charleston, SC 29403
  (803) 722-1219

Business Assistance Network
181 East Evans Street
Florence, SC 29501
  (803) 664-2800

Control Data Bus. & Technology Center
David Perkins
181 East Evans Street
Florence, SC 29501
  (803) 664-2800

Enterprise Park
38 Westfield Street
Greenville, SC 29601
  (803) 232-4252

Greenville New Business Center
Greenville Chamber of Commerce
P.O. Box 10048
Greenville, SC 29603
  (803) 242-1050

Ocean Pines Development Corporation
P.O. Box 3326
Myrtle Beach, SC 29578
  (803) 238-0849

Business and Technology Center
802 East Martintown Road
North Augusta, SC 29841
  (803) 827-2205

Business and Technical Center
454 South Anderson Road, BTC-513
Rock Hill, SC 29730
  (803) 329-7099

Control Data Bus. & Technology Center
David Vipperman
454 South Anderson Road
Rock Hill, SC 29730
  (803) 329-9700

Rock Hill Economic Development Corp.
P.O. Box 11706
Rock Hill, SC 29731
  (803) 591-4210

SOUTH DAKOTA

Brookings Economic Development Center
2308 Sixth Street, P.O. Box 431
Brookings, SD 57006
   (605) 692-6125

Enterprise Development Center
Dakota State University
820 North Washington
Madison, SD 57042
   (605) 256-5156

Business Incubator Economic Development
SD School of Mines and Technology
Rapid City, SD 57702

TENNESSEE

Business Development Center
100 Cherokee Boulevard
Chattanooga, TN 37405
   (615) 265-0991/756-2121

Knox County Government
Fairview Incubation Center
400 Main, Room 603, City/County Building
Knoxville, TN 37902

Matrix Business Incubator
The Moses Center
220 Carrick Street
Knoxville, TN 37921
   (615) 515-6310

Memphis Biomedical Resource Zone
740 Court Avenue
Memphis, TN 38105
   (901) 526-1165

Memphis Chamber of Commerce
555 Beale Street
Memphis, TN 38103

Airport South Business Center
The Watson & Taylor Companies
Suite 103, 501 Metrophex Drive
Nashville, TN 37211
   (615) 832-7752

Nashville Business Incubation Center
10th & Charlotte Avenues
Nashville, TN 37203
   (615) 251-1180

Tennessee Innovation Center, Inc.
P.O. Box 607
Oak Ridge, TN 37831
   (615) 482-2440

TEXAS

Advanced Dynamics Corporation
Office Services Division
2000 East Lamar Boulevard
Arlington, TX 76006
   (817) 274-6363

Austin Technology Incubator, Austin
P.O. Box 7459
Austin, TX 78713-7459
   (512) 471-1616

Southeast Business Incubator, Austin
2020 East St. Elmo
Austin, TX 78744
   (512) 385-5087

Beaumont Business Incubator
Suite N-F, 1090 South Fourth Street
Beaumont, TX 77701
   (409) 835-1554

Corpus Christi Enterprise Center
"Incubator Without Walls"
1201 North Shoreline
Corpus Christi, TX 78403
   (512) 888-4227

K. Wolen Industrial Incubator Building
200 North 12th Street
Corsicana, TX 75151
  (214) 872-4811

Dallas County Community College Dist.
Suite 0101, 311 South Akard
Dallas, TX 75202

The Dallas Business Incubator
2811 McKinney
Dallas, TX 75204
  (214) 953-1656

Gulf Coast Small Bus. Develop. Center
University of Houston
401 Louisiana, 8th Floor
Houston, TX 77002
  (713) 223-1141

The City of Houston
Business and Technology Center
5330 Griggs
Houston, TX 77021
  (712) 845-2420

Board of City Development
2005 Broadway
Lubbock, TX 79417

Midland Chamber of Commerce
P.O. Box 1890
Midland, TX 79702

Control Data Bus. & Technology Center
Robert McKinley
301 South Frio
San Antonio, TX 78207
  (512) 270-4500

Victoria Incubator Foundation
University of Houston/Victoria
Suite 102, 700 Main Center
Victoria, TX 77901
  (512) 575-8944

Business Resource Center
4601 North 19th
Waco, TX 76708

Heart of TX Bus. Resource Cntr. Incubator
4601 North 19th Street
Waco, TX 76708
  (512) 754-8898

UTAH

Research Technology Park
Utah State University
Suite 104, 1780 North Research Park Way
Logan, UT 84321
  (801) 750-6924

Institutional Development Association
Suite 200, 200 North Main
Salt Lake City, UT 84103
  (801) 328-1504

Research park Development
University of Utah
505 Wakara Way
Salt Lake City, UT 84108
  (801) 581-8133

Utah Innovation Center
Suite 206, 419 Wakara Way
Salt Lake City, UT 84108
  (801) 584-2500

VERMONT

Chace Mill Associates
One Mill Street
Burlington, VT 05401

Pine Square
266 Pine Street
Burlington, VT 05401

The Davis Company
Maltex Building, 431 Pine Street
Burlington, VT 05401

Cambridge Incubator
P.O. Box 455
Morrisville, VT 05640

Newport Incubator
RFD #1, Box 125G
Newport, VT 05855

Bennington County Industrial Corp.
P.O. Box 357
North Bennington, VT 05257
  (802) 442-8975/447-0750

Precision Valley Development Corp.
P.O. Box 477
Springfield, VT 05156
  (802) 885-2138

Stedley Partnership
93 South Main Street
Waterbury, VT 05676

VIRGINIA

NOVA/Center for Bus. & Govern. Services
Northern Virginia Community College
4001 Wakefield Chapel Road
Annandale, VA 22003

University of Virginia
Thornton Hall
Charlottesville, VA 22901

University Business Innovation Center
Booker House, 3rd Fl., P.O. Box 9023
Charlottesville, VA 22906
  (804) 924-6310

Entrep. Center, Exp. & Domestic Programs
George Mason University
4400 University Drive
Fairfax, VA 22030
  (703) 323-3751/3799

George Mason University
School of Business Administration
4400 University Drive
Fairfax, VA 22032

Longwood Small Business Development
School of Business and Economics
Longwood College
Farmville, VA 23901

Rockingham Innovation Center, Inc.
James Madison University
Wine-Price Hall, Room G-1
Harrisonburg, VA 22807
  (703) 434-3235

Hopewell Technology Center, Inc.
End of Main Street
15 Terminal Street
Hopewell, VA 23860
  (804) 452-1000

City of Lynchburg
Economic Development Office
P.O. Box 60
Lynchburg, VA 24505
  (804) 847-1732

Southwest Virginia Community College
Office of the President
P.O. Box SVCC
Richland, VA 24641

Southwest Virginia Community College
Economic Development/Technology Transfer
P.O. Box SVCC
Richlands, VA 24641
  (703) 964-2555

Richmond Tech, and Enterprise Center
18 South 22nd Street
Richmond, VA 23223
  (804) 648-7832

City of Roanoke
Economic Development and Grants
Room 355, Municipal Building
215 Church Avenue, S.W.
Roanoke, VA 24011
  (703) 981-2344

City of Roanoke - Economic Development
Room 355, Municipal Building
215 Church Avenue, S.W.
Roanoke, VA 24011
  (703) 981-2344

Winchester-Frederick County Economic
  Development Commission
12 Rouss Avenue
Winchester, VA 22601
  (703) 665-0973

WASHINGTON

Port of Skagit County
P.O. Box 348
Burlington, WA 98233
  (206) 757-0013

TRICO Economic Development District
121 West Astor
Colville, WA 99114
  (509) 684-4571

Kittitas County Action Council, Lead Agency
City of Ellensburg
115 West Third
Ellensburg, WA 98632
  (509) 925-1448

Center for Bus. & Employment Develop.
917 134th S.W.
Everett, WA 98204
  (206) 743-9669

Snohomish County Airport
Paine Field, Terminal Building
Everett, WA 98204
  (206) 353-2110

Port of Kennewick Development Building
Port of Kennewick
One Clover Island
Kennewick, WA 99336
  (509) 545-2293

Kent Business Development Center
Venture Center
P.O. Box 301
Kent, WA 98032
  (206) 854-8744

Incubator Steering Committee
Lower Columbia College
1600 Maple
Longview, WA 98632
  (206) 577-2336

Lower Columbia Comm. Action Council
P.O. Box 2129
Longview, WA 98632
  (206) 425-3430

Thurston County EDC/Evergreen CDA
721 South Columbia
Olympia, WA 98501
  (206) 754-6320

Okanogan Cnty Council for Econ. Develp.
P.O. Box 1067
Omak, WA 98840
  (509) 422-4041

Washington State Univ. Res. & Tech. Park
NE 1615 Eastgate Boulevard
Pullman, WA 99164-1802
  (509) 335-5526

Raymond/South Bend Area
545 Ballentine
Raymond, WA 98577
  (206) 942-3112

Port of Benton Development Building
2952 George Washington Way
Richland, WA 99352
  (509) 545-2380

Tri-Cities Enterprise Center
City of Richland
P.O. Box 190
Richland, WA 99352
  (509) 943-9161, ext. 359

Evergreen CDA Incubator-Thurston Co.
Evergreen CDA
2122 Smith Tower
Seattle, WA 98104
  (206) 622-3731

Spokane Business Incubation Center
P.O. Box 19206
Spokane, WA 99219
  (509) 458-6340

Tacoma-Eastside Business Incubator
3203 Portland Avenue East
Tacoma, WA 98404
  (206) 272-0068

Tacoma-Pierce County Bus. Devel. Center
1121 South "K" Street
Tacoma, WA 98405
  (206) 597-6433

WEST VIRGINIA

Bluefield Business Center
821 Bluefield Avenue
Bluefield, WV 24701
  (703) 322-3233

Charleston Enterprise Center
1116 Smith Street
Charleston, WV 25301
  (304) 340-4250

1st Step Enterprise Center of Randolph Cnty.
Suite 10, Seneca mall
Elkins, WV 26241
  (304) 636-0066

1st Step Enterprise Center of Marshall Cnty.
#1 Bridgeville Plaza, S. Lafayette Ave.
Moundsville, WV 26041
  (304) 845-2045

Business Hatchery
701 Main Street
Princeton, WV 24740
  (304) 425-4323

1st Step Enterprise Cntr of St. Albans
86 Olde Main Plaza
St. Albans, WV 25177
  (304) 722-6250

WISCONSIN

DJ Bordini Tech. Innovation Cntr. OP
Fox Valley Technical College
P.O. Box 2277
Appleton, WI 54913
  (414) 735-2537

Chippewa Valley Incubation Center, Inc.
917 Harris Street
Eau Claire, WI 54701
  (715) 836-2842

ADVOCAP Business Center
19 West First Street, P.O. Box 1108
Fond du lac, WI 54936-1108
  (414) 922-7760/9881

Advance Business Development Center
835 Potts Avenue
Green Bay, WI 54303
  (414) 496-9010/9001

Gateway Technical College
Gateway Enterprise Center
3520 30th Avenue
Kenosha, WI 53142-1690

Coulee Region Business Center, Inc.
2615 George Street
LaCrosse, WI 54603
  (608) 781-2722

Derse Schroeder Associates
Derse & Schroeder, Ltd.
1202 Ann Street
Madison, WI 53711
  (608) 273-2494

Laboratory Associated Businesses
1202 Ann Street
Madison, WI 53711
  (608) 251-3005

Madison Business Incubator
210 North Bassett Street
Madison, WI 53703
  (608) 258-7070

Madison Enterprise Center
100 South Baldwin Street
Madison, WI 53703
  (608) 256-6565

Madison Incubator for Tech. Develop.
3802 Packers Avenue
Madison, WI 53704
  (608) 249-1234

Indianhead Enterprises
1426 Indianhead Drive
Menomonie, WI 54751
  (715) 235-9058

UW-Stout Incubator
University of Wisconsin-Stout
206 Fryklund Hall
Menomonie, WI 54751
  (715) 232-1252

Community Enterprise of Greater Milwaukee
3118 North Teutonia Avenue
Milwaukee, WI 53206

DePaul Sertoma Industries, Inc.
3450 West Hopkins Street
Milwaukee, WI 53211
  (414) 447-1600

Metroworks
4767 North 32nd Street
Milwaukee, WI 53209
  (414) 871-7500

Milwaukee Business Ventures
1125 West National Avenue
Milwaukee, WI 63204
  (14) 643-7740

Milwaukee Business Ventures
1125 West National Avenue
Milwaukee, WI 53204
  (414) 643-7740 or 781-6067

Milwaukee Enterprise Center
2821 N. 4th Street, P.O. Box 12077
Milwaukee, WI 53212
  (414) 372-3609/3936

Rapids Business Center
1509 Rapids Drive
Racine, WI 53404
  (414) 632-7711

Richland County Economic Devel. Corp.
P.O. Box 49
Richland Center, WI 53581
  (608) 647-4310

Richland County Economic Devel. Corp.
P.O. Box 49
Richland Center, WI 53581
  (608) 647-4310

Sheboygan County Enterprise Center
824 South 8th Street
Sheboygan, WI 53801

Waukesha Area Incubator Committee
2029 Cobblestone Court
Waukesha, WI 53188
  (414) 542-3966

Marathon County Economic Devel. Council
P.O. Box 569
Wausau, WI 54401
  (715) 845-6231

CAPsell Center
205 East Main, #1
Wautoma, WI 54982
  (414) 787-3949

Business Development Center
5317 West Burnham Street
West Allis, WI 53219
  (414) 643-8720

WYOMING

Enterprise Center
Laramie County Community College
1400 East College Drive
Cheyenne, WY 82001
  (307) 635-5853

Small Business Incubator
Small Business Development Center
P.O. Box 1028
Douglas, WY 82633
  (307) 358-4090

PUERTO RICO

Producir, Inc.
P.O. Box 1660
Canovanas, PR 00629
  (809) 876-7150

Asociacion de Pequenos Agricultores Del
  Rabanal, Inc.
P.O. Box 849
Cidra, PR 00639
(809) 745-6415

Desarrollos Metalarte
P.O. Box 1494
Coamo, PR 00640
  (809) 825-1508

APPENDIX B

SAMPLE LOAN FORMS

Form FmHA 449-1
(Rev. 5-16-83)

UNITED STATES DEPARTMENT OF AGRICULTURE
FARMERS HOME ADMINISTRATION

FORM APPROVED
OMB NO. 0575-0021
EXPIRES 10-31-85

APPLICATION FOR LOAN AND GUARANTEE
(Business and Industry)

FmHA Case Number

General Information: The "Application for Loan and Guarantee" is to provide information needed for the analysis and loan determination process. Tear at perforations for ease in use. Specific references are made in this application to sections of the Business and Industrial Loan Instruction. For complete guidance, see FmHA Instruction 1980-A and 1980-E and related FmHA forms.

Part A – is to be completed by the proposed borrower. The original and two copies with attachments will be submitted to the proposed lender.

Part B – is to be completed by the lender. Upon completion, the original and one copy and attachments of Part A and B will be filed with the FmHA State Office.

PART A

Instructions to Proposed Borrower: Complete items one through 20. Submit original and two copies of this application and all supporting documents to the lender. If additional space is required, provide for by an attachment. Additional information may be obtained from any FmHA Office.

1. NAME: *(Show official name without abbreviations unless the abbreviation is a part of the official name. For proprietor or partnership, show name(s) followed by d/b/a and trade name used, if any, and attach a copy of the partnership agreement).*

Street		City	County
State	ZIP Code	Telephone Number	Amount of Loan Requested $
Project Location: City	Population *(Last Census)*	County	State

Franchise ☐ Yes ☐ No   If Yes, submit copy

2. TYPE OF BUSINESS:	Applicant's Tax Identification Number	SIC Number

3. THIS PROJECT IS: Date Enterprise Established:
    ☐ A new business venture   ☐ Other *(Explain)*
    ☐ A new branch of facility   ☐ An expansion of an existing facility
    ☐ Refinancing debts   ☐ Transfer of Ownership

4. VETERAN - For individual or partner indicate if veteran   ☐ Yes ☐ No
    If yes, indicate service from   to   Branch

5. CITIZENSHIP - Do you meet the citizenship requirements in FmHA Instruction 1980.403?   ☐ Yes ☐ No

6. HISTORY OF BUSINESS - Provide a brief description and history of the business *(attach additional sheets if necessary).*

_____

_____

_____

_____

7. COMMUNITY BENEFITS - Comment on the benefits the community will receive if the loan is made *(i.e., taxes, jobs and any other benefits).*

_____

_____

_____

Information requested by this form is collected for determining program eligibility and project analysis. Completion of this form is required to obtain the benefit of an FmHA Business and Industry loan guarantee. This statement is furnished pursuant to P. L. 96-511.

- 2

8.   PREVIOUS FEDERAL, STATE, OR LOCAL FINANCING - List assistance received, requested, or any pending applications. *(Include direct, participation, insured, or guarantee loans and grants from any Federal, State, or local sources).*

9.   LITIGATIONS - List details of any pending or final disciplinary or legal *(civil or criminal)* action against the proposed borrower, guarantors, partners, principal stockholders and directors.

10.   NAMES OF ATTORNEYS, ACCOUNTANTS, AND OTHER PARTIES - List the names of all attorneys, accountants, appraisers, packagers, agents, and all other parties *(whether individuals, partnerships, associations)* engaged by or on behalf of the proposed borrower *(whether on a salary, retainer or fee basis and regardless of the amount of compensation)* for the purpose of rendering professional or other services of any nature whatever to proposed borrower, in connection with the preparation or presentation of this application to a lender. List all fees or other charges or compensations **paid or to be paid** for any purpose in connection with this application or disbursement of the loan whether in money or other property of any kind whatever, by or for the account of the proposed borrower together with a description of such services rendered or to be rendered with complete justification for such purposes. **NOTE: all fees and charges are subject to FmHA review and approval and may, in some cases, be paid out of loan proceeds. (See FmHA Instruction 1980.411 and 1980.414).**

Name and Address *(Include ZIP Code)*	Description of Service Rendered or to be Rendered with complete Justification	Total Compensation Agreed to be Paid*	Compensation Already Paid

Enter specific dollar amounts or hourly rates. "Unknown," "Undetermined," or other imprecise terms are not sufficient.

11.   SUBSIDIARIES AND AFFILIATES - (1) List the name and addresses of all concerns that are subsidiaries, parent organizations, or affiliates of the proposed borrower, including concerns in which the proposed borrower holds a controlling *(but not necessarily a majority)* interest:

(2) List all other concerns that are in any way affiliated, by stock ownership, management contracts, or otherwise, with the proposed borrower. The proposed borrower should comment briefly regarding the trade relationship between the proposed borrower and such subsidiaries or affiliates and if the proposed borrower has no subsidiary or affiliate, a statement to this effect should be made. Signed and dated balance sheets, operating statements and reconcilement of net worth *(all not more than 60 days old)* must be submitted for all subsidiaries, parent organizations, and affiliates in the same manner as required of the proposed borrower.

_____

_____

_____

_____

_____

12. PURCHASE AND SALES RELATIONS WITH OTHERS - Does proposed borrower buy from, sell to or use the services of, any concern in which an officer, director, major stockholder, or partner, or proprietor of the proposed borrower has a substantial interest? ☐ Yes ☐ No   If, "Yes" give names of such officer, director, stockholder, and partners, names of such concerns and explain the nature of the transaction(s).

_____

_____

_____

_____

_____

13. RECEIVERSHIP - BANKRUPTCY - Has the proposed borrower or any officer or, partner or director of the proposed borrower, affiliates or any other concern with which such person has been connected ever been in receivership or adjudicated bankrupt? ☐ Yes ☐ No   If "Yes" give names, dates and details.

_____

_____

_____

_____

14. DISCLOSURE OF SPECIAL INFORMATION REGARDING PRINCIPALS - (a) List below the names of any FmHA employees who are related by blood, marriage, or adoption, or who have any present or have had any past, direct or indirect, financial interest in or association with, the proposed borrower, or any of its partners, officers, directors, principal stockholders including such interest in other enterprise; (b) When the proprietor, or any partner, officer, director, or their spouse, is an employee of the U.S. Government including members of the armed forces, detailed information shall be submitted with the application. Check box(s) if (a) or (b) is not applicable.   ☐ (a)   ☐ (b)

NAMES AND ADDRESS *(Include ZIP Code)*	Details of Relationship or Interest

- 4

15. MANAGEMENT - Enter names of (a) all owners, partners, key officers, directors or stockholders and their annual compensation, including salaries, fees, withdrawals, etc., (b) hired manager, and (c) all other stockholders having 20 percent or more interest in the proposed borrower. Elected officials and managers on applications for loans from public bodies are excluded. Personal guarantees from major stockholders or owners having a major interest in a corporation, and all partners of partnerships usually will be required. If guarantor cannot provide such guarantee due to existing contractual or legal restrictions, explain in an attachment. Final determinations will be made by the FmHA. Attach, in the case of personal guarantee, current financial statements not over 60 days old at time of filing, and for any corporate guarantee, current financial statements not over 90 days old at time of filing and certified by an officer of the corporation. Additional updated financial statements may be required depending on processing time.

(a) Name	(b) Position or Title	(c) Annual Compensation $	(d) % Owner- ship	(e) Outside Net Worth $	(f) Personal Guarantee Offered* (Yes or No)	(g) Insurance Carried For Benefit of Applicant

*If none offered, provide full explanation why guarantee cannot be offered. *(See FmHA Instruction 1980.443 (b)).*

16. REGULATORY AGENCIES - List all regulatory agencies *((National, State, or Local)* which affect this business or project and explain if there are any pending matters with such regulatory agencies. Indicate if permits, licenses or clearance are necessary and their status. *(See FmHA Instruction 1980.45 and 1980.451)*

_____

_____

_____

_____

17. INSTRUCTION TO PROPOSED BORROWER - Attach to this application the following supporting documents. Reference for 1980-A include section 1980.1 thru 1980.100 and reference for 1980-E include sections 1980.401 thru 1980.500:

(a) Comments from state and local governments, if not already submitted. *(See FmHA Instruction 1980.451 (f) (8)).*

(b) Form FmHA 449-4, "Statement of Personal History," if not already submitted. *(See FmHA Instruction 1980.451 (f) (3)).*

(c) Form FmHA 449-22, "Certification of Non-Relocation and Market and Capacity Information," if applicable. *(See FmHA Instruction 1980.412 (c) and (d).*

(d) Financial data for new or existing businesses are required in accordance with FmHA Instruction 1980.451 (i) (7) and (8).

(e) Aging of accounts receivable and payable. *(Use 30, 60, 90 days with individual account explanation of items over 90 days old). (See FmHA Instruction 1980.451 (i) (15)).*

(f) For companies listed on major stock exchanges and subject to the Securities and Exchange Commission regulations, a copy of the latest SEC 10K report. *(See FmHA Instruction 1980.451 (i) (16)).*

(g) Provide supporting documentation for your projections, including economic factors, markets, management, etc. For loans in excess of $1 million see FmHA Instruction 1980.442 .

(h) If construction is involved, *(See FmHA Instruction 1980.451 (i) (11)).* Final plans and specifications must be submitted to the lender for approval prior to the commencement of construction. Architectural or engineering plans, if applicable, need be attached. *(See FmHA Instruction 1980.451 (i) (4) and 1980.454 (d)).*

(i) If construction is involved, provide applicable equal opportunity and nondiscrimination forms. *(See FmHA Instruction 1980.41).*

(j) Form FmHA 449-10, "Applicant's Environmental Impact Evaluation." *(See FmHA Instruction 1980.40 and 1980.451 (i) (3)).*

(k) Evidence whether the project is located in a flood or mudslide hazard area. *(See FmHA Instruction 1980.42 and 1980.451 (i) (17)).*

(l) Provide a written statement of effect project would have on Historic Places, if any. *(See FmHA Instruction 1980.44 and 1980.451 (i) (15)).*

(m) If application is for health care facility, attach a "Certificate of Need," from appropriate regulatory agency having jurisdiction over the project. *(See FmHA Instruction 1980.451 (k)).*

(n) If loan is in excess of $100,000, provide certification and notices as required for the Clean Air Act and Water Pollution Control Act. *(See FmHA Instruction 1980.43).*

(o) Document utilities availability with letter of commitment from utilities, energy, water, sewer, fire and police protection.

(p) For all persons listed under MANAGEMENT, item 15, provide a brief description of education, technical training, employment and business experience *(resumes may be used).*

(q) Provide a detailed debt schedule correlated to the latest balance sheet reflecting the name of the creditors, loan purpose, original loan amount and loan balance, date of loan, interest rate, maturity date, monthly or annual payments, payment status and collateral that secures such loans. You may use Form FmHA 449-29 Attachment I.

18. POLICY AND REGULATIONS CONCERNING REPRESENTATIVES AND THEIR FEES:

(a) A proposed borrower may obtain the assistance of any attorney, engineer, appraiser, or other representative to aid it in the preparation of its application, however, such representation is not mandatory. In the event a loan is approved, the services of an attorney may be necessary to assist in the preparation of closing documents, title examination, etc.

(b) There are no "authorized representatives" of FmHA, other than our regular salaried employees. Payment of any fee or gratuity to FmHA employees is illegal and will subject the parties to such a transaction to prosecution.

(c) FmHA will not approve placement or finder's fees for the use or attempted use of influence in obtaining or trying to obtain a loan.

(d) Fees which will be approved will be limited to reasonable sums for services actually rendered in connection with the application or the closing, based upon the time and effort required, and the nature and extent of the services rendered by such representative.

(e) It is the responsibility of the proposed borrower to set forth in Section 10 of this application the names of all persons or firms engaged by or on behalf of the proposed borrower. Proposed borrowers are also required to advise FmHA in writing of the names and fees of any representatives engaged by the proposed borrower subsequent to the filing of the application. Failure to so notify FmHA constitutes "misrepresentation" and will cause FmHA to contest the guarantee if lender had knowledge of this omission.

(f) Any proposed borrower having any question concerning the payment of fees, or the reasonableness of fees, should communicate with FmHA before the application is filed for a loan guarantee.

19. AGREEMENT OF NONEMPLOYMENT OF FmHA PERSONNEL. In consideration of FmHA guaranteeing any part of the loan applied for in this application, the proposed borrower hereby agrees with FmHA that proposed borrower will not, for a period of two years after date of guarantee of any part of the loan, employ or tender any office or employment to, or retain for professional services, any person who, on the date of such disbursement, or within one year prior to said date, (a) shall have served as an officer, attorney, agent, or employee of FmHA and (b) as such, shall have occupied a position or engaged in activities which FmHA shall have determined, or may determine, involved discretion with respect to the granting of assistance under the Consolidated Farm and Rural Development Act and other acts administered by FmHA from time to time.

20. CERTIFICATION - The proposed borrower hereby certifies that:

(a) The Proposed borrower has read FmHA policy and regulations concerning representatives and their fees *(18 above)* and has not paid or incurred any obligation to pay, directly or indirectly, any fee or other compensation for obtaining the loan hereby applied for other than for services and expenses authorized pursuant to paragraph 18 above.

(b) The proposed borrower has not paid or incurred any obligation to pay any Government employee or special Government employee any fee, gratuity or anything of value for obtaining the assistance hereby applied for. If such fee, gratuity, etc. has been solicited by any such employee, the proposed borrower agrees to report such information to the Office of Inspector General, USDA, Washington, D.C. 20250.

(c) Information contained above and in exhibits attached hereto are true and complete to the best knowledge and belief of the proposed borrower and are submitted for the purpose of requesting FmHA to guarantee a loan by a lender to the proposed borrower. Whether or not the loan herein applied for is approved, the proposed borrower agrees to pay or reimburse the lender for the cost of any surveys, title or mortgage examinations, appraisals, etc., performed by nonlender personnel with consent of the proposed borrower.

(d) The proposed borrower hereby covenants, promises, agrees and gives herein the ASSURANCE that in connection with any loan to the proposed borrower which FmHA may guarantee as a result of this application, it will COMPLY with the requirements of Executive Order 11245 regarding Equal Credit Opportunity. Proposed borrower further agrees that in the event it fails to comply with said applicable provision, FmHA may cancel, terminate, accelerate repayment of or suspend in whole or in part the financial assistance provided or to be provided by FmHA, and that FmHA or the United States Government may take any other action that may be deemed necessary or appropriate of this ASSURANCE OF COMPLIANCE. These requirements prohibit discrimination on the grounds of race, religion, color, sex, marital status or national origin recipients of Federal financial assistance, including but not limited to employment practices, and require the submission of appropriate reports and access to books and records. These requirements are applicable to all transferees and successors in interest.

NOTICE: **In accordance with 5 U.S.C. 552a, the Privacy Act of 1974, any individual should be provided a copy of Form FmHA 410-9, "Statement Required by the Privacy Act," at the time this application is completed.**

- 6

The proposed borrower hereby agrees to provide the lender and FmHA timely periodic financial statements including the annual financial statement required by FmHA Instruction 1980.451 (i)(13). Failure to provide such reports will be considered a default of the loan in accordance with Form FmHA 449-35, "Lender's Agreement," which is a part of Subpart E of Part 1980, Title 7 CFR.

WARNING: Section 1001 of Title 18, United States Code provides: "Whoever, in any matter within the jurisdiction of any department or agency of the United States knowingly and willfully falsifies, conceals or covers up a material fact, or makes any false, fictitious or fraudulent statements or representations, or makes or uses any false writing or document knowing the same to contain any false, fictitious or fraudulent statement or entry, shall be fined not more than $10,000 or imprisoned not more than 5 years, or both."

Misrepresentation of material facts may also be the basis for denial of credit by the Farmers Home Administration.

*Proposed Borrower Name:

_____

_____

CORPORATE SEAL

By _____

Title _____

Attest: _____

Date Signed: _____ , 19___

_____

(Title)   (Title)

Proposed Borrower's Contact Person

_____

Name

_____

Address

*(Individual, general partner, trade name, or corporation name).

_____

Telephone

- 7

PART B

INSTRUCTIONS: Lender completes item 21 through 33 and submits the original and one copy of this application and all supporting documents to FmHA.

21.   **REQUEST FOR GUARANTEE**:   LENDER TAX IDENTIFICATION
      (For use only by lender)   NO. _____

We propose to make and service a loan to the proposed borrower named on page 1 of this application. We request an FmHA
loan guarantee subject to the provisions of the applicable FmHA Instructions.

22.   **TERMS AND CONDITIONS OF LOAN**:   Percent of Guarantee Requested _____%
      (1) Type   Amount   Terms (yrs.)   Interest*   Monthly Payments

Real Estate $ _____   _____ yrs.   _____ % $_____
Machinery and Equipment $ _____   _____ yrs.   _____. % $_____
Working Capital $ _____   _____ yrs.   _____ % $_____
Other _____ $ _____   _____ yrs.   _____ % $_____

            TOTAL $ _____ $_____

*If the variable rate, follow by a "v" and identify base rate used and what interest differential is added to base rate. If multi-
rates are used provide overall effective interest rate for the entire loan: _____%. NOTE: Guaranteed borrower must
have the right to prepay their loans. Prepayment penalties are permitted if reasonable and approved by FmHA. Attach
amortization schedule for loan.

23.   (a) SOURCE AND USE OF FUNDS: Loan funds will be disbursed and used for the following purposes, in the following
           amounts.
           Building and Improvements $ _____   Machinery and Equipment $ _____
           Land and Rights   _____   Contingencies   _____
           Fees *(List below)*   _____   Debt Refinancing*   _____
           Legal and Engineering Fees _____   Working Capital   _____
           Interim Interest   _____   Other *(Specify)* _____ _____

                                                                                  $ _____

*Attach complete justification for the request *(include long and short term debt)*
      (b) Describe in detail the source and use of funds from (a) above and any other source of funds for the project and its
           amount and indicate whether the amounts and sources are proposed or definite.

24.   COLLATERAL AND LIEN POSITION:(Describe collateral in detail, show whether now owned or to be acquired). (Use
                                   Form FmHA 449-2 with appropriate appraisal reports and indicate any prior
                                   liens that may exist on the collateral).

25.   PLANNED DISBURSEMENTS: Record plans for distributing the loan. *(See FmHA Instruction11980.60 and 1980.454)*.

26.   (a) PERSONAL AND/OR CORPORATE GUARANTEES RECOMMENDED: *(See FmHA Instruction 1980.443)*.
      (b) COLLATERAL OFFERED FOR PERSONAL AND/OR CORPORATE GUARANTEES:

27.   INSURANCE: (List requirements for Life, Hazard, Federal Flood, and Liability).

28. COMMENTS OF LENDER: *(Attach additional sheets, if necessary).*

(a) Evaluate proposed borrower's management, past record, repayment ability and other financial analysis.

_____

_____

_____

_____

(b) State whether any officer, director, stockholder, or employee of the lender has a financial interest in the proposed borrower or vice versa. If so, give details:

_____

_____

_____

_____

_____

(c) Is proposed borrower indebted to lender? ☐ Yes ☐ No   If yes, provide history of debt repayment and other details:

_____

_____

_____

_____

(d) List all fees and charges for the loan, including those for preparation of application, servicing, etc. Indicate whether the guarantee fee will be passed on to proposed borrower. *(See FmHA Instruction 1980.411 and 1980.414).*

_____

_____

_____

_____

(e) Provide loan servicing plans, including field inspections, frequency of obtaining periodic and annual financial statements and their analysis, use of correspondents or other outside consultants, location of office servicing the loan, and complying with servicing responsibilities set forth in the "Lender's Agreement," Form FmHA 449-35.

_____

_____

_____

_____

-9

29. LOAN AGREEMENT: Attach proposed lender and borrower loan agreement *(See FmHA Instruction 1980.451 (i) (13)).*

30. LENDER'S EXPERIENCE WITH FmHA:
    (a) Have you made any loans guaranteed by FmHA?   ☐ Yes ☐ No
        If yes, check program area: ☐ Farmer Programs   ☐ Rural Housing   ☐ Business and Industry.
    (b) If proposed borrower has or had a loan(s) with you, has such loan(s) appeared in regulatory examination report?
        ☐ Yes   ☐ No   If yes, explain.

_____

_____

    (c) Have you ever been debarred from participation in FmHA programs? If yes, explain.

_____

_____

31. Verify and comment on proposed borrower's debt schedule: _____

_____

_____

_____

32. PLANS FOR CONSTITUTING THE LOAN: *(See Form FmHA 449-35, "Lender's Agreement," paragraph III A).*

    (a) Will retain entire loan   ☐ Yes ☐ No
    (b) Will utilize secondary market for guaranteed portion *(indicated by check).*
        Assignment _____   Participation _____   Multi-note _____
    (c) Participation of unguaranteed portion ☐ Yes   ☐ No
        (Lender must retain 5% of the unguaranteed portion of loan in its portfolio).

33. OPINION: In our opinion, the loan has repayment ability, appears feasible and all FmHA requirements in FmHA Instruction 1980-A and 1980-E will be met.

WARNING: **Section 1001 of Title 18, United States Code provides: "Whoever, in any matter within the jurisdiction of any department or agency of the United States knowingly and willfully falsifies, conceals or covers up a material fact, or makes any false, fictitious or fraudulent statements or representations, or makes or uses any false writing or document knowing the same to contain any false, fictitious or fraudulent statement or entry, shall be fined not more than $10,000 or imprisoned not more than 5 years, or both."**

Misrepresentation of material facts may also be the basis for FmHA not issuing a Loan Note Guarantee.

LENDER:

_____

Contact Person _____

_____

Telephone Number _____

_____

Date _____ , 19____

_____

By : _____
                                         Authorized Officer

_____
                                           Title

OMB Approval No. 3245-0016
Expiration Date: 10-31-87

U.S. Small Business Administration

Application for Business Loan

Applicant	Full Address

Name of Business	Tax I.D. No.

Full Street Address	Tel. No. (Inc. A/C)

City	County	State	Zip	Number of Employees (Including subsidiaries and affiliates)

Type of Business	Date Business Established	At Time of Application _____

Bank of Business Account and Address	If Loan is Approved _____
	Subsidiaries or Affiliates _____ (Separate from above)

Use of Proceeds: (Enter Gross Dollar Amounts Rounded to Nearest Hundreds)	Loan Requested	SBA USE ONLY
Land Acquisition		
New Construction/ Expansion/Repair		
Acquisition and/or Repair of Machinery and Equipment		
Inventory Purchase		
Working Capital (Including Accounts Payable)		
Acquisition of Existing Business		
Payoff SBA Loan		
Payoff Bank Loan (Non SBA Associated)		
Other Debt Payment (Non SBA Associated)		
All Other		
Total Loan Requested		
Term of Loan		

Collateral

If your collateral consists of (A) Land and Building, (D) Accounts Receivable and/or (E) Inventory, fill in the appropriate blanks. If you are pledging (B) Machinery and Equipment, (C) Furniture and Fixtures, and/or (F) Other, please provide an itemized list (labeled Exhibit A) that contains serial and identification numbers for all articles that had an original value greater than $500. Include a legal description of Real Estate offered as collateral.

	Present Market Value	Present Loan Balance	SBA Use Only Collateral Valuation
A. Land and Building	$	$	$
B. Machinery & Equipment			
C. Furniture & Fixtures			
D. Accounts Receivable			
E. Inventory			
F. Other			
Totals	$	$	$

PREVIOUS SBA OR OTHER GOVERNMENT FINANCING: If you or any principals or affiliates have ever requested Government Financing, complete the following:

Name of Agency	Original Amount of Loan	Date of Request	Approved or Declined	Balance	Current or Past Due
	$			$	
	$			$	

SBA Form 4 (2-85) Previous Editions Obsolete

INDEBTEDNESS: Furnish the following information on all installment debts, contracts, notes, and mortgages payable. Indicate by an asterisk (*) items to be paid by loan proceeds and reason for paying same (present balance should agree with latest balance sheet submitted).

To Whom Payable	Original Amount	Original Date	Present Balance	Rate of Interest	Maturity Date	Monthly Payment	Security	Current or Past Due
	$		$			$		
	$		$			$		
	$		$			$		
	$		$			$		

MANAGEMENT (Proprietor, partners, officers, directors and all holders of outstanding stock — <u>100% of ownership must be shown</u>). Use separate sheet if necessary.

Name and Social Security Number	Complete Address	% Owned	*Military Service From	To	*Race	*Sex

* This data is collected for statistical purposes only. It has no bearing on the credit decision to approve or decline this application.

ASSISTANCE   List the name(s) and occupation(s) of any who assisted in preparation of this form, other than applicant.

Name and Occupation	Address	Total Fees Paid	Fees Due
Name and Occupation	Address	Total Fees Paid	Fees Due

Signature of Preparers if Other Than Applicant

THE FOLLOWING EXHIBITS MUST BE COMPLETED WHERE APPLICABLE. ALL QUESTIONS ANSWERED ARE MADE A PART OF THE APPLICATION.

For Guaranty Loans please provide an original and one copy (Photocopy is Acceptable) of the Application Form, and all Exhibits to the participating lender. For Direct Loans submit one original copy of application and Exhibits to SBA.

Submit SBA Form 1261 (Statements Required by Laws and Executive Orders). This form must be signed and dated by each Proprietor, Partner, Principal or Guarantor.

1. Submit SBA Form 912 (Personal History Statement) for each person e.g. owners, partners, officers, directors, major stockholders, etc.; the instructions are on SBA Form 912.

2. Furnish a signed current personal balance sheet (SBA Form 413 may be used for this purpose) for each stockholder (with 20% or greater ownership), partner, officer, and owner. Social Security number should be included on personal financial statement. Label this Exhibit B.

3. Include the statements listed below: 1, 2, 3 for the last three years; also 1, 2, 3, 4 dated within 90 days of filing the application; and statement 5, if applicable. This is Exhibit C (SBA has Management Aids that help in the preparation of financial statements.) All information must be signed and dated.

   1. Balance Sheet   2. Profit and Loss Statement
   3. Reconciliation of Net Worth
   4. Aging of Accounts Receivable and Payable
   5. Earnings projections for at least one year where financial statements for the last three years are unavailable or where requested by District Office.
      (If Profit and Loss Statement is not available, explain why and substitute Federal Income Tax Forms.)

4. Provide a brief history of your company and a paragraph describing the expected benefits it will receive from the loan. Label it Exhibit D.

ALL EXHIBITS MUST BE SIGNED AND DATED BY PERSON SIGNING THIS FORM.

SBA Form 4 (2-85) Previous Editions Obsolete

5. Provide a brief description of the educational, technical and business background for all the people listed under Management. Please mark it Exhibit E.

6. Do you have any co-signers and/or guarantors for this loan? If so, please submit their names, addresses and personal balance sheet(s) as Exhibit F.

7. Are you buying machinery or equipment with your loan money? If so, you must include a list of the equipment and cost as quoted by the seller and his name and address. This is Exhibit G.

8. Have you or any officers of your company ever been involved in bankruptcy or insolvency proceedings? If so, please provide the details as Exhibit H. If none, check here: ☐ Yes ☐ No

9. Are you or your business involved in any pending lawsuits? If yes, provide the details as Exhibit I. If none, check here: ☐ Yes ☐ No

10. Do you or your spouse or any member of your household, or anyone who owns, manages, or directs your business or their spouses or members of their households work for the Small Business Administration, Small Business Advisory Council, SCORE or ACE, any Federal Agency, or the participating lender? If so, please provide the name and address of the person and the office where employed. label this Exhibit J. If none, check here: ☐ Yes ☐ No

11. Does your business, its owners or majority stockholders own or have a controlling interest in other businesses? If yes, please provide their names and the relationship with your company along with a current balance sheet and operating statement for each. This should be Exhibit K.

12. Do you buy from, sell to, or use the services of any concern in which someone in your company has a significant financial interest? If yes, provide details on a separate sheet of paper labeled Exhibit L.

13. If your business is a franchise, include a copy of the franchise agreement and a copy of the FTC disclosure statement supplied to you by the Franchisor. Please include it as Exhibit M.

CONSTRUCTION LOANS ONLY

14. Include a separate exhibit (Exhibit N) the estimated cost of the project and a statement of the source of any additional funds.

15. File the necessary compliance document (SBA Form 601).

16. Provide copies of preliminary construction plans and specifications. Include them as Exhibit O. Final plans will be required prior to disbursement.

DIRECT LOANS ONLY

17. Include two bank declination letters with your application. These letters should include the name and telephone number of the persons contacted at the banks, the amount and terms of the loan, the reason for decline and whether or not the bank will participate with SBA. In cities with 200,000 people or less, one letter will be sufficient.

EXPORT LOANS

18. Does your business presently engage in Export Trade? Check here ☐ Yes ☐ No

19. Do you plan to begin exporting as a result of this loan? Check here ☐ Yes ☐ No

20. Would you like information on Exporting? Check here ☐ Yes ☐ No

AGREEMENTS AND CERTIFICATIONS

Agreements of Nonemployment of SBA Personnel: I/We agree that if SBA approves this loan application I/We will not, for at least two years, hire as an employee or consultant anyone that was employed by the SBA during the one year period prior to the disbursement of the loan.

Certification: I/We certify: (a) I/We have not paid anyone connected with the Federal Government for help in getting this loan. I/We also agree to report to the SBA office of the Inspector General, 1441 L Street N.W., Washington, D.C. 20416 any Federal Government employee who offers, in return for any type of compensation, to help get this loan approved.

(b) All information in this application and the Exhibits are true and complete to the best of my/our knowledge and are submitted to SBA so SBA can decide whether to grant a loan or participate with a lending institution in a loan to me/us. I/We agree to pay for or reimburse SBA for the cost of any surveys, title or mortgage examinations, appraisals etc., performed by non-SBA personnel provided I/We have given my/our consent.

I/We understand that I/We need not pay anybody to deal with SBA. I/We have read and understand Form 394 which explains SBA policy on representatives and their fees.

If you make a statement that you know to be false or if you over value a security in order to help obtain a loan under the provisions of the Small Business Act, you can be fined up to $5,000 or be put in jail for up to two years, or both.

If Applicant is a proprietor or general partner, sign below:

By: _____
                                                          Date

If Applicant is a Corporation, sign below:

_____
Corporate Name and Seal   Date

_____

By: _____
                        Signature of President

Attested by: _____
                        Signature of Corporate Secretary

ALL EXHIBITS MUST BE SIGNED AND DATED BY PERSON SIGNING THIS FORM.

OMB Approval No. 3245-0188
Exp. Date: 10-31-89

PERSONAL FINANCIAL STATEMENT

As of _____ 19 ____

Complete this form if 1) a sole proprietorship by the proprietor; 2) a partnership by each partner; 3) a corporation by each officer and each stockholder with 20% or more ownership; 4) any other person or entity providing a guaranty on the loan.

Name	Residence Phone

Residence Address

City, State, & Zip

Business Name of Applicant/Borrower

ASSETS (Omit Cents)	LIABILITIES (Omit Cents)
Cash on hand & in Banks.................$_____	Accounts Payable ....$_____
Savings Accounts........................ _____	Notes Payable (to Bk & Others
IRA...................................... _____	(Describe in Section 2).................. _____
Accounts & Notes Receivable	Installment Account (Auto)
(Describe in Section 6) .... _____	Mo. Payments $_____ _____
Life Insurance—Cash	Installment Account (Other)
Surrender Value Only .... _____	Mo. Payments $ _____ _____
Stocks and Bonds	Loans on Life Insurance .... _____
(Describe in Section 3) .... _____	Mortgages on Real Estate................
Real Estate	(Describe in Section 4)................. _____
(Describe in Section 4) .... _____	Unpaid Taxes
Automobile—Present Value .... _____	(Describe in Section 7).................. _____
Other Personal Property	Other Liabilities
(Describe in Section 5) _____	(Describe in Section 8)................. _____
Other Assets	
(Describe in Section 6) .... _____	Total Liabilities.......................... _____
	Net Worth .... _____
Total.......................$_____	Total.......................$_____

Section 1. Source of Income   Contingent Liabilities

Salary .... $_____	As Endorser or Co-Maker ....$_____
Net Investment Income .... _____	Legal Claims & Judgments .... _____
Real Estate Income .... _____	Provision for Fed Income Tax........................ _____
Other Income (Describe)* .... _____	Other Special Debt .... _____

Description of Items Listed in Section I _____

*(Alimony or child support payments need not be disclosed in "Other Income" unless it is desired to have such payments counted toward total income.)

Section 2. Notes Payable to Banks and Others

Name & Address of Noteholder	Original Balance	Current Balance	Payment Amount	Terms (Monthly-etc.)	How Secured or Endorsed—Type of Collateral

SBA Form 413 (10-87)   Use 10-86 edition until exhausted   Refer to SOP 50   10

(Response is required to obtain a benefit)

Section 3. Stocks and Bonds: (*Use separate sheet if necessary*)

No. of Shares	Names of Securities	Cost	Market Value Quotation/Exchange	Date Amount

Section 4. Real Estate Owned. (*List each parcel separately. Use supplemental sheets if necessary. Each sheet must be identified as a supplement to this statement and signed*).

Address—Type of property	Title is in name of	Date Purchased	Original Cost	Present Value	Mortgage Balance	Amount of Payment	Status of Mortgage

Section 5. Other Personal Property. (*Describe, and if any is mortgaged, state name and address of mortgage holder and amount of mortgage, terms of payment, and if delinquent, describe delinquency.*)

Section 6. Other Assets, Notes & Accounts Receivable (*Describe*)

Section 7. Unpaid Taxes. (*Describe in detail, as to type, to whom payable, when due, amount, and what, if any, property the tax lien attaches*)

Section 8. Other Liabilities. (*Describe in detail*)

Section 9. Life Insurance Held (*Give face amount of policies—name of company and beneficiaries*)

SBA/Lender is authorized to make all inquiries deemed necessary to verify the accuracy of the statements made herein and to determine my/our creditworthiness.
(I) or (We) certify the above and the statements contained in the schedules herein are a true and accurate statement of (my) or (our) financial condition as of the date stated herein. This statement is given for the purpose of: (*Check one of the following*)

☐ Inducing S.B.A. to grant a loan as requested in the application, to the individual or firm whose name appears herein.
☐ Furnishing a statement of (my) or (our) financial condition, pursuant to the terms of the guaranty executed by (me) or (us) at the same time S.B.A. granted a loan to the individual or firm, whose name appears herein.

Signature	Signature	Date

SOCIAL SECURITY NO.	SOCIAL SECURITY NO.

SBA Form 413 (10-87)

GPO 931-151

Return Executed Copies 1, 2 and 3 to SBA

OMB APPROVAL NO. 3245-0178
Expiration Date: 5-31-90

United States of America

SMALL BUSINESS ADMINISTRATION

STATEMENT OF PERSONAL HISTORY

Please Read Carefully - Print or Type

Each member of the small business concern requesting assistance or the development company must submit this form in TRIPLICATE for filing with the SBA application. This form must be filled out and submitted by:

1. If a sole proprietorship by the proprietor.
2. If a partnership by each partner.
3. If a corporation or a development company, by each officer, director, and additionally by each holder of 20% or more of the voting stock.
4. Any other person including a hired manager, who has authority to speak for and commit the borrower in the management of the business.

Name and Address of Applicant (Firm Name) (Street, City, State and ZIP Code)

SBA District Office and City

Amount Applied for:

1. Personal Statement of: (State name in full, if no middle name, state (NMN), or if initial only, indicate initial). List all former names used, and dates each name was used. Use separate sheet if necessary.

First   Middle   Last

2. Date of Birth: (Month, day and year)

3. Place of Birth: (City & State or Foreign Country).

U.S. Citizen? ☐ YES ☐ NO
If no, give alien registration number:
#

4. Give the percentage of ownership or stock owned or to be owned in the small business concern or the Development Company.

Social Security No.

5. Present residence address:

From: To: Address:

City   State

Home Telephone No. (Include A/C):

Business Telephone No. (Include A/C):

Immediate past residence address:

From: To: Address:

BE SURE TO ANSWER THE NEXT 3 QUESTIONS CORRECTLY BECAUSE THEY ARE IMPORTANT.

THE FACT THAT YOU HAVE AN ARREST OR CONVICTION RECORD WILL NOT NECESSARILY DISQUALIFY YOU. BUT AN INCORRECT ANSWER WILL PROBABLY CAUSE YOUR APPLICATION TO BE TURNED DOWN.

6. Are you presently under indictment, on parole or probation?

☐ Yes ☐ No   If yes, furnish details in a separate exhibit. List name(s) under which held, if applicable.

7. Have you ever been charged with or arrested for any criminal offense other than a minor motor vehicle violation?

☐ Yes ☐ No   If yes, furnish details in a separate exhibit. List name(s) under which charged, if applicable.

8. Have you ever been convicted of any criminal offense other than a minor motor vehicle violation?

☐ Yes ☐ No   If yes, furnish details in a separate exhibit. List name(s) under which convicted, if applicable.

9. Name and address of participating bank

The information on this form will be used in connection with an investigation of your character. Any information you wish to submit, that you feel will expedite this investigation should be set forth.

Whoever makes any statement knowing it to be false, for the purpose of obtaining for himself or for any applicant, any loan, or loan extension by renewal, deferment or otherwise, or for the purpose of obtaining, or influencing SBA toward, anything of value under the Small Business Act, as amended, shall be punished under Section 16(a) of that Act, by a fine of not more than $5000, or by imprisonment for not more than 2 years, or both.

Signature

Title

Date

It is against SBA's policy to provide assistance to persons not of good character and therefore consideration is given to the qualities and personality traits of a person, favorable and unfavorable, relating thereto, including behavior, integrity, candor and disposition toward criminal actions. It is also against SBA's policy to provide assistance not in the best interests of the United States, for example, if there is reason to believe that the effect of such assistance will be to encourage or support, directly or indirectly, activities inimical to the Security of the United States. Anyone concerned with the collection of this information, as to its voluntariness, disclosure or routine uses may contact the FOIA Office, 1441 ''L'' Street, N.W., and a copy of §9 ''Agency Collection of Information'' from SOP 40 04 will be provided.

SBA FORM 912 (5-87) SOP 9020 USE 6-85 EDITION UNTIL EXHAUSTED

1. SBA FILE COPY

GLOSSARY

Basket Clause: A provision specifying the amount of public pension funds that may be placed in investments not included on a state's legal list. (See "Legal List.")

Blue Chip Security: A low-risk, low-yield security representing an interest in a very stable company.

Blue Sky Laws: General term which denotes various states' laws regulating securities.

Business Development Corporation (BDC): A business financing agency, usually comprising financial institutions in an area or state that are organized to help finance industrial enterprises unable to obtain such assistance through normal channels. The risk is spread among various BDC members; interest rates may vary from those charged by the member institutions.

Business and Industrial Development Company (BIDCO): A private, for-profit financing corporation chartered by the state to provide both equity and long-term debt capital to small business owners.

Capital: (1) Assets less liabilities, representing the ownership interest in a business; (2) A stock of accumulated goods, especially at a specified time and in contrast to income received during a specified time period; (3) Accumulated goods devoted to the production of goods; (4) Accumulated possessions calculated to bring in income.

Certified Development Company (CDC): A local area or statewide corporation or authority—for profit or nonprofit, depending on the situation—that packages SBA, bank, state and private money into a financial assistance package for existing business capital improvement. The SBA holds the second lien on its maximum share of 40 percent involvement. Each state has at least one CDC. See also SBA 503/504 loans.

Collateral: Securities, evidence of deposit, or other property pledged by a borrower to secure repayment of a loan.

Common Stock: The most-frequently used instrument for purchasing ownership in private or public companies. It generally carries the right to vote on certain corporate actions and can pay dividends (although it rarely does in venture investments). In liquidation, common stockholders are the last to share in the proceeds from the sale of assets of a corporation--bond holders and preferred shareholders have priority. Common stock is often used in first-round start-up financing.

Community Development Corporation: A corporation established to develop economic programs for a community and, in most cases, to provide financial support for such development.

Consortium: A coalition of organizations—such as banks and corporations—set up to fund ventures requiring large capital resources.

Convertible Securities: A feature of certain bonds, debentures, or preferred stocks that allows them to be exchanged by the owner for another class of securities at a future date and in accordance with any other terms of the issue.

Convertible Preferred Stock: A class of stock that pays a reasonable dividend and is convertible into common stock. Generally, the convertible feature may be exercised only after being held for a stated period of time. This arrangement is usually considered second round financing when the company needs equity to maintain its cash flow.

Debenture: (1) A certificate given as acknowledgement of a debt secured by the general credit of the issuing corporation; (2) A bond, usually without security, issued by a corporation and sometimes convertible to common stock.

Debt: Something owed by one person to another. Debt securities, such as bonds and notes, are simply loans that provide a specified rate of return for a specified period of time. Short-term debt is an obligation which matures within one year. Mid-term debt matures within one to five years and long-term debt is any obligation which matures in a period that exceeds five years.

Equity: An ownership interest in a business. Equity securities such as stocks, for example, afford ownership in a company without any guaranteed return, but with the opportunity to share in the company's profits.

Equity Midrisk Venture Capital: An unsecured investment in a company. Usually a purchase of ownership interest in a company that occurs in the later stages of a company's development.

Equity Partnership: A limited partnership arrangement for providing start-up and seed capital to businesses.

General Obligation Bond: A municipal bond secured by the taxing power of the municipality. The Tax Reform Act of 1986 limits the purposes for which those bonds may be issued and establishes volume limits on the extent of their issuance.

Incubator: A facility designed to encourage entrepreneurship and minimize obstacles to new business formation and growth, particularly for high technology firms, by housing a number of fledgling enterprises that share an array of services. These shared services may include meeting areas, secretarial services, accounting services, research library, on-site financial and management counseling, and word processing facilities.

Industrial Development Authority: The financial arm of a state or other political subdivision established for the purpose of financing economic development in an area. Usually this takes the form of loans to nonprofit organizations, which in turn provide facilities for manufacturing and other industrial operations.

Industrial Revenue Bond (IRB): A tax-exempt bond issued by a state or local government agency to finance industrial or commercial projects that serve a public good. The bond usually is not backed by the full faith and credit of the government that issues it, but is repaid solely from the revenues of the project and requires a private sector commitment for repayment.

Innovation: Introduction of a new idea into the marketplace in the form of a new product or service, or an improvement in organization or process.

IRB: See Industrial Revenue Bond.

Job Training Partnership Act (JTPA): Federal law, passed in 1983, providing for publicly financed training from private-sector experts for economically disadvantaged adults and youth.

Legal List: A list of securities selected by a state in which certain institutions and fiduciaries (such as pension funds, insurance companies, and banks) may invest. Securities not on the list are not eligible for investment. Legal lists typically restrict investments to high-quality securities meeting certain specifications. Generally, investment is limited to U.S.

securities and investment-grade "blue chip" securities.

Limited Partnerships: (See "Venture Capital Limited Partnerships.")

Liquidity: The ability to convert a security or any asset into cash promptly.

Local Development Corporation: An organization, usually made up of local citizens of a community, designed to improve the economy of the area by inducing business and industry to locate and expand there. A local development corporation establishes a capability to finance local growth.

Maturity: The date upon which the principal or stated value of a bond or other indebtedness becomes due and payable. (See "Term.")

Minority-Owned Businesses: Generally businesses owned by persons of African, Hispanic, American Indian or Asian descent. The definition may vary from state to state.

Net Worth: Assets less liabilities. (See "Capital.")

Pension: A series of payments made monthly, semiannually, annually, or at other specified intervals during the lifetime of the pensioner. The term is sometimes used to denote the portion of the retirement allowance financed by the employer's contributions.

Pension Fund: A fund established to provide for the payment of pension benefits; the collective contributions made by all of the parties to the pension plan.

Procurement Assistance: Programs or services offered by government to aid small businesses in bidding on government procurement contracts. Such assistance can take the form of counseling, procurement service centers, set-asides, and sheltered-market bidding.

Product Liability: Type of tort, or civil liability that applies to product manufacturers and sellers.

Prompt Payment Act: Federal law that requires federal procuring agencies to pay interest to contractors on bills not paid within 30 days of invoicing or completion of work.

Prudent Investor Rule or Standard: A legal doctrine that requires fiduciaries to make investments using the prudence, diligence, and intelligence that would be used by a prudent person in making similar investments. Because fiduciaries make investments on behalf of third-party beneficiaries, the standard results in very conservative investments. Until recently, most state regulations required the fiduciary to apply this standard to each investment. Newer, more progressive regulations permit fiduciaries to apply this standard to the portfolio taken as a whole, thereby allowing a fiduciary to balance a portfolio with higher-yield, higher-risk investments. In states with more progressive regulations, practically every type of security is eligible for inclusion in the portfolio of investments made by a fiduciary, provided that the portfolio investments, in their totality, represent those of a prudent person.

Rate of Return: The yield obtained on a security or other investment based on its purchase price or its current market price. The total rate of return is current income plus or minus capital appreciation or depreciation. (See "Yield.")

Regulation D: A vehicle by which small businesses make small offerings and private placements of securities with limited disclosure requirements. It was designed to ease the burdens imposed on small businesses utilizing this method of capital formation.

Regulatory Flexibility Act: Federal law that requires federal agencies to evaluate the impact of their regulations on small businesses before the regulations are issued and to consider less burdensome alternatives.

SBA 503/504 Loans: Two economic development loan programs offered by the SBA and administered by Certified Development Companies certified by the SBA. See also Certified Development Company.

SBIC: See Small Business Investment Company.

SBIR: See Small Business Innovation Research Program.

Secondary Market: A market established for the purchase and sale of outstanding securities following their initial distribution.

Section 8(a) Program: A program designed to assist socially and economically disadvantaged small firms to become more competitive. The SBA provides for business development by entering into contracts with federal agencies to supply goods and services, and then subcontracts the actual performance of this work to 8(a) certified firms. To be eligible for 8(a) certification, a company must be managed, controlled, and at least 51-percent-owned by American citizens who are socially and economically disadvantaged individuals.

Small Business Development Centers (SBDCs): University-based programs, organized and financed by the SBA and run in conjunction with individual states and state universities, that provide faculty and student counseling to small business owners.

Small Business Innovation Research (SBIR) Program: Program mandated by the federal Small Business Innovation Development Act of 1982, requiring federal agencies with $100 million or more of extramural R & D obligations to set aside 1.25 percent of these funds for small businesses. Contract awards are made in three phases: Phase I awards up to $50,000 for feasibility studies; Phase II awards up to

$500,000 for product development of Phase I projects; Phase III involves private funds for commercial marketing of Phase II projects.

Small Business Institute (SBI): Small business counseling program, offered nationally at 530 colleges and universities, that provides indepth management counseling to small businesses by student teams under faculty guidance.

Small Business Investment Company (SBIC): A privately owned institution licensed by the SBA. The SBIC operates under SBA regulations, but its transactions with small companies are private arrangements and have no direct connection with the SBA. An SBIC may be formed by three or more parties, and must be chartered by the state in which it is formed. No individual bank may own more than 49 percent of an SBIC. Minimum initial private capitalization is $1 million. An SBIC may lend or invest a maximum of 20 percent of its initial private capital to any one company. After 75 percent of the initial private capital has been loaned out, the SBIC may then borrow additional capital from the SBA at an average rate of $3 for each $1 loaned out.

Surety Bonding Assistance: An SBA program that helps qualified small businesses to obtain bid, payment or performance bonds on government and commercial contracts otherwise unobtainable from commercial sources.

Targeted Jobs Tax Credit: Federal legislation enacted in 1978 that provides a tax credit to an employer who hires structurally unemployed individuals.

Taxable Bonds: An interest-bearing certificate of public or private indebtedness. Bonds are issued by public agencies to finance economic development. Taxable bonds may be used for a far greater variety of purposes than Industrial Revenue Bonds.

Term: The length of time for which a loan is made. (See "Maturity.")

Terms of a Note: The conditions or limits of a note. The terms of a note include the interest rate per annum, the due date, and transferability and convertibility features, if any.

Time Deposit: A bank deposit that may not be withdrawn before a specified future time.

Treasury Bills: Investment tender issued by the Federal Reserve Bank in amounts of $10,000, maturing in 91 to 182 days.

Treasury Bonds: Long-term notes with maturity dates of not less than seven nor more than twenty-five years.

Treasury Notes: Short-term notes maturing in less than seven years.

Unfunded Accrued Liability: The excess of total liabilities, both present and prospective, over present and prospective assets.

Venture Capital: Money used to support new or unusual commercial undertakings; equity, risk, or speculative investment capital. This funding is provided to new or existing firms that exhibit above-average growth rates, a significant potential for market expansion, and are in need for additional financing to sustain growth or further research and development. Sources of venture capital financing include public and private pension funds, commercial banks and bank holding companies (which have separate venture financing activities), Small Business Investment Companies licensed by the SBA, private venture capital firms, insurance companies, investment management companies, bank trust departments, industrial companies seeking to diversify their investments, and investment bankers acting as intermediaries for other investors or directly investing on their own behalf.

Venture Capital Limited Partnerships: Designed for business development, these partnerships are an institutional mechanism for providing capital for young, technology-oriented businesses. The investors' money is pooled and invested in money market assets until venture investments have been selected. The general partners are experienced investment managers who select and invest the equity and debt securities of firms with high growth potential and the ability to go public in the near future.

Venture Capital Network (VCN): A computer database that matches investors with entrepreneurs.

Yield: The rate of income returned on an investment, expressed as a percentage. Income yield is obtained by dividing the current dollar income by the current market price of the security. Net yield or yield to maturity is the current income yield minus any premium above par or plus any discount from par in purchase price, with the adjustment spread over the period from the date of purchase to the date of maturity. (See "Rate of Return.")

INDEX

The Business Bookshelf

These books have been carefully selected as the best on these subjects. **Your satisfaction is guaranteed or your money back.**

To order, call toll-free 1-800-255-5730 ext. 110. In Colorado, call (303) 872-8924 ext. 110. Please have your Visa, Mastercard, American Express, or Discover card ready.

Small Time Operator:
How to Start Your Own Business, Keep Your Books, Pay Your Taxes, and Stay Out of Trouble

By Bernard Kamoroff, C.P.A. The most popular small business book in the U.S., it's used by over 250,000 businesses. Easy to read and use, Small Time Operator is particularly good for those without bookkeeping experience. Comes complete with a year's supply of ledgers and worksheets designed especially for small businesses, and contains invaluable information on permits, licenses, financing, loans, insurance, bank accounts, etc.

ISBN 0-917510-06-2 190 pages 8-1/2 x 11 paperbound $12.95

The Business Planning Guide
Creating a Plan for Success in Your Own Business

By Andy Bangs. *The Business Planning Guide* has been used by hundreds of banks, colleges, and accounting firms to guide business owners through the process of putting together a complete and effective business plan and financing proposal. The *Guide* comes complete with examples, forms and worksheets that make the planning process painless. With over 150,000 copies in print, the *Guide* has become a small business classic.

ISBN 0-936894-10-5 149 pages 8-1/2 x 11 paperbound $16.95

Free Help from Uncle Sam to Start Your Own Business (*or Expand the One You Have*) Revised Edition

By William Alarid and Gustav Berle. *Free Help* describes over 100 government programs that help small business and gives dozens of examples of how others have used this aid. Included are appendices with helpful books, organizations and phone numbers.

ISBN 0-940673-91-X 208 pages 5-1/2 x 8-1/2 paperbound $11.95

Marketing Without Advertising

By Michael Phillips and Salli Rasberry. A creative and practical guide that shows small business people how to avoid wasting money on advertising. The authors, experienced business consultants, show how to implement an ongoing marketing plan to tell potential and current customers that yours is a quality business worth trusting, recommending and coming back to.

ISBN 0-87337-019-8 200 pages 8-1/2 x 11 paperbound $13.95

Call Toll Free and Order Now

1-800-255-5730 Extension 110

he Business Bookshelf

— continued —

Advertising in the Yellow Pages: *How to Boost Profits and Avoid Pitfalls*

By W. F. Wagoner. Written by a top Yellow Pages salesman, trainer and manager, this one-of-a-kind manual for advertisers in the Yellow Pages teaches you proven methods for making Yellow Pages advertising pay off

ISBN 0-940969-00-9 174 pages 5-1/2 x 8-1/2 paperbound $12.95

The Partnership Book

By attorneys Dennis Clifford and Ralph Warner. When two or more people join to start a small business, one of the most basic needs is to establish a solid, legal partnership agreement. This book supplies a number of sample agreements which you can use as is. Buy-out clauses, unequal sharing of assets, and limited partnerships are all discussed in detail.

ISBN 0-87337-041-4 221 pages 8-1/2 x 11 paperbound $18.95

Small Business Guide to Federal R & D Funding Opportunities

By the National Science Foundation Office of Small Business Research and Development. Each year, more than one billion dollars of federal money goes to small companies for research and development. This report has a primer on finding and pursuing these opportunities and contains hundreds of program descriptions of Uncle Sam's needs.

104 pages 8-1/2 x 11 paperbound $17.95

Money Sources For Small Business: How You Can Find Private., State, Federal, and Corporate Financing

By William Alarid. Contains hundreds of government programs, venture capital clubs, networks, and companies that want to help you finance your small business. Contains examples of forms required by government lenders.

ISBN 0940673-51-7 224 pages 8-1/2 X 11 paperbound $19.95

FOR CREDIT CARD ORDERS

Call Toll-Free 1-800-255-5730 ext. 110.
In Colorado, call (303) 872-8924 ext. 110.

Please have Visa, Mastercard, American Express, or Discover card ready.

Puma Publishing, 1670 Coral Drive Suite R, Santa Maria, California 93454.

Sales Tax: Please add 6.75% for shipping to California addresses.

Shipping: $2.00 for first book and $1.50 for each additional book. (Surface shipping may take three to four weeks)

Air Mail: $4.00 for first book and $2.00 for each additional book

Your Satisfaction is Guaranteed or Your Money Back!

Puma Publishing ● 1670 Coral Drive, Suite R
Santa Maria, California 93454